Fabergé: Lost and Found

Fabergé: Lost and Found

The Recently Discovered Jewelry Designs from the St. Petersburg Archives

By A. Kenneth Snowman

Harry N. Abrams, Inc.
Publishers

EDITOR: *Margaret Rennolds Chace*
DESIGNER: *Judith Michael*

ON PAGE 2:

The Orange Tree Egg was presented to the Dowager Empress Marie Feodorovna by Nicholas II. Based on a solid block of nephrite and surrounded by four gold-mounted nephrite pillars connected by chains of translucent emerald-enameled gold leaves half covering pearls. A white quartz tub, set with cabochon rubies and pearls, trellised in gold and decorated with chased gold swags, is filled with hammered gold soil. The naturalistically modeled gold tree trunk supports the foliage composed of carved nephrite leaves. Set among the leaves are white opaque enameled flowers with brilliant diamond centers and various gemstones (citrines, amethysts, pale rubies, and champagne diamonds) representing fruit. When a small button is pressed, the top leaves spring up, and a feathered gold bird rises from the interior of the tree, sings, and then automatically disappears. Engraved "Fabergé 1911" on front bottom edge of tub. Height 10½" (26.7 cm). Forbes Magazine Collection, New York.

ON PAGE 6:

A photograph of the Tsarina Alexandra Feodorovna signed in her hand in 1899. She wears a diamond tiara in the form of a kokoshnik *and holds a fan by Fabergé. Below is a working watercolor drawing of a gold fan to be enameled translucent rose* guilloché *and set with brilliant and rose diamonds. Length of fan in drawing, 13¼" (33.6 cm). Wartski, London.*

ON PAGES 10–11:

Diadem, convertible to a necklace, with brilliant and rose diamonds mounted in silver and gold designed as a row of cyclamen flowers and leaves, made in the Fabergé workshop of Albert Holmström, 1908–17. 3⅛ × 11" (8 × 28 cm). Her Grace the Duchess of Westminster. The diadem is shown here photographed in front of the pencil design for the piece, and appearing opposite is a signed watercolor drawing for the same diadem.

LIBRARY OF CONGRESS CATALOGING-IN-PUBLICATION DATA

Snowman, A. Kenneth (Abraham Kenneth), 1919–
Fabergé, lost and found : the recently discovered jewelry designs from the St. Petersburg Archives / by A. Kenneth Snowman.
p. cm.
Includes bibliographical references and index.
ISBN 0-8109-3307-1
1. Faberzhe (Firm) 2. Fabergé, Peter Carl, 1846–1920—Notebooks, sketchbooks, etc. 3. Jewelry—Russia (Federation)—History—20th century—Drawings. 4. Jewelry—Russia (Federation)—History—20th century—Design. 5. Archives—Russia (Federation)—Saint Petersburg. 6. Nicholas II, Emperor of Russia, 1868–1918—Art patronage. I. Fabergé, Peter Carl, 1846–1920. II. Title.
NK7398.F32S62 1993
739.2′092—dc20 92-45822
CIP

Published in 1993 by Harry N. Abrams, Incorporated, New York
A Times Mirror Company

Printed and bound in Italy

Contents

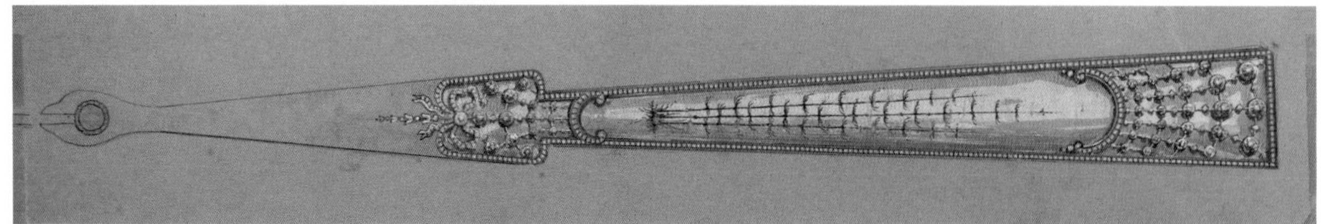

Preface and Acknowledgments

The spark that fired the idea for this book was ignited by a telephone call from Jacqueline Kennedy Onassis—it was received, naturally enough, with both surprise and delight. She had read an article about the Fabergé record books of designs that I had written for *Apollo* magazine in September 1987 and suggested that the subject matter warranted expansion in the form of an illustrated book.

A request to Anna Somers Cocks, the Editor at the time of the magazine in question, who had asked me to produce the article in the first place, was unhesitatingly granted, and I was thus free to repeat and substantially extend the material I had used.

I should like therefore to acknowledge my debt to the imagination and generosity of these two delightful ladies.

The article was included earlier in Géza von Habsburg's catalogue compiled for the memorable exhibition "Fabergé: Hofjuwelier der Zaren," organized by the Bavarian National Museum at the Kunsthalle in Munich in 1986–87; and I very much appreciate their allowing me the same freedom. Finally, I am particularly grateful to Paul Gottlieb at Abrams for his friendly enthusiasm and understanding and to his talented staff who have made this book a reality, especially my editor, Margaret Chace, and Judith Michael, the designer.

Having devoted several books and catalogues and numerous essays to the work of Carl Fabergé and his craftsmen, the sudden appearance of the design books was, for me, an extremely exciting event, and the discovery of so many of the original drawings and paintings for jewels I had actually seen and handled over the years understandably evoked a very special joy. Seen as a collection these designs vividly demonstrate how far Fabergé's inventive imagination was in advance of that of the conventional jeweler in Russia and, for a moment, in the whole of Europe. Although I find myself being reminded daily of the solemn verity set down by the aging Arnold Schönberg, "Things will always find a way of becoming worse, somehow," and despite the profundity of this undeniable truth, something, somehow, has nevertheless turned up which is actually *better* and indeed, quite simply, good news.

Among the treasures was a small mosaic watercolor drawing, the inspiration as we now know for the Imperial Easter Egg presented to the Tsarina in 1912, which I have called the Mosaic Egg and which now forms part of the collection of Queen Elizabeth II. I should like to record my thanks to Her Majesty for having, with characteristic generosity, allowed me to photograph the egg resting on the page upon which the relevant design is painted. This photograph was specifically composed for the cover of the handbook of the Burlington Fair of 1987, the original Antique Dealers' Fair founded in 1934, which took place every two years in the 1980s as an international event at the Royal Academy in London's Burlington House under the enlightened presidency of Sir Hugh Casson. On this occasion the Mosaic Egg, among other royal loans, was displayed with the design books for the first time.

Although most rational persons would regard yet another publication on the theme of Fabergé at this stage, when barely three months are allowed to go by without some further work being offered to the public, as singularly foolhardy, I have nevertheless taken courage, faced with the surprising emergence of this new "seed-corn" evidence, since it really does add something fresh to our picture of this astonishing man.

I want to thank my friend Kip Forbes for having both the imagination and the generosity, upon the occasion of the splendid exhibition of Fabergé Easter eggs in San Diego in 1989–90, to have thought of photographing the gold model of the imperial yacht *Standart*, which rests in the Kremlin's rock-crystal and lapis lazuli Easter egg, in front of the preliminary drawing that was made for it. The happy result of this creative inspiration appears on page 166. Gordon Roberton of Messrs. A. C. Cooper in London has, as always, proved the most intelligent and patient of photographers.

Svetlana Lloyd, with her invaluable knowledge of Russian, has ensured that the captions in the volumes have been properly translated, and I am grateful for this help.

My colleagues Geoffrey Munn and Stephen Dale have leapt eagerly upon this new source material, and their research has brought many rewards, which are evidenced in the pages that follow; June Trager and Katherine Purcell have carefully checked my every move and I thank them all for their help.

I am particularly indebted to my wife, Sallie, who with her command of Russian has as always proved an invaluable ally.

ФАБЕРЖЕ

Fabergé: Lost and Found

The Fabergés were of Huguenot descent and were obliged to leave their native Picardy when the Edict of Nantes was revoked in 1685. As victims of religious persecution, they had fled through Eastern Europe, and many years later Gustav Fabergé, Carl's father, who had been born in Pernau in 1814, opened up in a small basement in St. Petersburg as a run-of-the-mill jeweler in 1842.

Peter Carl Fabergé, whose work concerns us here, was born in 1846. His father had ensured that he received the most careful education, which included visits to all the principal museums and collections in Europe. He proved an exceptional student who became increasingly attracted to the art of the goldsmith and the

possibilities of this craft as exemplified in the treasures he saw during visits to Dresden, Florence, Paris, and London.

In 1870, at the age of only twenty-four, he accepted the responsibility of running the business so that his father could retire. Fired with enthusiasm, Carl Fabergé brought about a quiet but decisive revolution in the applied arts of Russia. This was the result of his fundamental belief that the value of a work of art lay in the inspiration of its design and the merit of its craftsmanship and not in the cost of the ingredients employed in its manufacture.

This philosophy was a complete reversal of what had gone before in imperial Russia, where ostentation and brilliance of effect had taken precedence over every other consideration.

Sir Roy Strong, director of the Victoria & Albert Museum in London at the time of the 1977 Fabergé exhibition celebrating the Queen's Silver Jubilee, wrote the following tribute in the catalogue of the event: "Fabergé is almost the last expression of court art within the European tradition which brings with it a passionate conviction of the importance of craftsmanship and inventiveness of design, aligned to a celebration of the virtues of wit and fantasy applied to everyday objects, that still has a relevance to the design of today."

As a result of a happy sequence of events, two of the original design books collated by the jewelry workshops at Fabergé's in St. Petersburg have come to light; more specifically, they turn out to be Albert Holmström's books, recording, it seems, every jewel made from March 6, 1909, to March 20, 1915. Albert had taken control of the workshops in 1903 after the death of his father, August Wilhelm Holmström, who had previously run them. Further valuable information emerged as a result of conversations and correspondence with Ulla Tillander-Godenhielm of Helsinki, at the time of the splendid exhibition "Fabergé: Hofjuwelier der Zaren" in Munich.[1]

The record books, containing a total of 1,221 large pages, each measuring 16⅛ by 10¼ inches, crammed with drawings in pen or pencil, the great majority washed with watercolor, show in

Osvald K. Jurisons (1892–1980), in a photograph taken in Latvia in the early 1930s.

meticulous detail exactly how each individual design has been carried out by the jeweler and, where necessary, the chaser, lapidary, or enameler working at Fabergé's. On the right of each of the colored diagrams that follow one another down the page, a neatly handwritten description of the materials, quantities of stones needed, with exact weights, is set out, and in some of the early entries the prices in code are given in the far right margin of the page. The cost of any work carried out in connection with the specific object illustrated is also supplied.

It is entirely as a result of the single-mindedness of one man, a diamond-setter from August Holmström's workshop, Osvald K. Jurisons, that these books have become available to us today, some seventy-five years after Fabergé's was closed down. Jurisons' best friend in the firm was Julius Rappaport, the workmaster who controlled the silver workshop. It was Jurisons, then a young man of thirty-three, who had the imagination and vision to appreciate their potential interest to future generations and carry them with him from St. Petersburg to Latvia in 1925. His son and daughter have appreciated the fascination the books exert on today's collectors and have welcomed the research that has been carried out on them.

No mark existed in Russia for stamping platinum, and it is quite clear, as one turns the pages of these books, that many platinum jewels by Fabergé—and there are hundreds of them here—must have often changed hands anonymously with neither the seller nor the buyer recognizing the distinguished provenance involved—a situation that presumably must prevail to this day.

A careful examination of the books has provided a fascinating insight into a technical process that, it appears, has not up to now been either recognized or discussed. On page 158 we have an illustration of the second volume open to pages 594 and 595, dated August 27, 1914, which show a total of eight brooches from a numbered collection of twelve, slightly varied in design, in the form of frost flowers all to be set with rose diamonds with occasionally a brilliant in the center. On the right of each of these carefully expressed drawings is the written description, each one of which concludes with the three vital words, "silver, gold, platinized."

In an attempt to discover exactly what these words implied and

Carl Fabergé, with his son Eugène, photographed at Pully near Lausanne, Switzerland, in July 1920, two months before Carl's death.

not having on hand any of these frost flowers for examination, I selected another jewel illustrated in the books and thought to have been similarly mounted and sent it to the Assay office at Goldsmiths' Hall in London for analysis. This brooch, set with a large white topaz and made three years earlier, in September 1911, appears on page 97 next to the original design.

The report after testing was precise—the brooch had been made from an alloy of silver and gold (of about six carats) and then platinized. This practice was clearly quite common at the time, and the technique must have been regarded as both practical and economical. The assumption would formerly have been that this unmarked brooch, not heavy enough to be platinum, was made of white gold. There must be in existence quite a considerable number of jewels made in this way.

A number of the designs in these books are frankly a touch conventional, and the possibility that the firm may have carried out work for other houses (trade commissions) cannot be dismissed. There are, for example, many designs for diamond-set wristwatches that one does not easily associate with what one knows of Fabergé's work. The workshops were extensive, the craftsmen numerous, and Fabergé, in addition to being a consummate artist himself, was a wise and practical man with a business to run, who, one imagines, would not have been above generating extra income to help finance his more imaginative, complicated, and possibly speculative projects. However, some of the designs for wristwatches in these books are so original (pages 117 and 146), that the question of their having been made for the House of Fabergé or for the trade seems to remain in the balance, especially since the majority were mounted

The interior of Albert Holmström's office, about 1912. Left to right: Evgeny Vasilyevitch Zvershinsky, accountant and cashier; Oskar Woldemar Pihl, artistic assistant responsible for sorting sketches of jewelry and filing them in the archives; Alma Pihl, designer; Albert Holmström at his desk; and Alma Holmström-Zvershinskaya, designer. The record books that form the subject of this volume may well be among those shown on top of the desk.

in platinum and thus lack any stamped identification. We know for certain of one striking example of a Fabergé design being carried out by another firm, in this instance, Fedor Lorié of Moscow; it is illustrated on page 77, where the drawing and the brooch are shown together.

Among the many joys to be found in this vast collection of drawings are quite a number of jewels one has actually known and, in some cases, handled in their finished form. To demonstrate just how faithfully the jewelry workshops followed the designs they were given, a number of the photographs show actual jewels resting upon the pages with the painted drawings from which they were created.

Included also within the jeweler's domain are meticulously detailed designs for gem-set tortoiseshell fans (page 84), cigarette holders (page 161), and an evening bag, as well as, less surprisingly, hair combs and cuff links, which are, after all, jewelry. This cross-fertilization is characteristic of Fabergé's method of work, which involved employing whoever was the most appropriate craftsman for the job in hand: a stone carving of an animal or a bird requiring gold additions such as legs, feet, claws, beak, or a perch or cage would be sent to Michael Perchin's workshop or, after his death in 1903, to Henrik Wigström's to be finished off.

Page 213 of the first volume is devoted to simple drawings of pendant frames and brooches designed to accommodate likenesses of selected members of the Siamese royal family, painted in enamel on platinum or gold panels (page 91). An additional happy discovery in our books is the inclusion of examples of far more elaborately designed frames which today form part of the Royal Collection in Bangkok (pages 128 and 129). King Chulalongkorn of Siam was, for

August Holmström (1829–1903).

Albert Holmström (1876–1925).

Holmström's workshop in the Fabergé premises at 24 Bolshaya Morskaya Street in St. Petersburg. The two figures standing at the back of this photograph are Albert Holmström on the left and, on the right, his experienced workmaster, the master goldsmith Lauri Ryynänen. The photograph was taken in 1903 to celebrate the latter's twenty-fifth anniversary with the firm.

a number of years, an enthusiastic patron of the House of Fabergé. A vividly colored book, published in Thailand, entitled *Fabergé*, the name inscribed on the spine—no title page, date, or author being vouchsafed (although we are given a charming foreword by Her Majesty the Queen)—nevertheless offers much fascinating new material, including an amusing double stone figure of Tweedledum and Tweedledee, to which Henry Bainbridge had made an oblique reference in his biography of Fabergé.[2]

It is a gross error to suggest that Carl Fabergé ever for a moment relinquished his role as artistic director of the firm. Every piece had to pass the rigorous test of his personal scrutiny and judgment before it was allowed to be cased up, put on display, and offered for sale. An extraordinary paragraph in the Thai book runs, "Fabergé's main job was not so much on the actual manufacturing side as in organization and management. This may explain why no piece can be proved to have come from Fabergé's own hand. It could be said that Fabergé saw himself not as an artist in his own right but as the leader and coordinator of a body of outstanding artists and craftsmen." The reason Fabergé never signed any of the works that he may have wholly or partly designed was quite simply that he was indeed a designer all his adult life and not a working goldsmith at the bench, or a workmaster. Indeed a number of the designs signed in his hand are illustrated in this very book. To relegate him to a managerial role and to call him "not an artist in his own right" is to misunderstand and denigrate one of the most lively artists in the recorded history of the goldsmith's art. As he himself made clear in an interview he gave in 1914 at the age of sixty-eight, he was not a merchant—he was, he emphasized, an artist-jeweler.

The repeating columns of small, exquisitely painted sketches of jewels, the seemingly infinite procession of pendants, brooches, rings, necklaces, diadems, earrings, tiepins, and clasps is interrupted quite without warning by a life-size drawing of one of Fabergé's characteristic flower studies, a generous spray of forget-me-nots in a vase (page 108). Occupying most of page 106 in the second book, and dated May 12, 1912, the painting indicates exactly how the flower was to be carried out: the flower heads to be composed of turquoise petals, with rose-diamond centers supported on lightly engraved gold stems, leaves of nephrite, the whole spray casually placed in a rock-crystal vase, the mandatory receptacle for these studies, carved by the lapidary to give the impression of being nearly filled with water.

The very fact that a flower design should figure among those for jewels seems to demonstrate that, although the stems of these studies are sometimes physically stamped with the marks of the goldsmith, their nature is, in a sense, ambiguous, growing in some sort of no-man's-land or neutral soil between *objet de vitrine* and jewel. The particular example in our book certainly calls upon the skill of the jeweler to a greater extent than is the case with most of the flowers, and this presumably accounts for its appearing in notable isolation in this context.

There are pages devoted to drawings for brooches, badges, tiepins, and so on, destined for what is designated here as "His Imperial Majesty's Cabinet," incorporating imperial ciphers and monograms set beneath the Romanoff crown designed by Jeremie Pauzié. To celebrate the Tercentenary of Romanoff sovereignty in 1913, a variety of pendants, decorations, cuff links, and tiepins were specially prepared by Fabergé, many of them including an elaborately chased and gem-set version of Peter the Great's sable-trimmed *shapka* or cap of Monomach (pages 126 and 127). Henry Bainbridge, writing about jewelry commemorating State occasions, notes that "there were large numbers of brooches and pendants with Imperial emblem designs made for the Coronation of the Tsar Nicholas II. In 1913, to commemorate the Tercentenary of Romanoff rule, brooches of diamonds, stones of color and pearls, in the shape of the Imperial Crown and emblems—all different, of course—were made for presentation to each of the Grand Duchesses and ladies of the court. The designs for these were based on the original drawings which the Tsarina Alexandra Feodorovna herself prepared and sent to Fabergé for elaboration."[3]

Ample evidence is provided of the legendary dinner parties given by Dr. Emanuel Nobel, the Stockholm petrol tycoon (and nephew of Alfred Nobel of dynamite and prize fame), at which every lady present found, cunningly concealed in the place setting before her, an ice jewel, normally composed of rock crystal and diamonds, by Fabergé. Several pages of the design books are devoted to veritable flurries of frost flower brooches and pendants that take the form of icicles, naturalistically carved drops of rock crystal sometimes burnished, sometimes matt (page 134), to which cling a twinkling diamond-set gossamer webbing of "frost." There are even a couple of bracelets carried out in this decor. This winter theme is further reflected in many of the designs for the miniature Easter eggs so beloved of Russian ladies.

On page 371 of the second book, under the date July 24, 1913, there is a small, carefully finished watercolor drawing of a circular

К. ФАБЕРЖЕ

ПРИДВОРНЫЙ ЮВЕЛИРЪ.

С.-Петербургъ.
Москва. ✻ Кіевъ. ✻ Одесса.
Нижегородская Ярмарка.
Лондонъ.

C. FABERGÉ

JOAILLIER DE LA COUR.

St. Pétersbourg.
Moscou. ✻ Kiev. ✻ Odessa.
Foire de Nijny-Novgorod.
Londres.

LONDON, 48, DOVER STREET,
W.

SPRING, 1907.

Mr. Fabergé has the honour to inform you that he has sent from St. Petersburg a new choice. An opportunity to show you this he would esteem.

PLEASE TURN OVER

OBJECTS IN ENAMEL, GOLD, CHISELLED SILVER, SIBERIAN STONES, ETC.

BONBONNIERES, ANIMALS, CLOCKS, FLOWERS IN VASES, FRAMES, PAPER KNIVES, SEALS, PENHOLDERS, GUM BOTTLES, BELL PUSHES, MECHANICAL BELLS, CIGARETTE LIGHTERS, CIGARETTE BOXES, ASH TRAYS, PENCILS, ETC.

FANS, LORGNETTES, HANDLES FOR UMBRELLAS, PARASOLS, STICKS AND WHIPS, HAT PINS, MOTOR PINS, TOILET BOXES, NOTE BOOKS, SMELLING SALT BOTTLES.

CIGARETTE CASES, MATCH BOXES, CIGARETTE HOLDERS (AND CASES FOR SAME), CARD CASES, ETC.

LINKS, BUTTONS, BUCKLES, CLASPS, FLOWER BROOCHES, LOCKETS, PENDANTS, NECKLACES, DIADEMS, TIE PINS, BROOCHES, BRACELETS, MUFF CHAINS, EASTER EGGS, ETC.

LARGE BOWLS (RUSSIAN STYLE) IN BEATEN SILVER AND IN ENAMEL.

A good idea of the normal stock-in-trade offered by the firm in the spring of 1907 is given on the card sent out from Fabergé's London branch, then at 48 Dover Street. These two photographs show the front and back views of the card. It is possible that more ordinary jewels were produced for home consumption in the same way that the House manufactured traditional silver objects in Moscow.

brooch (page 142) to be carried out by the setter in colored gemstones in mosaic technique, with surrounding borders composed of half pearls and enamel. This provided the germ for what was to become the Mosaic Egg, presented in 1914 to Alexandra Feodorovna by the Tsar, and now in the collection of Her Majesty Queen Elizabeth II (page 143). This beautiful object, as we now know, thanks to the careful research of Ulla Tillander-Godenhielm and Christina Ehrnrooth in Helsinki, was designed in the workshops of August Holmström by his granddaughter Alma Theresia Pihl (page 133), the daughter of the Fabergé workmaster Knut Oscar Pihl and Fanny Florentina Holmström. She had already designed the Winter Egg, one of Fabergé's most ravishing creations, for presentation to the Tsarina the previous year, 1913. At the time of writing, the whereabouts of this egg are, alas, in doubt. The catalogue of the memorable exhibition "Carl Fabergé and His Contemporaries," held in Helsinki in 1980,[4] records that Alma Pihl was employed by her uncle, Albert Holmström, the son of August, who ran the workshop after his father's death in 1903. We learn that she "was first employed by her uncle to draw ornaments and other precious articles for the archives. . . . Alma Pihl was exceptionally talented. She was equal to the most demanding challenges . . . she quickly taught herself to calculate how much material and what precious stones would be needed for any particular article so that she could reckon its cost before it was made. After her marriage in 1912 she was allowed to continue as a designer with Holmström, since she wasn't much good in the kitchen." Our two books are presumably part of what is referred to in the catalogue as "the archives," and it seems clear from the clue of this gem-mosaic alone that they formed an integral part of Holmström's workshops.[5] On December 30, 1986, Miss Tillander (as she is professionally known) wrote to me:

> The Holmström sketch books are a thrilling discovery. I talked to my old friend Miss Pihl, here in Helsinki, who for years literally sat at the side of her Aunt Alma Klee, listening to her stories from the workshop of uncle Albert's. She says having read your article in the Munich catalogue, "The text of the sketch books seems to be in Alma's handwriting. Her job in 1909 and in 1910 at Holmström's was to sketch the ready-made pieces of the workshop into the books. In 1911 she got a chance to do designs of her own. Alma remembered very vividly the day there was an order from the Nobel Office, very urgently to make up forty small pieces, preferably brooches, in a *new* design. The pieces were not to be valuable, the material, such that if the pieces were broken up, there would be no mentionable value to them. These pieces were not to be understood as bribes. Alma got her chance to make the designs to this order. As ice crystals were very frequent on the draughty window panes in those days, she suddenly got her inspiration from those. This is how the Nobel snowflakes came about." The year was 1911 or 1912.

Following a visit to London, where she was able to study the books in some detail, Miss Tillander writes on February 4, 1987, as follows:

> Alma's handwriting and sketches end December *1911*. Somebody else took over this mechanic [*sic*] work of copying pieces into the books. Six different models of snowflake brooches were pictured in the books early in the year 1912. If the number on the side of each piece 6 (7) for the fourth model means that altogether thirty-seven brooches were made, the above story told by Miss Pihl seems to be correct.
>
> After the first snowflake brooches comes an absolute mass production based on the same idea and I noted with interest how the idea developed,

finally to become very stereotyped and to be a boring chore for the poor designer.

As far as the sketch-books and their purpose goes I noted . . . that Holmström's had the same system as our firm still had a few years back, in the glorious past when one could afford to have a big staff.

A piece made at our workshop was submitted to the following "paper work".

1. designer's sketch

2. entered into production book and given a production number

3. entered into a new book, the inventory book and scratched with the inventory number. Drawing of piece in the inventory book all details of piece noted

4. parallel to this a "stock card" was made with all the details of the piece and a good sketch of the piece

5. a so called sketch book was compiled, chronologically the piece was nicely sketched, a few details of the piece were added. This book was compiled more or less to be of service to the retail shop and in order to plan the production.

It seems to me that the Holmström sketch books are of category 5.

Most of the designs of these books are of great distinction and in many cases stylistically ahead of their time. This, remembering the inventiveness of Fabergé's *objets de vertu*, is hardly surprising. That every one of the drawings is precisely dated is of inestimable value to the historian. For example, some of the brooch designs (pages 144 and 145) look as though they were conceived and created in the late 1920s in Paris, whereas in fact they date from 1913. It is not difficult to understand why, therefore, the Cartiers always retained a healthy respect for the creative energy of the House of Fabergé, as the late Hans Nadelhoffer has reminded us in his splendid book dedicated to that firm, *Cartier: Jewelers Extraordinary*. One of his early chapters is frankly entitled "Under the Spell of Fabergé." On the other hand, it is quite clear that more ordinary and even banal jewels were produced for home consumption, rather in the way that a great number of traditional silver objects were manufactured in the Moscow house for the same clientele.

Although the great bulk of the material contained in these record books is anonymous, there are some exceptions. The names or initials of particular members of the firm presumably responsible, in one way or another, for many of the examples illustrated for just over a fortnight in December 1913, and for part of the following year, appear above the descriptions of these objects. The name recurring most frequently at these particular times, which date from December 5–23, 1913, and later from June 19 to November 27, 1914, is that of Ivan Antony, a Balt and one of the first managers of the Odessa branch of the firm, which had opened in 1890. Judging by the frequent appearance of his signature, Ivan Antony seems to have been virtually in charge of the studios during these periods. Antony has not hitherto been assessed nor even identified as a designer, and we still cannot pronounce with any certainty upon his main function in the business, though it does seem to have been, in essence, managerial.

The mystery surrounding his role is further compounded by the discovery that the several entries under the name Antony appearing during that first fortnight in December 1913 are prefixed not by the initial I for Ivan, as is the case during the subsequent five-month period dating from June 1914, but by the initial G or sometimes by no initial at all. Almost identical frost flowers, one signed with the name G. Antony and dated December 19, 1913, and no fewer than twelve others with the name I. Antony and dated August 27, 1914, are certainly from the same hand, namely that, we now know, of Alma Pihl, who actually designed them. Any imagined father-and-son theory seems highly unconvincing here, especially in view of the following evidence. The majority of the names (four in number) in this shorter period are given this same initial G, which may stand for any Christian name, but also for the Russian title *Gospodin* or Mister.

The name K. Gust, presumably short for Karl Gustavovitch Fabergé, appears in this early period, but he, after all, was the governor and would in all probability not be set down in the same form as the others, just as Ev. Karl and Ag. Karl, which also figure at this same time, must stand for Eugène Karlovitch Fabergé and Agathon Karlovitch Fabergé, Carl's eldest son and younger brother, respectively.

Nothing being known of any books from before 1909, this fortnight appears to be the very first time names of individuals were set down at all, and the preferred style to be employed had evidently not yet been finally settled. In addition to the Russian initials *КР* and *ВП* (translating as K.R. and V.P.), the names G. Antony, G. Gurié, and G. Kazak are found (referred to in the 1914 period as, respectively, Ivan Antony, M. Gurié, and A. Kazak), as well as that of G. Piggott, who would have been entitled to his G. on both counts since his name was George. He was a Moscow Englishman recorded as an early manager of the Odessa branch.

The most distinguished of the personalities, so vividly brought to life in the later section of the books covering five months of 1914, is that of the master himself: the initials, in Cyrillic characters,

Photographs of ladies at court formally dressed and appropriately bejeweled.

standing for Karl Gustavovitch Fabergé, appear above eighteen jewel designs that must surely have been of his own inspiration. Three others appear beneath the signature E. Fabergé, and one other with the initials E.K.F., all expressed in Cyrillic. They are those of Carl's son Eugène (the initials standing for Eugène Karlovitch Fabergé), whose main function, as he explained during the course of many conversations with the author of this text, was designing. Bainbridge confirms this cooperation between father and son: "Eugène devoted himself almost entirely to designing, thus following in the tradition of his uncle Agathon. Quiet and unassuming, he worked behind the partition in the shop, in collaboration with his father, on initial ideas."[6]

The other most significant name or initials to appear (eight times) during this brief and not necessarily typical span of five months was that of Fabergé's chief designer, François Birbaum. It should perhaps be pointed out here that these few months of what might be called the nomenclature now strike us as being entirely arbitrary in the face of the earlier years of complete anonymity. Some sort of policy decision must have been taken at this point: could it have been Ivan Antony's on being given a new, possibly administrative, responsibility? We shall probably never know.

One thing is certain, however: seemingly random cross sections of this nature cannot be taken as reliable guides to the composition of the design studios over a period of a generation. Neither are we entitled to reject out-of-hand the possibility that the signatures merely point to some administrative responsibility for the project currently under way—after all, we do not even know for certain from whose hand or hands all the drawings derive. To judge by the discernibly varied techniques employed, it would seem that a group of different artists was involved. Eugène has stated that both he and his genial brother Alexander spent much of their time creating and carefully executing just such designs.

The name or initials of Paul Blomerius, referred to by Bainbridge as of Swedish extraction, extremely international in outlook and known as the live wire at Fabergé's, but with never a hint of his being a designer, appears, either in full (once) or with initials P.B. or P.P.B., above fourteen designs. The other names, not previously mentioned, which are set down are I. Akvam and V. Pugolovki, in addition to the initials F.B. and N.R. Unfortunately we know nothing of these men or women.

Pressing inquiries in Russia over forty years ago had seemed to preclude the possibility of material of this nature ever turning up and becoming available for study. Research into this particular area was not encouraged at that time since objects of unashamed luxury epitomized precisely that which was anathema to the young socialist republic—they were scornfully rejected as toys for the rich, which they unarguably were and, happily, continue to be. Things have taken a turn for the better of late, at least in this regard, and Marina Lopato of the Hermitage, the most recent of a small band of scholars, has done valuable work in this documentary field, as evidenced in her article in the January 1984 issue of *Apollo* magazine.[7]

A third volume containing Fabergé designs, a very exalted scrapbook not connected with the two books we have been discussing (although acquired by the author at the same time), is packed with original drawings and painted designs pasted cheek by jowl on each of its fifty-five pages. These are true designs, not pictorial records. These working drawings and paintings on card, which may be compared to engineers' "jigs," were consulted and handled by the craftsmen at the bench at every stage as the work proceeded. I have included a small number of the drawings from this third book, since they were understandably deemed worthy of rescue by the redoubtable Osvald Jurisons along with the bound records we have been discussing. Two elegant drawings of the same subject (pages 10 and 11) depict a particularly romantic conception: it is composed of a row of cyclamen flowers and leaves to be expressed in brilliant and rose diamonds mounted in silver and gold. It was designed to be worn either as a diadem fitted on a prepared mount or as a flexible necklace. The original jewel has been found and was included in the 1986–87 exhibition in Munich. Finally, a working drawing for the model of the royal yacht *Standart* is shown from three different angles with a suggestion as to how it was to be accommodated within the rock-crystal shell of an Easter egg (page 166). This is the preparatory design for what is now referred to as the *Standart* Egg of 1909, one of the imperial eggs in the permanent collection of the Armory Museum in the Kremlin in Moscow (page 167). When confronted by the finished composition, this beautifully made nineteeth-century miniature steamer afloat on its aquamarine sea, imprisoned within an equally beautifully made Renaissance-revival oviform casket based on a design by the sixteenth-century goldsmith Jürg Ruel, really does strike a distinctly eccentric note.

Henry Bainbridge, in his invaluable book *Peter Carl Fabergé*, writes of the well-known and very similar Easter egg, also in the Armory and dated 1891, containing a comparable model of the cruiser *Pamiat Azova* made by August Holmström, "exact in every detail of guns, chains, anchor and rigging, in which Nicholas II when heir to the throne made his voyage around the world."[8] Our *Standart* drawing comes from the same studio, not from the hand of August Holmström, who had died six years earlier, but, in all probability, from that of his son Albert who, in Bainbridge's words, "continued in the fine tradition of his father." Convincing evidence of that fine tradition is happily preserved in these two books of Fabergé revelations.

The transmitting of pleasure was the aim of the designers working for Fabergé, and these recently discovered record books document for us, with elegance and precision, the proof of their success.

Thomas Traherne, born in or about 1637, the son of a Hereford shoemaker and later to become a parish priest, composed during a short life his wonderful *Poems of Felicity*. One of these, "Wonder," seems to describe exactly, if anachronistically, two centuries before Fabergé's time, the breathtaking wonder of coming across a group of tempting twinkling treasures by Karl Gustavovitch:

Rich Diamond and Pearl and Gold
In evry Place was seen;
Rare Splendors, Yellow, Blew, Red, White and Green,
Mine Eys did evry where behold,
Great Wonders clothd with Glory did appear,
Amazement was my Bliss.

Fabergé: Lost and Found

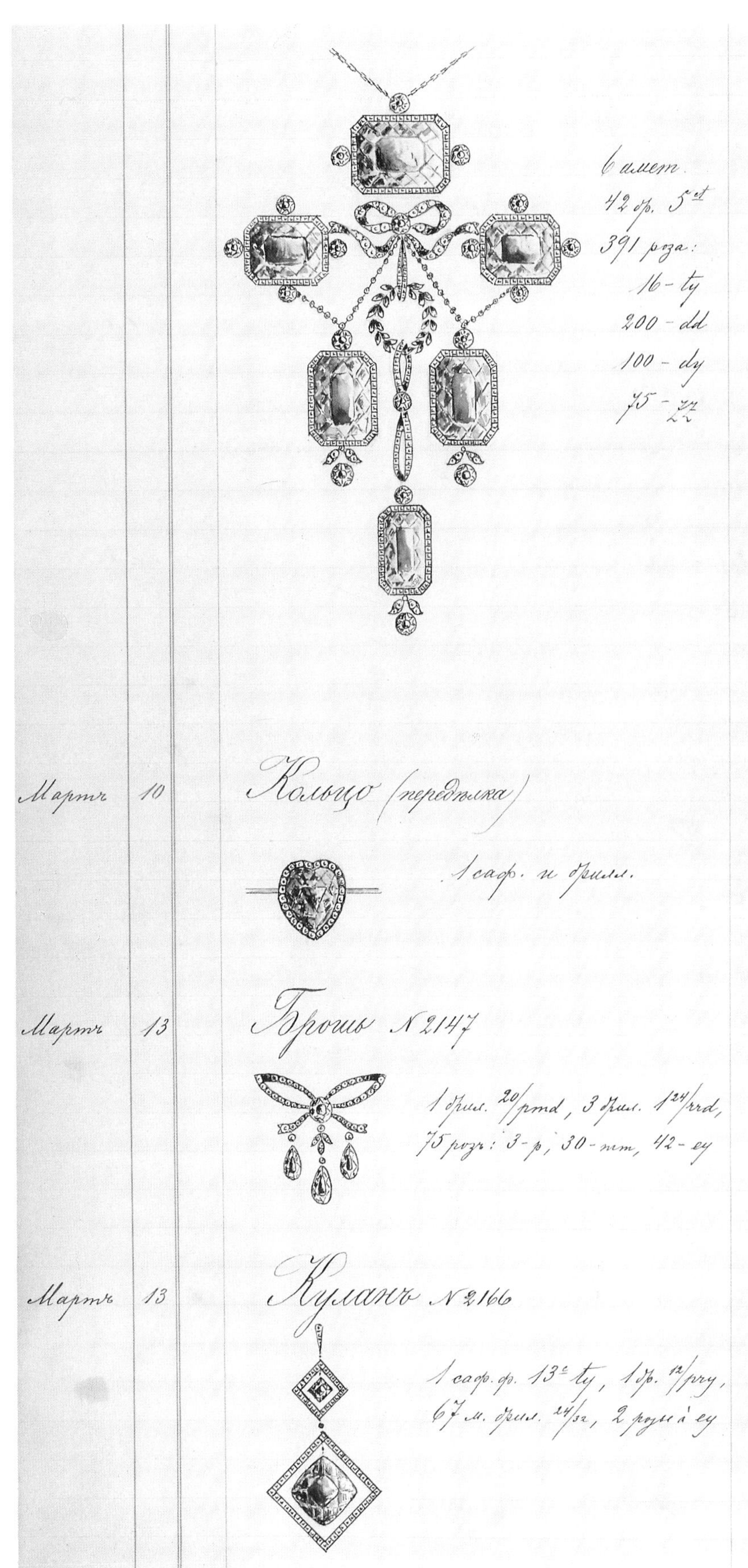

An elaborate amethyst and diamond pendant with 42 brilliant and 391 rose diamonds, a sapphire and diamond ring, a diamond brooch, and a sapphire and diamond pendant. Dated March 10–23, 1909.

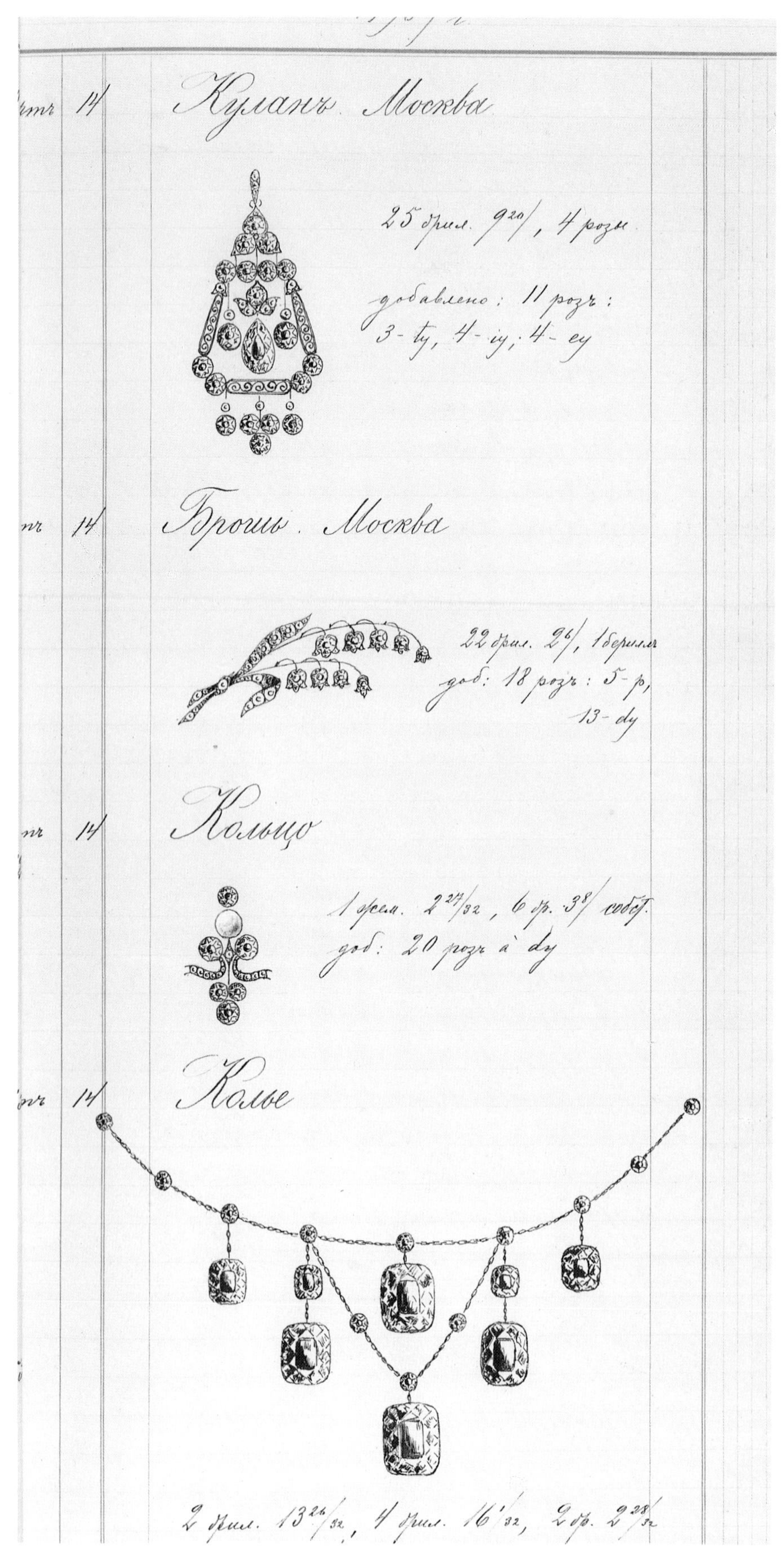

From top: diamond pendant, floral brooch, a pearl and diamond ring, and a diamond necklet. Dated March 14, 1909.

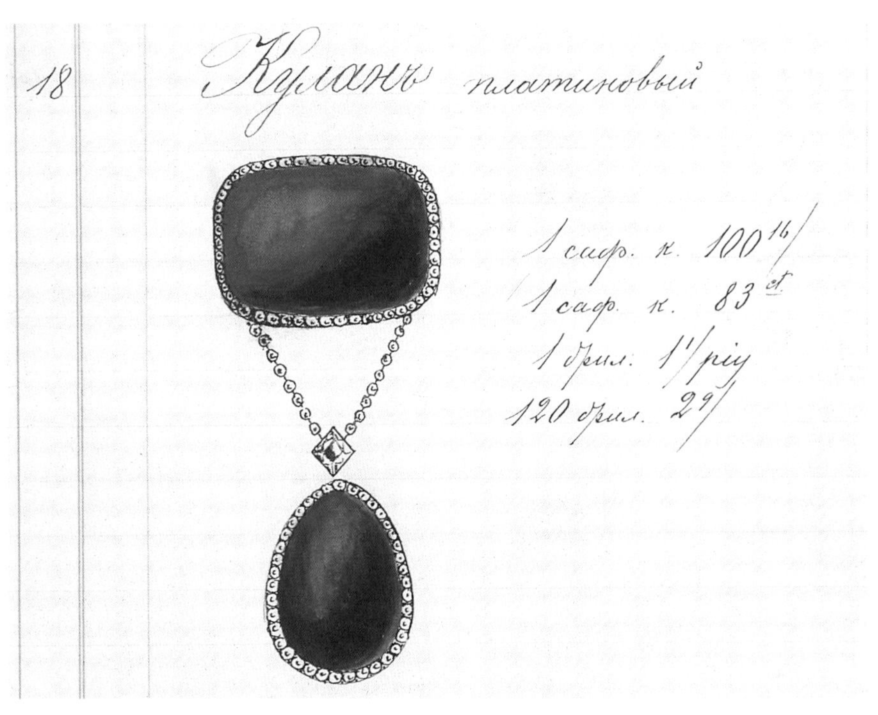

ABOVE:

A very large cabochon sapphire pendant, one stone weighing just over one hundred carats, the other eighty-three carats, set in platinum with brilliant diamonds. Designed for the Moscow House. Dated March 18, 1909.

RIGHT:

Pendant composed of brilliant diamonds both white and of champagne color and rose diamonds, designed as a vase of flowers with foliage. Designed for the Moscow House. Dated April 10, 1909.

OPPOSITE:

From the top: small gold elephant pendant set with tiny emerald eyes, the howdah with square-cut rubies and diamonds; one of a pair of large single-stone brilliant diamond earrings; a cabochon ruby ring mounted in gold; and a scrolling and floral diadem set with brilliant and rose diamonds and nine oriental drop pearls. Dated April 25–30, 1909.

…рѣля 25 **Слонъ** кп

50 руб. □ 19/32
обр. 14 руб. 6/32
36 руб. 13/32
52 брил. 22/
4 розы à ср
2 изумруда

…рѣля 25 **Серьги** tr

2 брил. 21 23/32

…рѣля 29 **Кольцо** te

1 руб. к. 9 11/32

…рѣля 30 **Diadема № 2160** ann

9 жем. 32 15/32
91 брил. 4 ct.
1387 розъ: 98 - iy
600 - dy
689 - ed

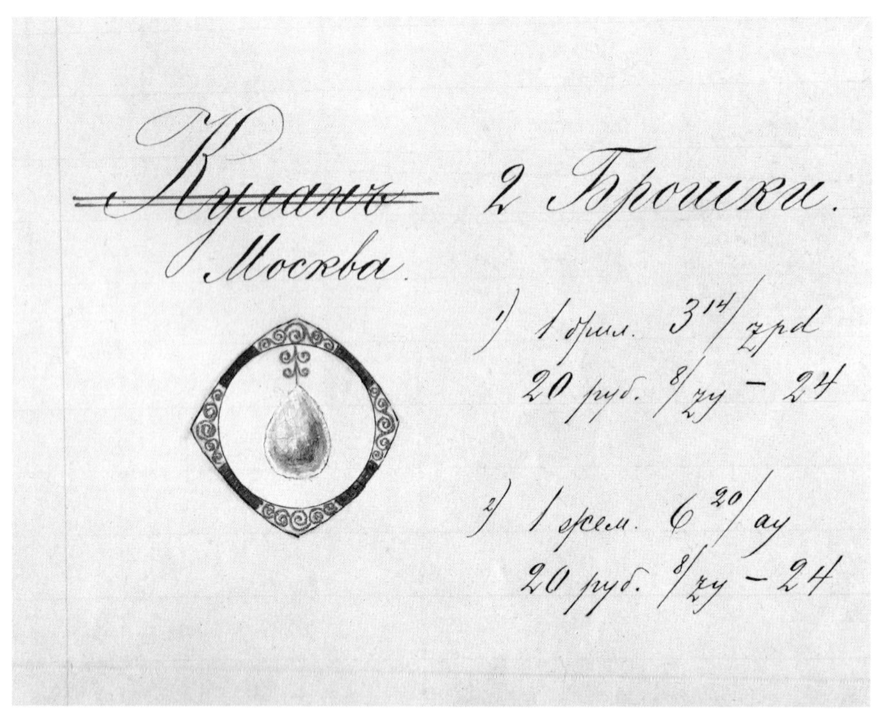

ABOVE:

Originally conceived as a pendant but subsequently to become two brooches, one with a drop pearl, the other with a drop diamond, each framed in a curved, four-sided scrolling mount set with calibré *rubies. Dated May 5, 1909.*

LEFT:

The actual brooch based on the design above, with a large diamond drop hanging freely from a scrolling gold frame set with calibré *rubies. Height 1³⁄₁₆″ (3 cm). Courtesy Albion Art, London, and Hakata, Japan.*

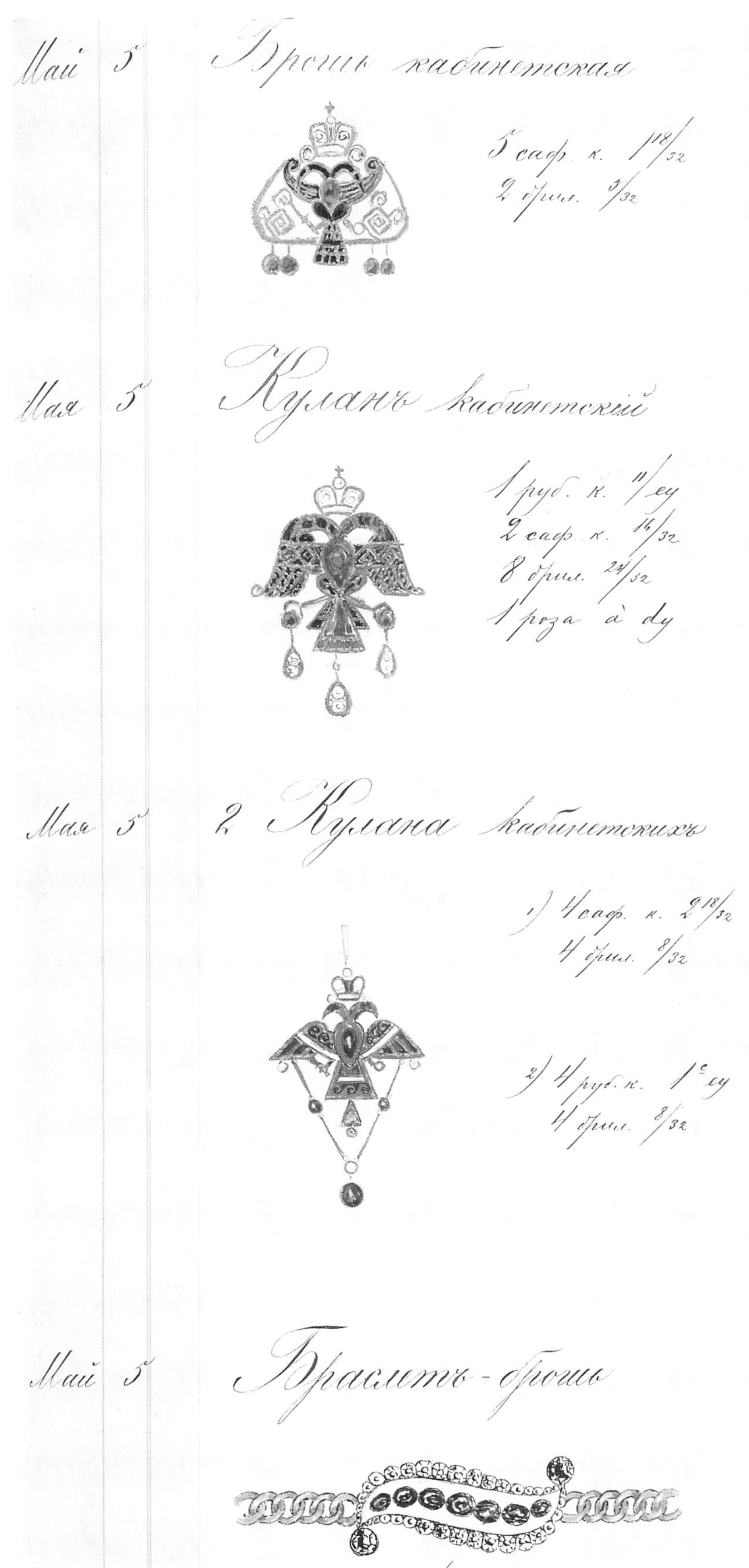

RIGHT:

From the top: three gold pendants designed as stylized Romanoff double-headed eagles, enameled and set with diamonds, sapphires, and a ruby, each with the Imperial Crown set with diamonds; a sapphire and diamond gold bracelet that converts into a brooch. Dated May 5, 1909.

OVERLEAF:

An open view of the first design book showing jewels made for the Private Cabinet, including two bracelets, three tiepins, and three cuff links incorporating the Imperial Crown, designed by Jeremie Pauzié, and the Romanoff double-headed eagle. To be enameled and set with rubies, sapphires, and diamonds. Dated May 5, 1909.

Мая 5 — 6 Браслетовъ кабин.
1) 2 саф. 15/32, 3 розы à тч
2) 2 саф. к. 13/32, 3 розы à тч
3) 2 саф. к. 15/32; 3 розы à тч
4) 2 руб. к. 13/32; 3 розы à тч
5) 2 руб. spin; 3 розы à іу
6) 2 руб. spin; 3 розы à іу

Мая 5 — 2 Браслета кабинетскихъ
1) 3 саф. к. 28/32; 92 розы à zp
2) 3 руб. к. 27/32; 95 розъ à zp

Мая 5 — 2 Булавки кабин.
1) 1 брил. 15/32
2) 1 брил. 15/32

Мая 5 — 2 Булавки кабин.
1) 1 брил. 16/32
2) 1 брил. 16/32

1909 г. Кредитъ

…ая	5	6 Булавокъ	
		1) 1 саф. к. 9/32, 4 брил. 7/32	22 —
		2) 1 саф. к. 9/32, 4 бр. 7/32	22 —
		3) 1 саф. к. 9/32; 4 бр. 7/32	22 —
		4) 1 руб. к. 10/32; 4 бр. 7/32	22 —
		5) 1 руб. к. 10/32; 4 бр. 7/32	22 —
		6) 1 руб. к. 10/32; 4 бр. 7/32	22 —
…ая	5	6 паръ запонокъ	
		1) 4 саф. ф. 6/32	32 —
		2) " " "	32 —
		3) " " "	32 —
		4) " " "	32 —
		5) " " "	32 —
		6) " " "	32 —
…Мая	5	6 паръ запонокъ	
		1)	30 —
		2)	30 —
		1) 6 брил. 5/32 3)	30 —
		14 розъ à ¼ 4)	30 —
		5)	30 —
		Во всѣхъ остальныхъ тоже 6)	30 —
…ая	5	6 паръ запонокъ	
		1) 2 саф. ф. 14/32 93 розы à ¼	45 —
		2) 2 саф. к. 15/32 77 розъ à ¼	45 —
		3) 2 саф. к. 15/32; 93 розы à ¼	45 —
		4) 2 руб. к. 10/32; 88 розъ à ¼	45 —
		5) 2 руб. грн. 12/32; 77 розъ à ¼	45 —
		6) 2 руб. ф. 10/32; 89 розъ à ¼	45 —

6 Колье de chien

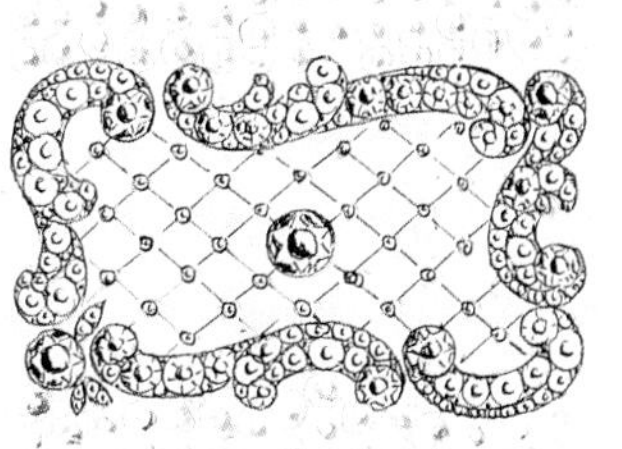

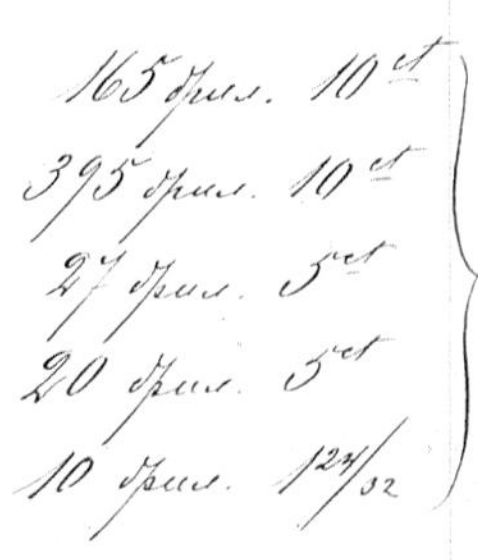

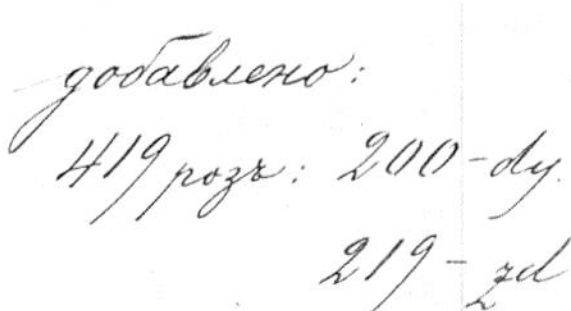

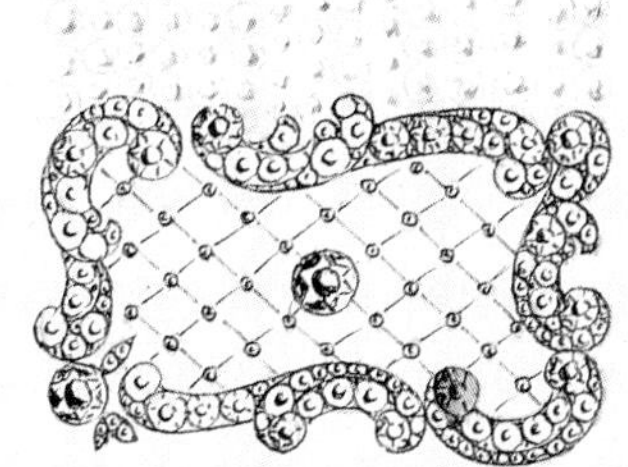

An elaborate dog collar composed of fifteen rows of pearls and a client's own brilliant and rose diamonds set in scrolling panels. Dated June 6, 1909.

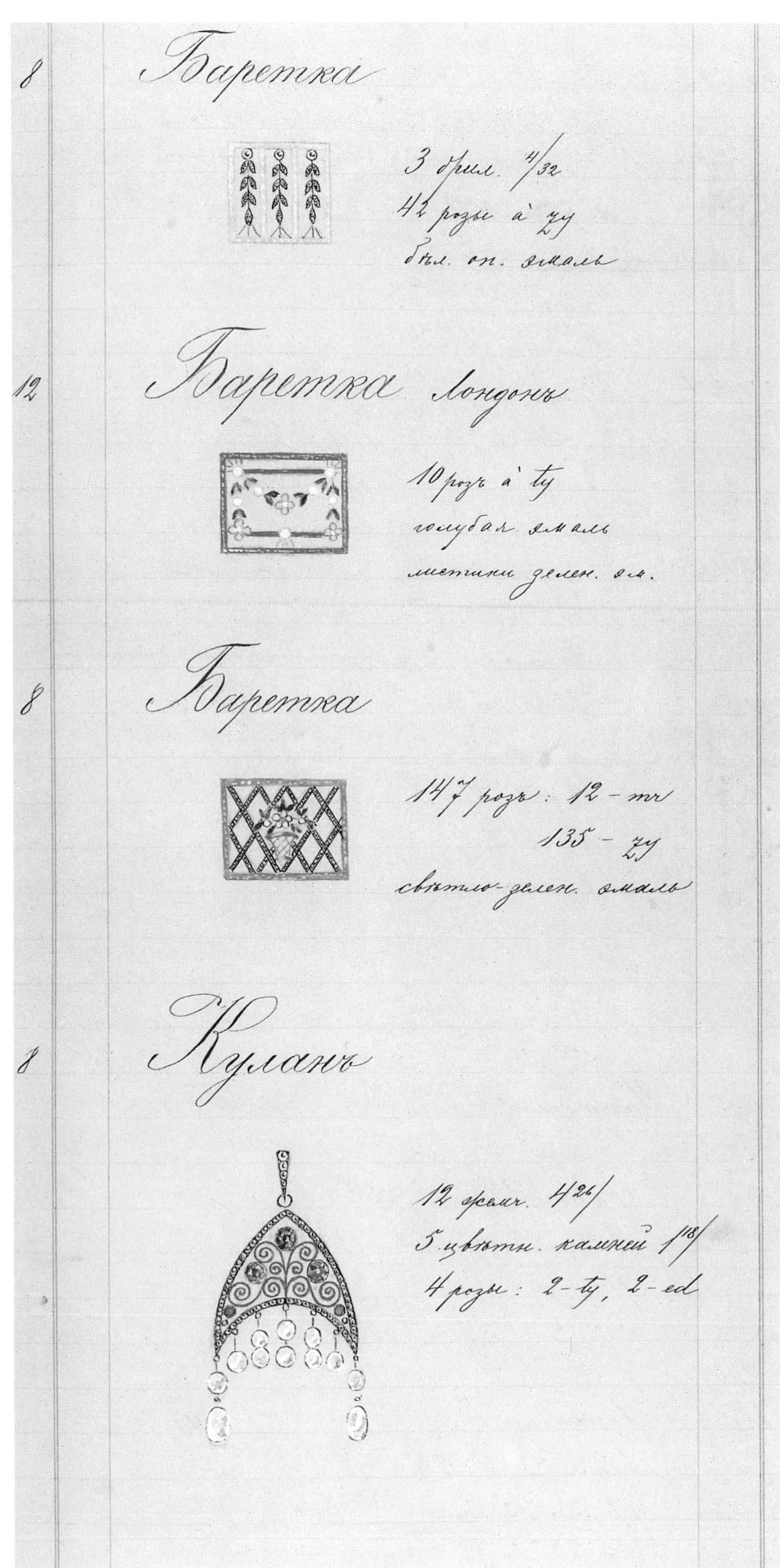

From the top: three designs for small gold hair slides to be carried out in diamonds, pearls, and enamels; a diamond-set pendant in the form of a kokoshnik *with gold scrolling, rubies and emeralds, and pearl drops. Dated June 8 and 12, 1909.*

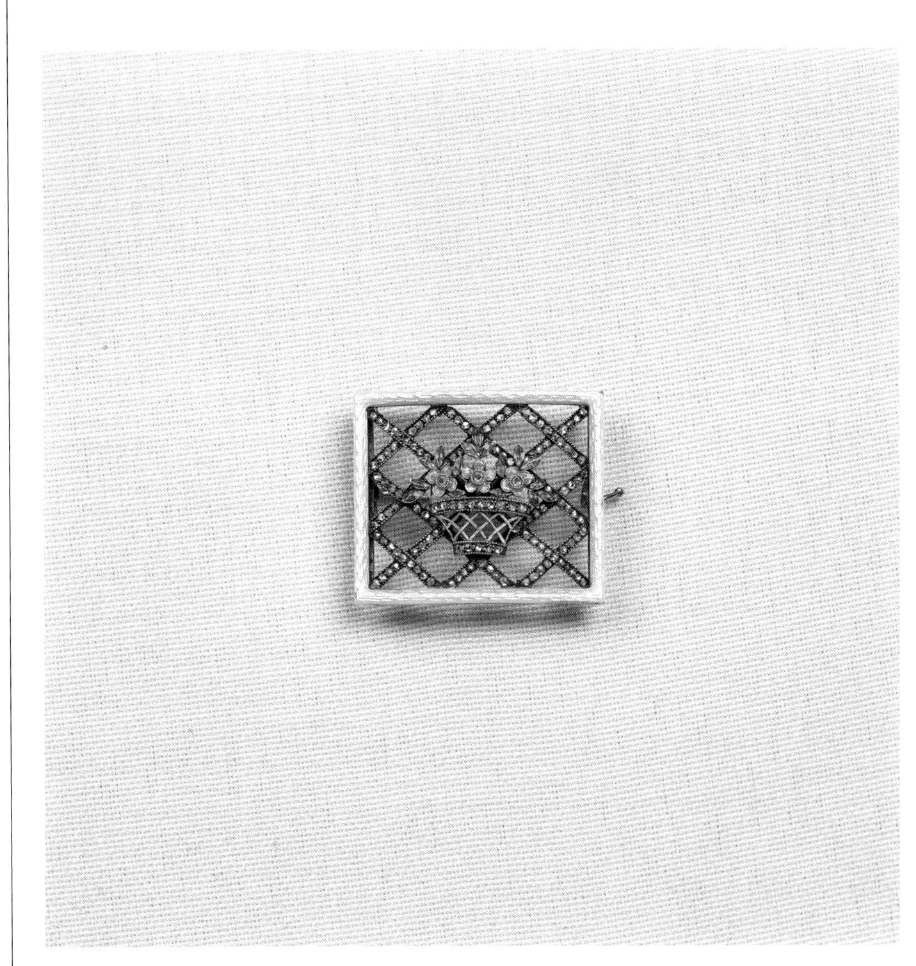

A hair slide deriving from the drawing in the center of the photograph shown opposite. Width 1 1/16″ (2.7 cm). A la Vieille Russie, New York.

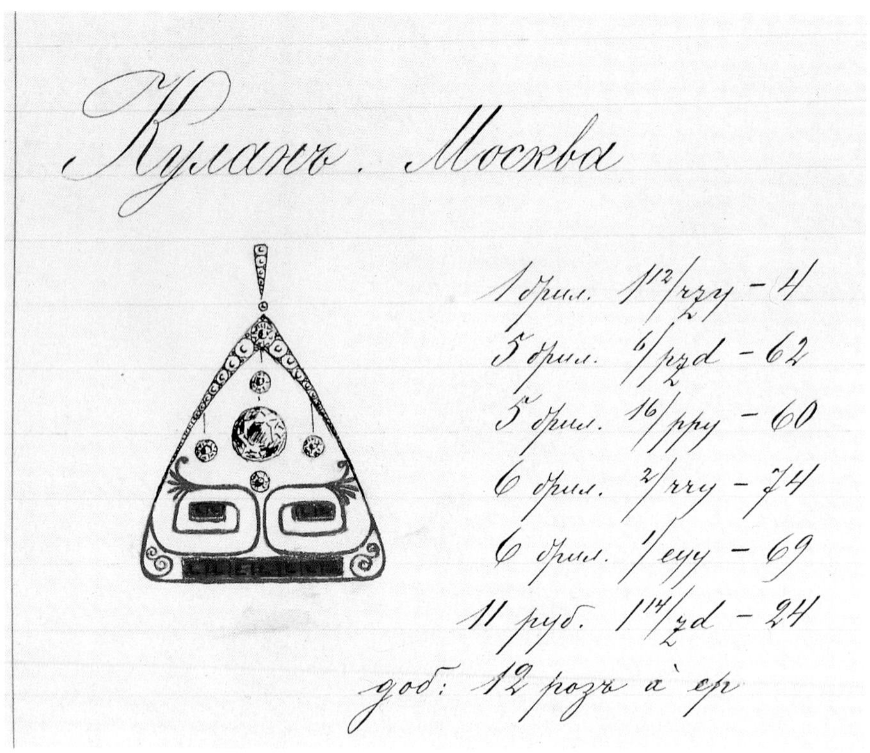

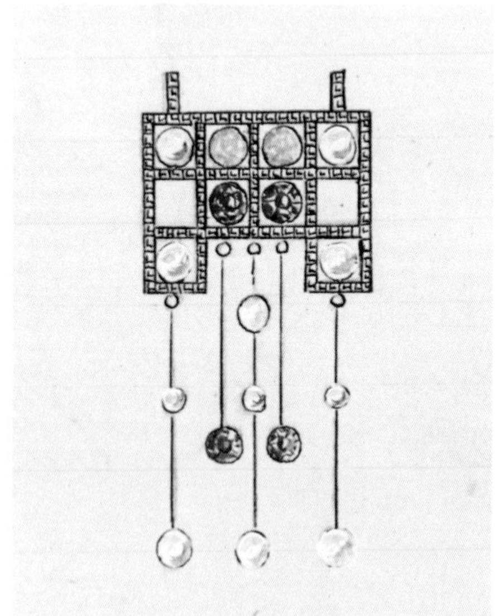

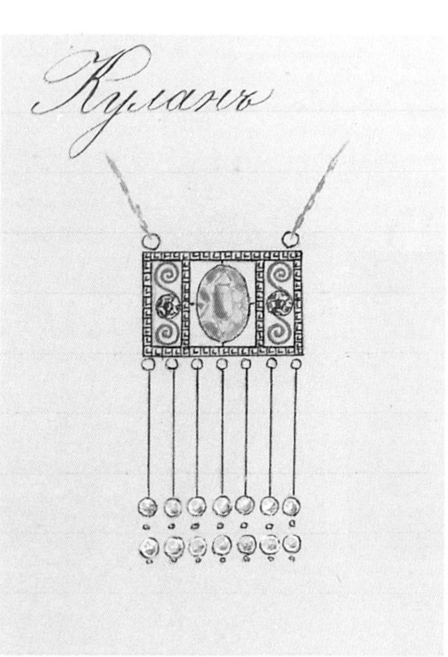

ABOVE:

A gold pendant of triangular form set with brilliant and rose diamonds and calibré rubies. Dated May 12, 1909.

LEFT:

Two pendants of geometric design composed of colored sapphires, pearls, and diamonds. Dated June 8, 1909.

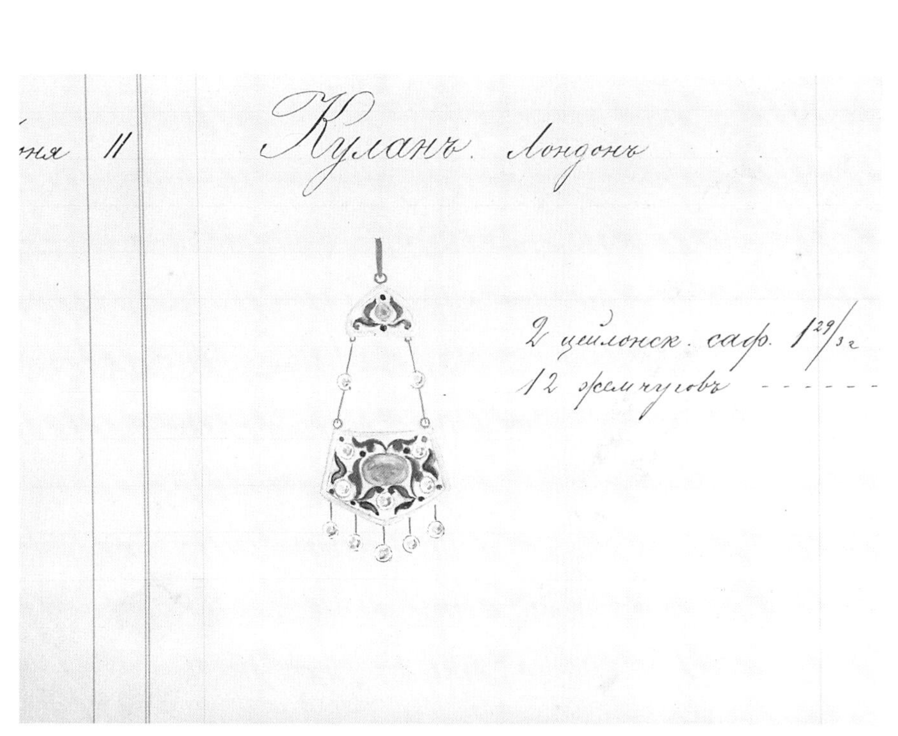

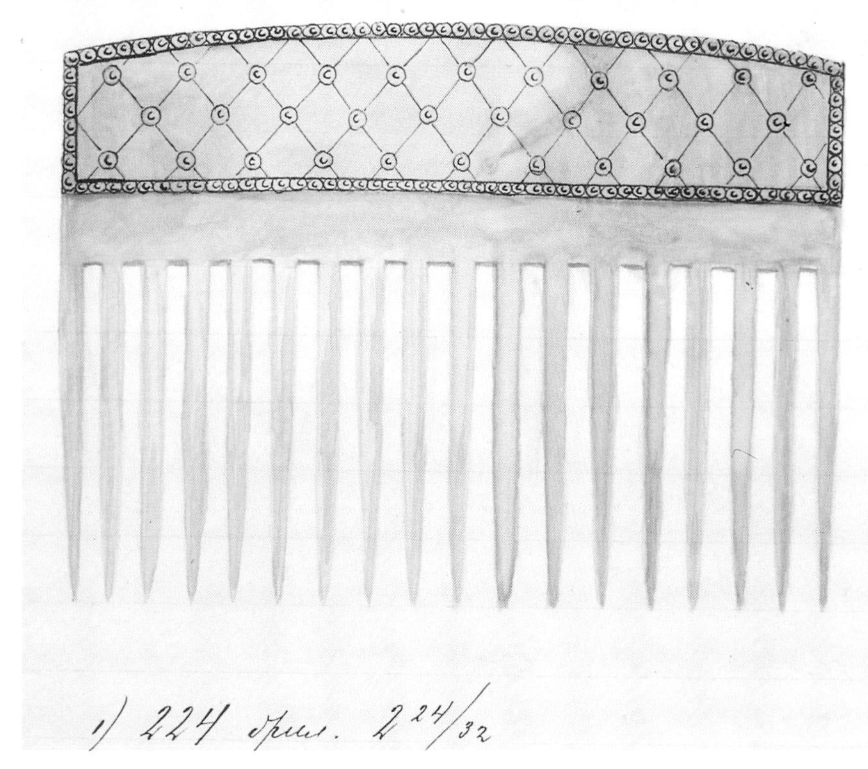

ABOVE:

An enameled pendant set with colored sapphires and pearls—a design very much in the spirit of the French designer Lucien Falize. Dated June 11, 1909.

RIGHT:

A tortoiseshell hair comb set with brilliant diamonds. Dated June 18, 1909.

From top: two pendants formed as baskets of flowers and another, in the center, as a flowering tree growing in a tub. All enameled and set with diamonds, blue and yellow sapphires, and pearls. Dated June 20, 1909. The central pendant appears to have provided the inspiration for the brooch shown in the photograph opposite and, eventually, the Imperial Easter egg known as the Orange Tree Egg illustrated on *page 2.*

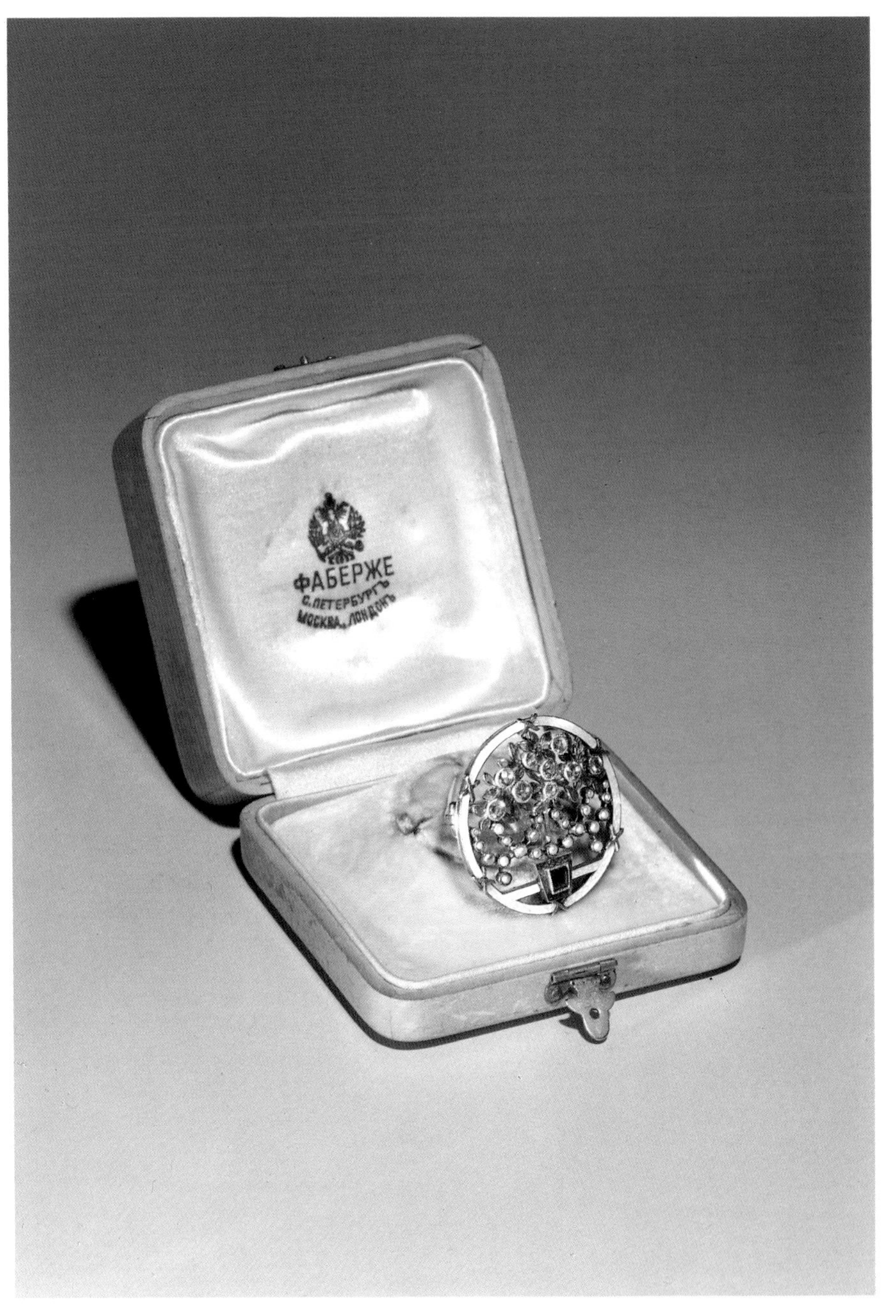

The circular brooch enameled translucent emerald with an opalescent oyster border and set with pearls, citrine, and a ruby. Stamped with the initials of Albert Holmström and the kokoshnik *in use from 1908 to 1917. Diameter 1 1/16" (2.7 cm). Wartski, London.*

LEFT:

One of the pendants for the Imperial Cabinet; three examples of this design were made in sapphires and diamonds, incorporating the crowned monogram of the Tsarina Alexandra Feodorovna. Dated July 8, 1909.

OPPOSITE:

A necklace composed of twelve chrysoprase carved cabochon alternating with brilliant and rose diamond motifs in the form of laurel wreaths and arrows. Dated June 8, 1909.

12 хризопр. à rd
36 брил. 29/32
953 розы : 75-dy
878 - zd

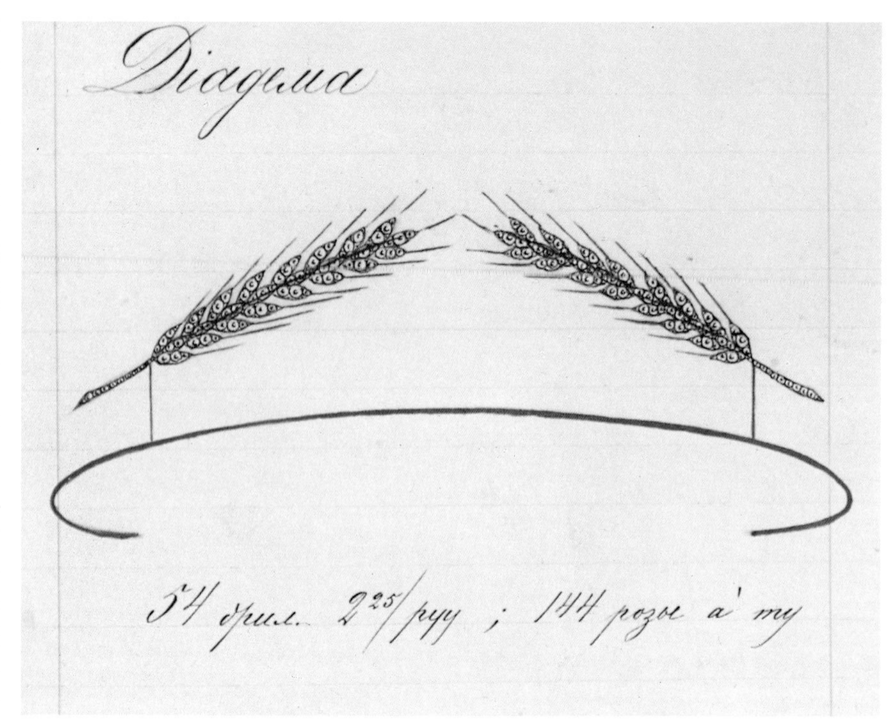

A diadem composed of two ears of wheat, set with brilliant and rose diamonds. Dated July 20, 1909.

Кулонъ кабинетский

1 брил. 10/32
3 брил. 7/32
27 сф. ф. 2 5/32
72 розы à md

Pendant for the Imperial Cabinet set with sapphires and diamonds, designed as the crowned monogram of the Dowager Empress Marie Feodorovna. The design specifies a platinum chain and a setting with ten sapphires. Dated July 29, 1909.

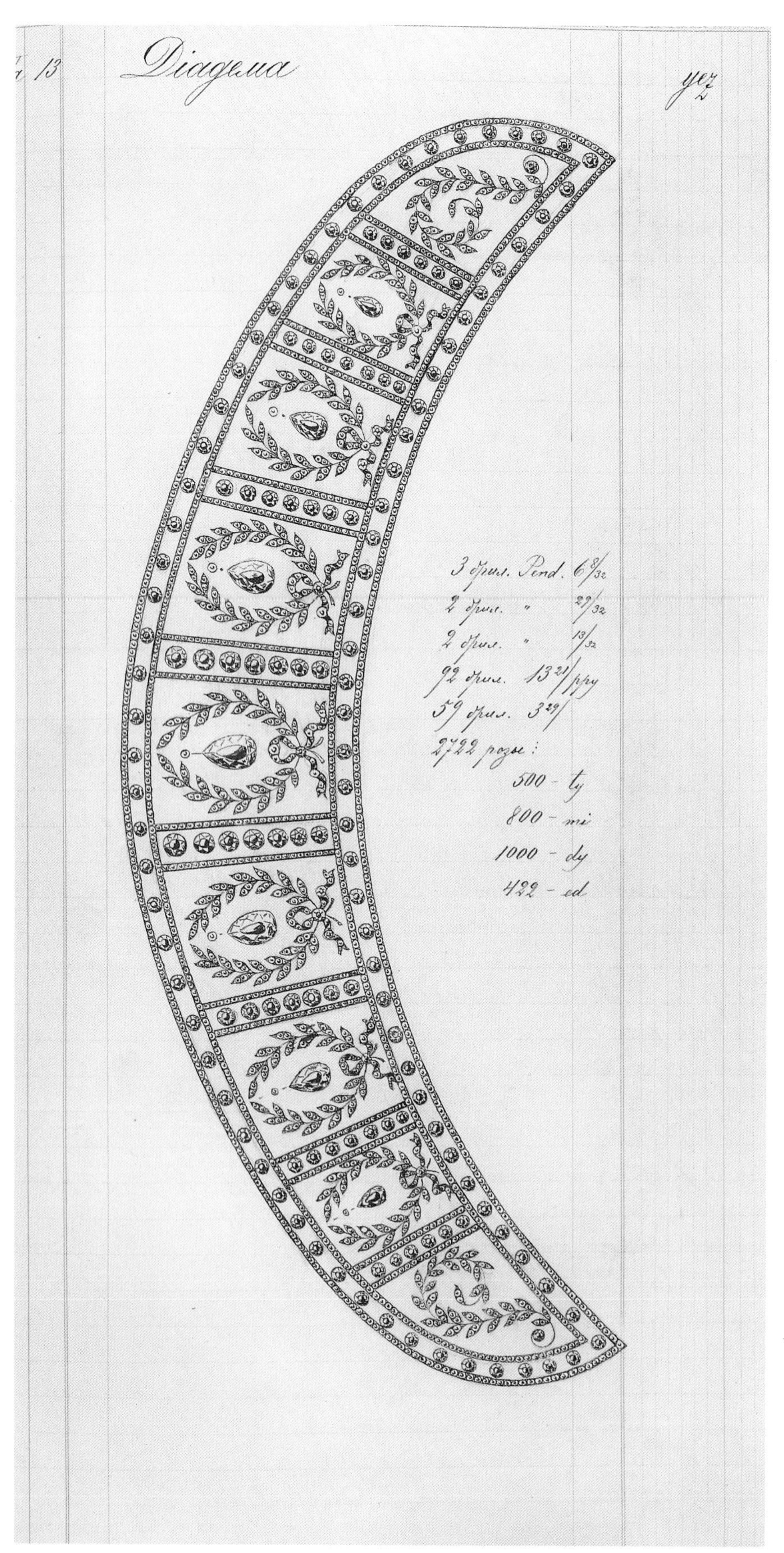

A diadem set with brilliant and rose diamonds divided into panels with laurel wreaths knotted with ribbon, each enclosing a pendant drop diamond. Dated August 13, 1909.

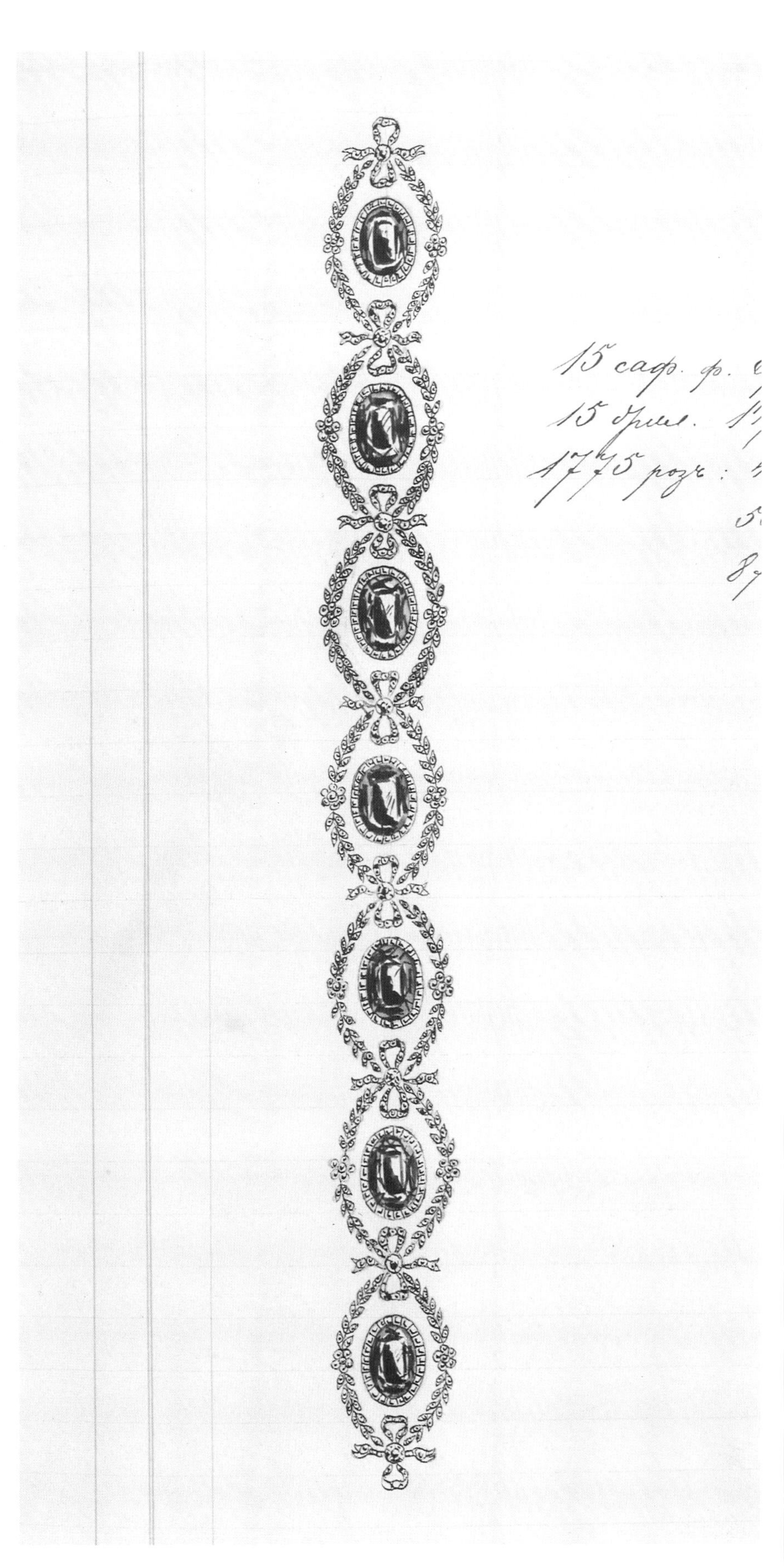

A necklace composed of fifteen sapphire and diamond clusters mounted in gold and silver within oval laurel frames connected by ribbon knots. The design shows only seven of the links destined for the completed necklace. Dated August 21, 1909.

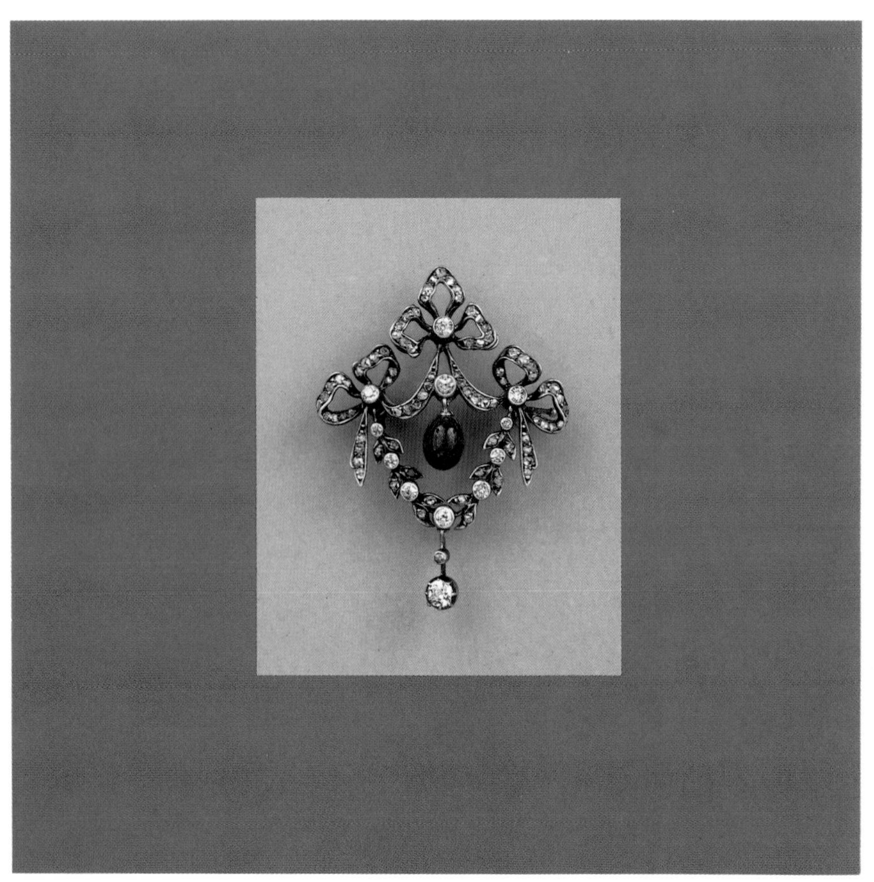

ABOVE:

A brooch-pendant set with brilliant and rose diamonds. Dated October 16, 1909.

LEFT:

A gold- and silver-mounted brooch broadly following the design above but with a gold Easter egg pendant enameled translucent strawberry over an engraved ground in place of the single brilliant diamond. Stamped with the initials of the workmaster August Hollming. Height 1¾" (4.5 cm). Wartski, London.

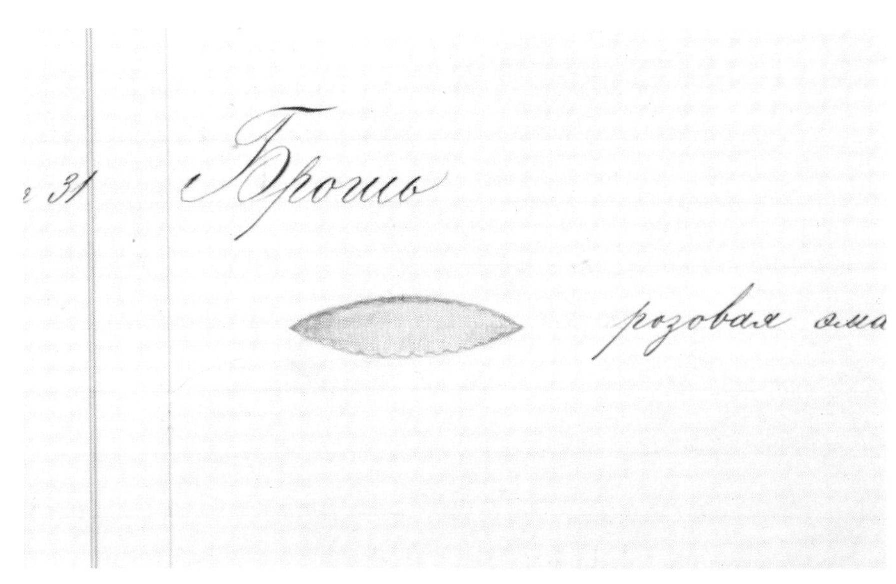

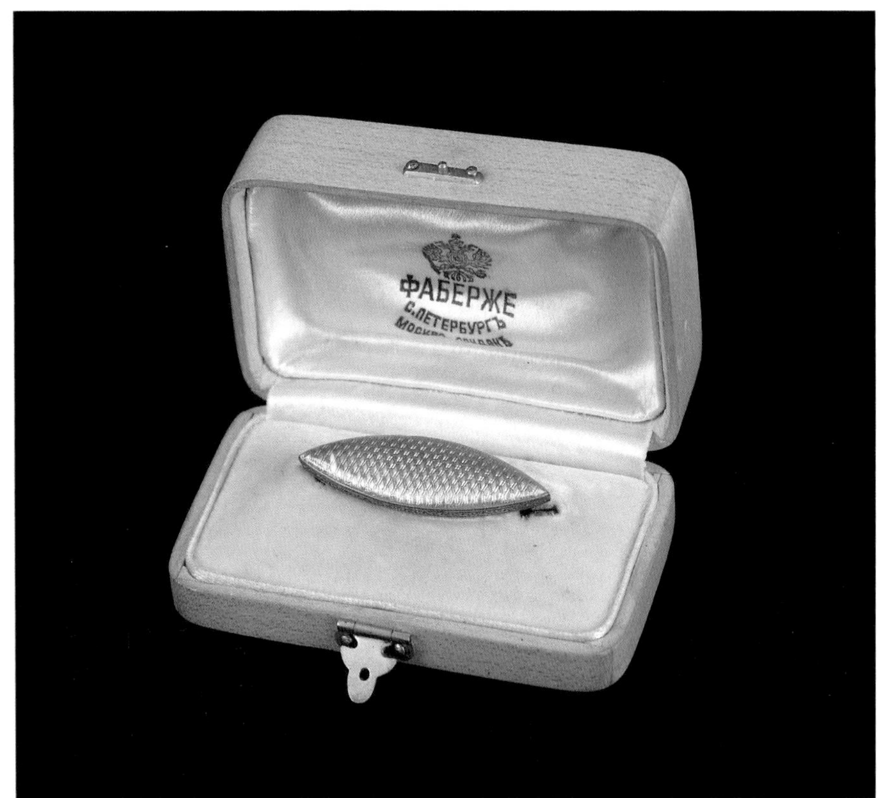

ABOVE:

A brooch of shuttle form to be enameled translucent rose over an engraved ground. Dated October 31, 1909.

LEFT:

A brooch based on the drawing above signed with the initials of the workmaster August Holmström, in its original case. Length $1\frac{3}{8}''$ *(3.4 cm). Collection Dr. E. Radlauer, New York.*

Bow brooch, made for the Moscow House, composed of 136 calibré *rubies and diamonds. Dated November 20, 1909.*

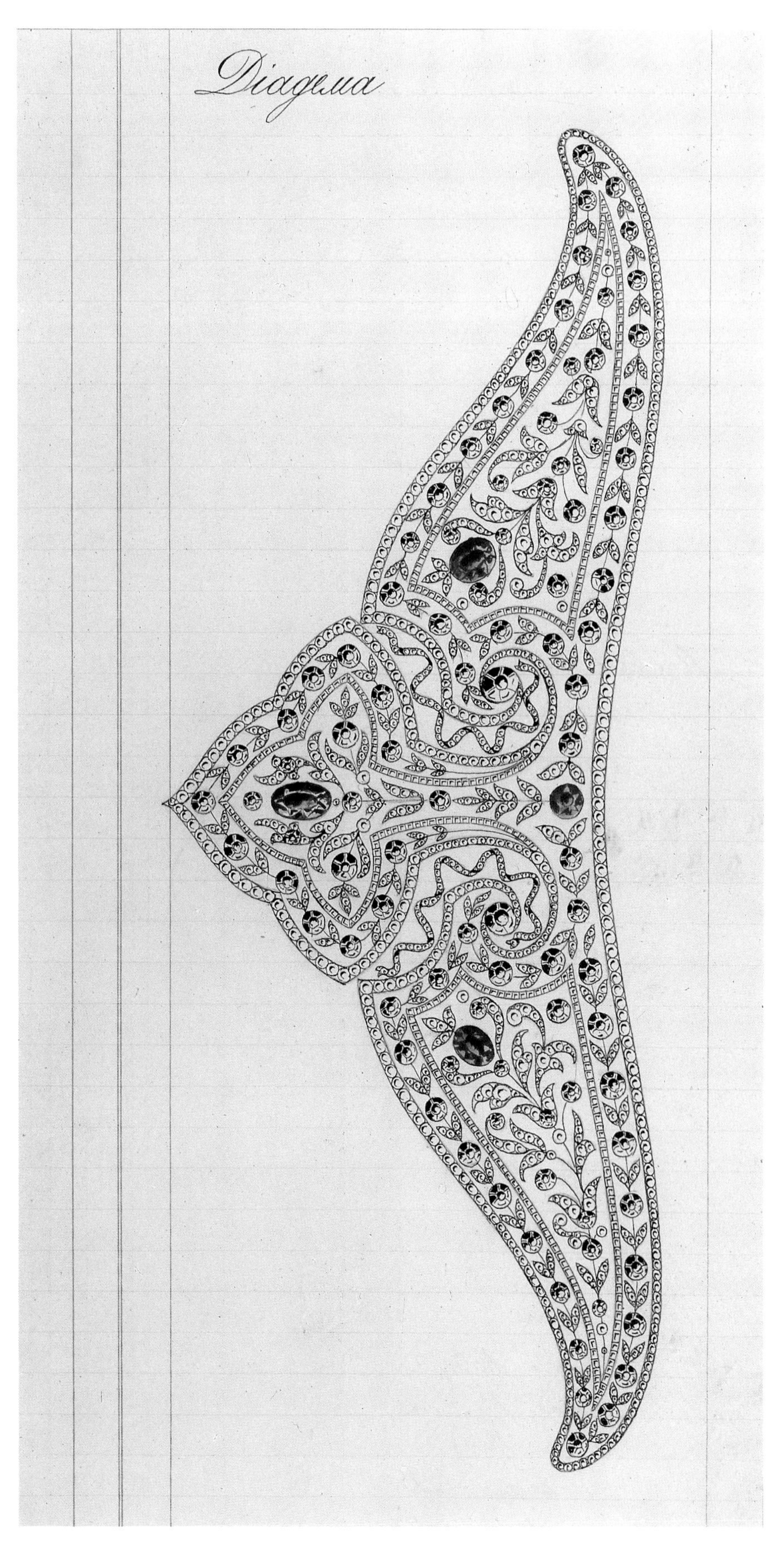

A diadem set with diamonds and four rubies in the form of a kokoshnik *with floral and foliate motifs. Not dated, but probably December 1 or 2, 1909.*

Кр.х 16 Браслетъ ten

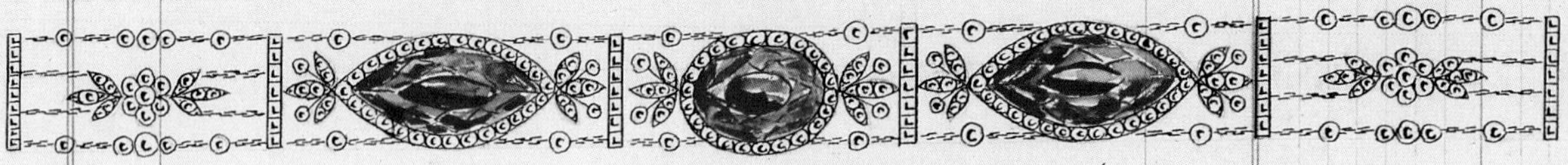

собств: { 3 руб. топ. 35 17/32
24 брил. 1 21/32

добавл: 20 брил. 1 18/ру

256 розъ: 48-аа, 60-iy

148-ее

Полировка топазовъ

Кр.х 16 Кулонъ-брошь ttn

3 руб. топаза 33 16/32 } собств
24 брил. 1 16/

добавл: 318 розъ:

40-аа

30-iy

50-da

198-ее

Полировка топазовъ

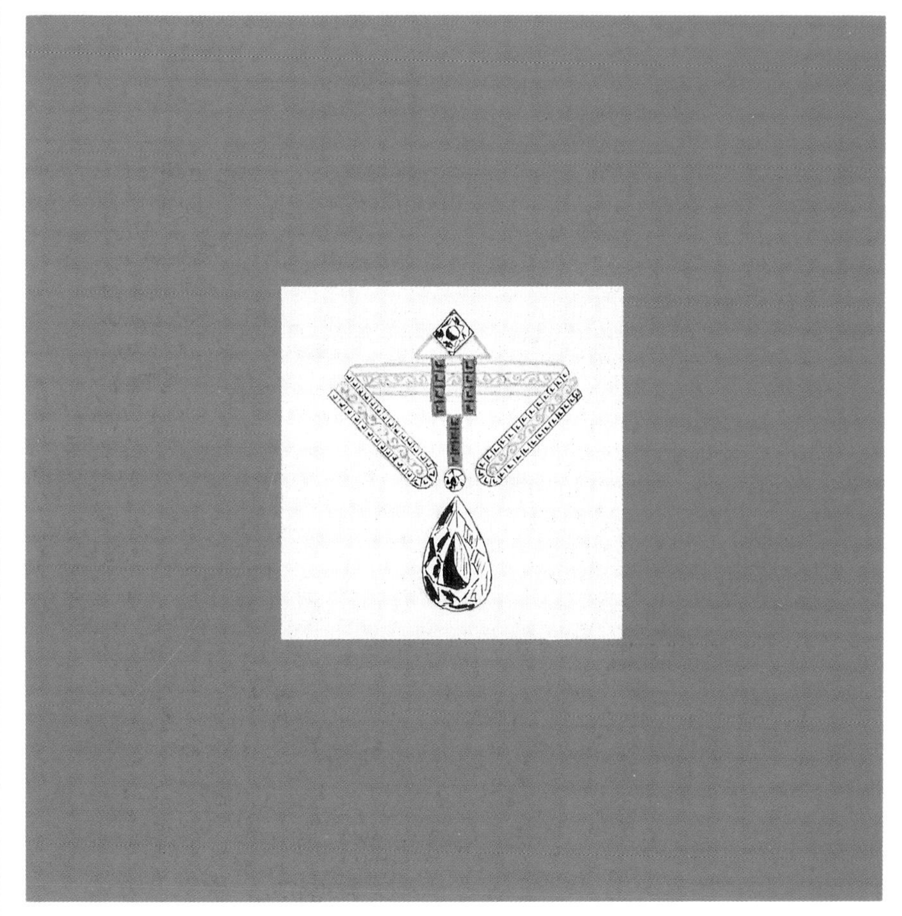

OPPOSITE:
A diamond bracelet of leaf and flower design set with a large oval and two navette-cut rubies within diamond borders. A diamond pendant-brooch composed of a laurel wreath and bowknots with three large navette rubies weighing together 33.50 carats. Both designs dated December 16, 1909.

ABOVE:
Circular hatpin set with brilliant and rose diamonds depicting a spiderweb with raindrops. Dated December 18, 1909.

RIGHT:
A brooch of geometric design incorporating a path of gold scrolling, set with brilliant and small square-cut diamonds, calibré *rubies, and a large diamond drop. For the Moscow House, dated January 15, 1910.*

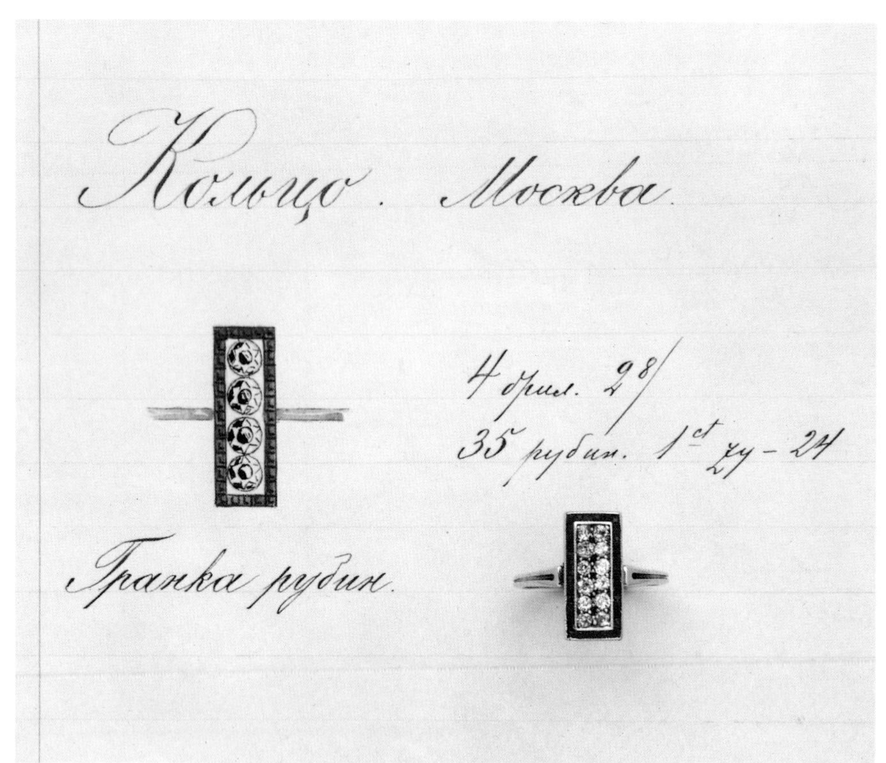

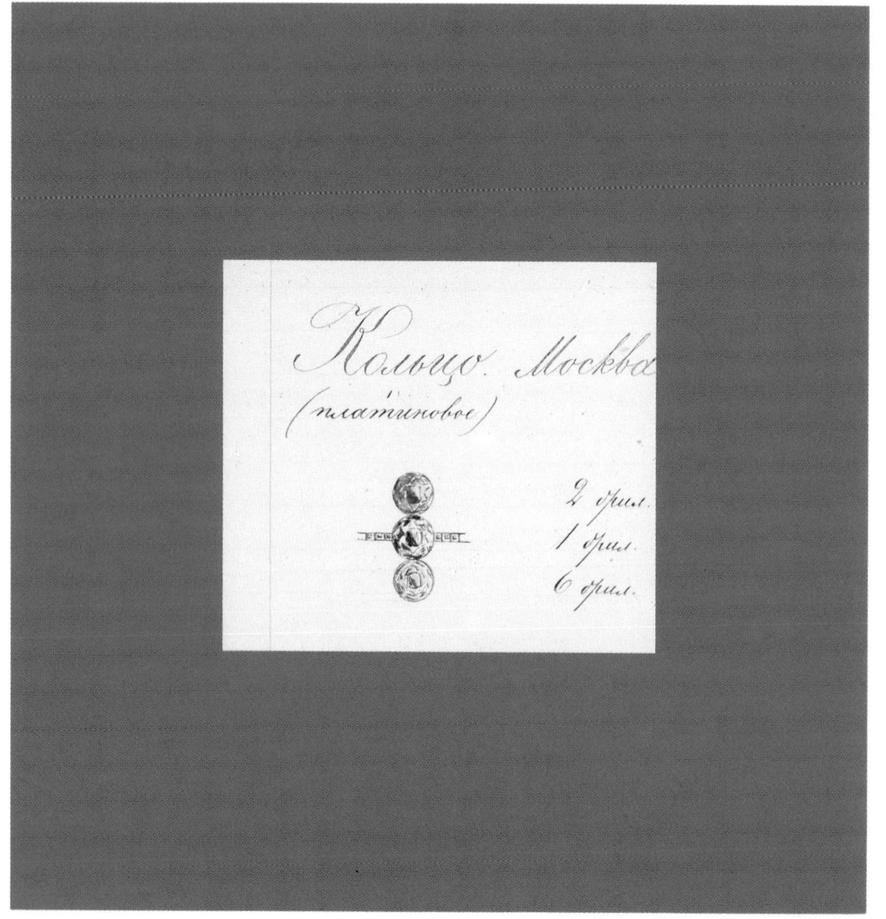

ABOVE:

Watercolor drawing of a rectangular gold-mounted ring composed of four brilliant diamonds bordered by calibré *rubies. Designed for the Moscow House, dated December 21, 1909. A ring probably based on this design is shown on the right, set, in this case, with small brilliant diamonds mounted in gold and platinum. With a carelessly stamped mark, evidently that of August Holmström. Height ⅝″ (1.5 cm). Collection Mrs. William Wood-Prince, Chicago.*

LEFT:

Platinum-mounted ring set with three large brilliant diamonds, that in the center white, with a brown and champagne stone on either side, the shank set with small square-cut diamonds. For the Moscow House, dated January 20, 1910.

Гребенка

5 брил. 13/руу
104 брил. 1¹¹/рау
185 розъ: 40 - dd
50 - ee
95 - ey

2 Баретки

1) бѣл. опал. эмаль
зелен. эмал. листики
58 розъ: 32 - ty,
26 - ee
2) темно голуб. эмаль
зеленые листики
58 розъ: 32 - ty
26 - ee

2 Баретки

1) бѣл. опал. эмаль
3 жем. 24/32
84 розы à ee
2) темно-голуб. эмаль
3 брил. 10/32
84 розы à ee

2 Баретки

1) бѣл. опал. эмаль
7 брил. 7/32
80 розъ à ee
2) розовая эмаль
7 брил. 7/32
80 розъ à ee

From the top: a blond tortoiseshell hair ornament with, at intervals, single scroll motifs set with brilliant and rose diamonds. Three designs for hair slides, all enameled and set with rose diamonds and one with three pearls. Two examples of each of these hair slides were made in different shades of enamel. Dated January 21, 1910.

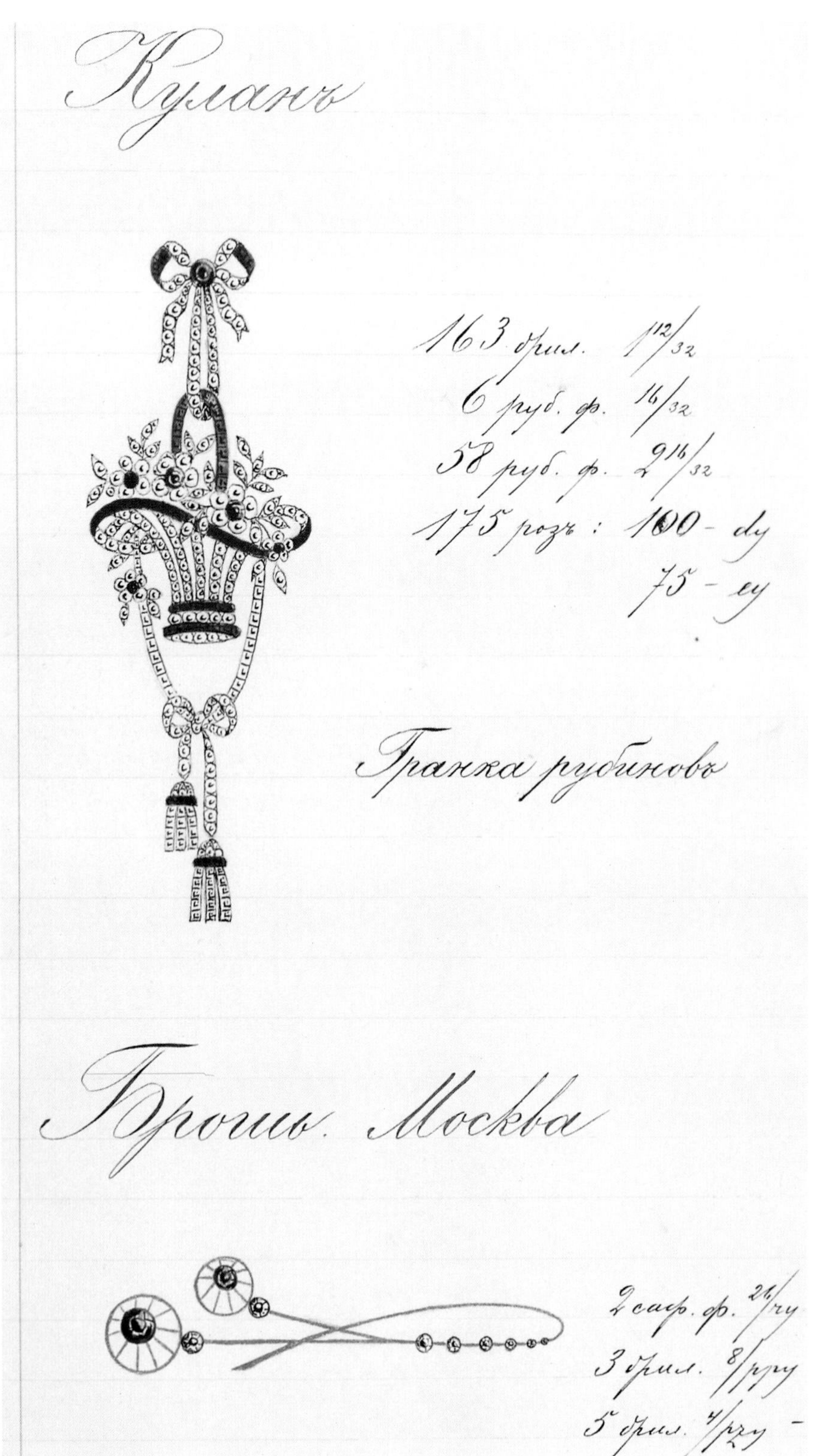

At top, a pendant designed as a basket of flowers suspended from a bowknot with attached cord and tassels set with brilliant, rose, and square-cut diamonds and rubies, both brilliant-cut and calibré. *Dated January 29, 1910. Below, a brooch of Jugendstil design, composed of two sapphires and brilliant diamonds. Dated January 27, 1910.*

ABOVE:
A chatelaine, depending from a gold link chain, comprising three rectangular moss agates, the natural dendritic inclusions suggesting grasses, set with square-cut diamond frames and connected by brilliant and rose diamond crossed mounts. Dated February 10, 1910.

CENTER:
An aquamarine of twenty carats to be mounted as a brooch bordered by small square diamonds and surmounted by a brilliant and rose diamond bow. Also specified are two other aquamarines of fifteen and eleven carats, respectively, similarly mounted as brooches. Dated March 24, 1910.

RIGHT:
Gold-mounted aquamarine and rose diamond brooch, surmounted by a bow set with a brilliant diamond. Signed by August Holmström. Width 7/8" (2.2 cm). Wartski, London.

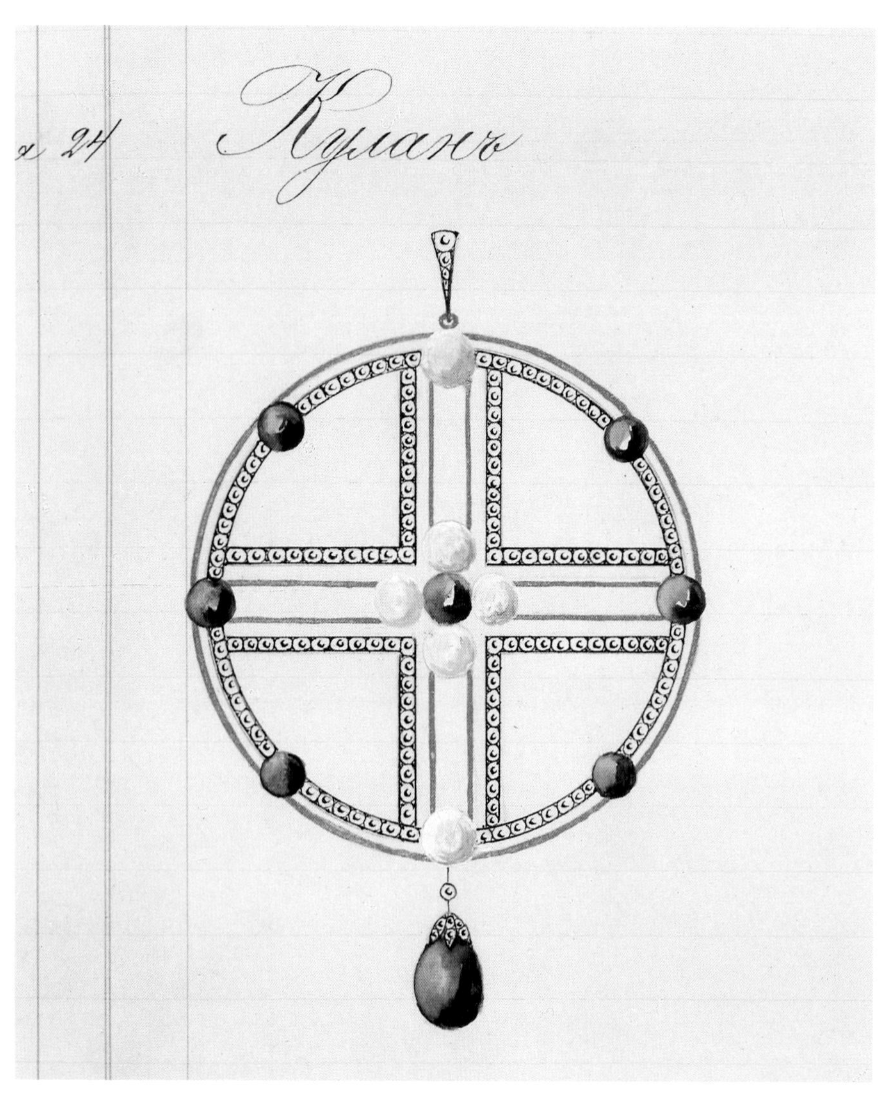

ABOVE:

A pendant of wheel form set with brilliant and rose diamonds, pearls, cabochon emeralds, and an emerald drop. Dated February 24, 1910.

OPPOSITE:

Two pendants set with large mecca stones and brilliant and rose diamonds. Dated March 7 and 8, 1910.

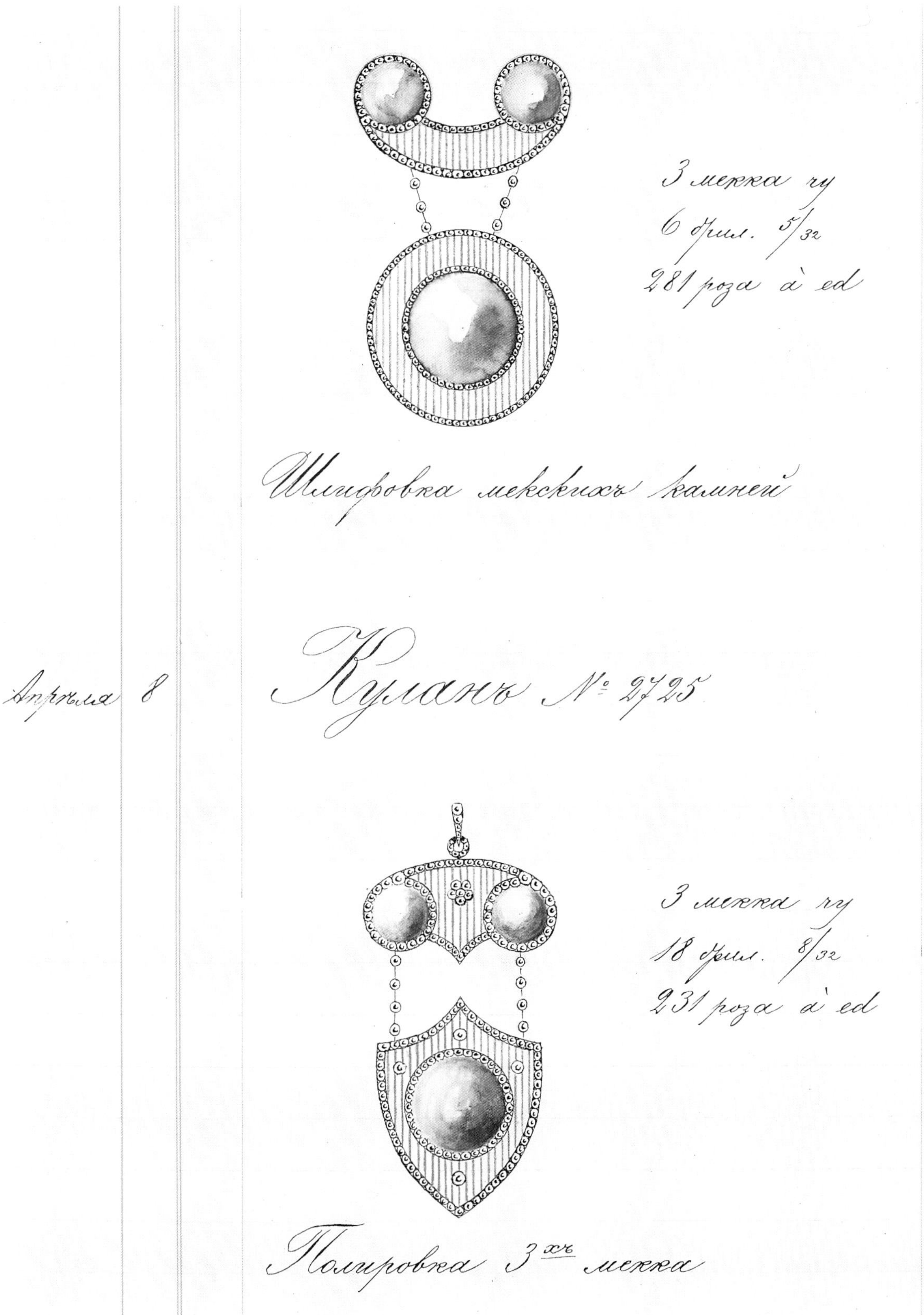

3 мекка чу
6 брил. 5/32
281 роза à ed

Шлифовка мекскихъ камней

Апрѣля 8

Кулонъ № 2725

3 мекка чу
18 брил. 8/32
231 роза à ed

Полировка 3хъ мекка

OPPOSITE:

Designs for a large blond tortoiseshell comb and a pair of smaller hair combs inlaid with brilliant and rose diamonds in foliate sprays. For the Moscow House, dated April 10, 1910.

10 Большой гребень. Москва

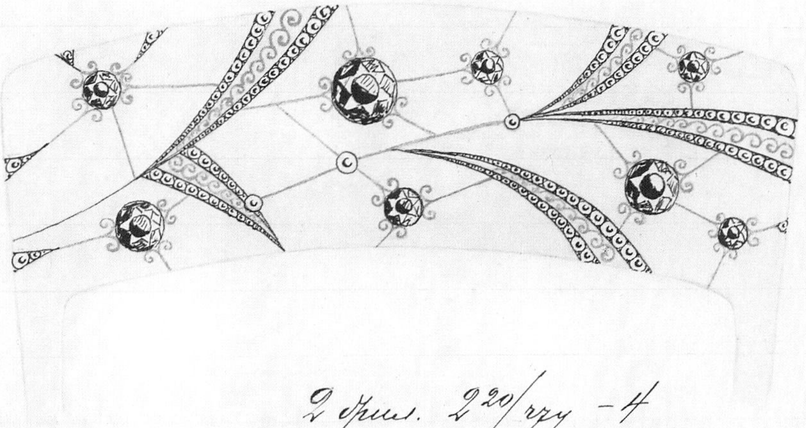

2 брил. 2^{20}/rzy – 4
2 брил. ^{30}/pid – 7
3 брил. ^{16}/pry – 64
4 брил. ^{6}/pzy – 62
доб: 165 розъ: 45-p, 40-iy, 80-ed

10 2 Шпильки. Москва

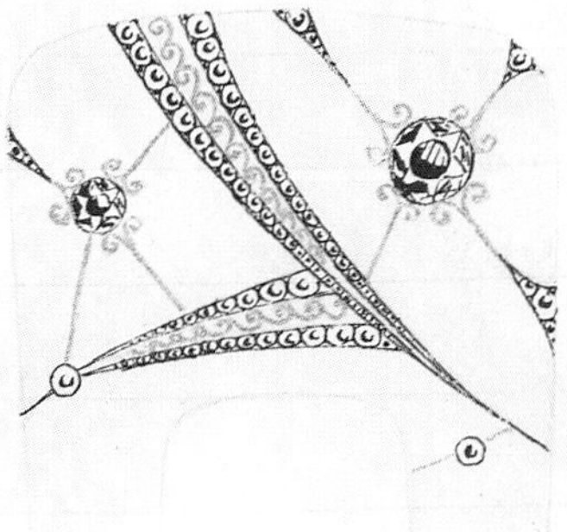

2 брил. 1^{16}/pid – 7
2 брил. ^{12}/pry – 64
4 брил. ^{4}/pzy – 62
доб: 165 розъ:
20 – p.
40 – iy
105 – ed

OPPOSITE:

Three carved Siberian nephrite pendants set with brilliant and rose diamonds. Dated June 24, 1910. A pendant broadly based on the design is shown to the right; the nephrite plaque mounted in platinum and gold set with a single brilliant and rose diamonds. Overall height 1¾″ (4.4 cm). Collection Lady Romsey.

Кулонъ

нефрит. кругъ
7 брил. 16/32
5 розъ : 2 - р. pd
3 - dy

Кулонъ

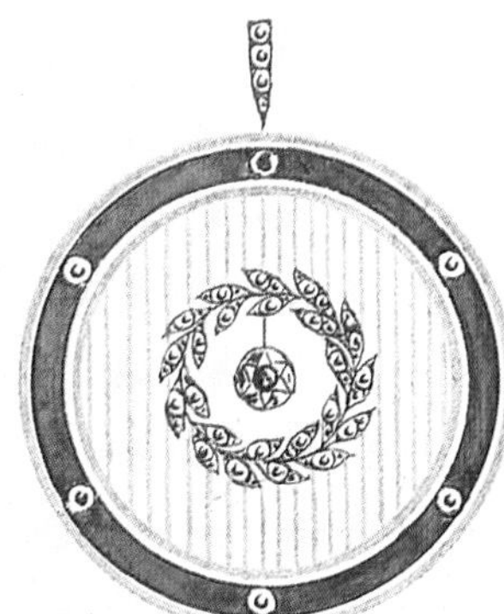

нефрит. кругъ
7 брил. 15/32
51 роза : 3 - р. pd
48 - dr

Кулонъ

нефрит. бляшка
1 брил. 4/32
104 розы : 3 - р. pd
12 - ny
89 - ed

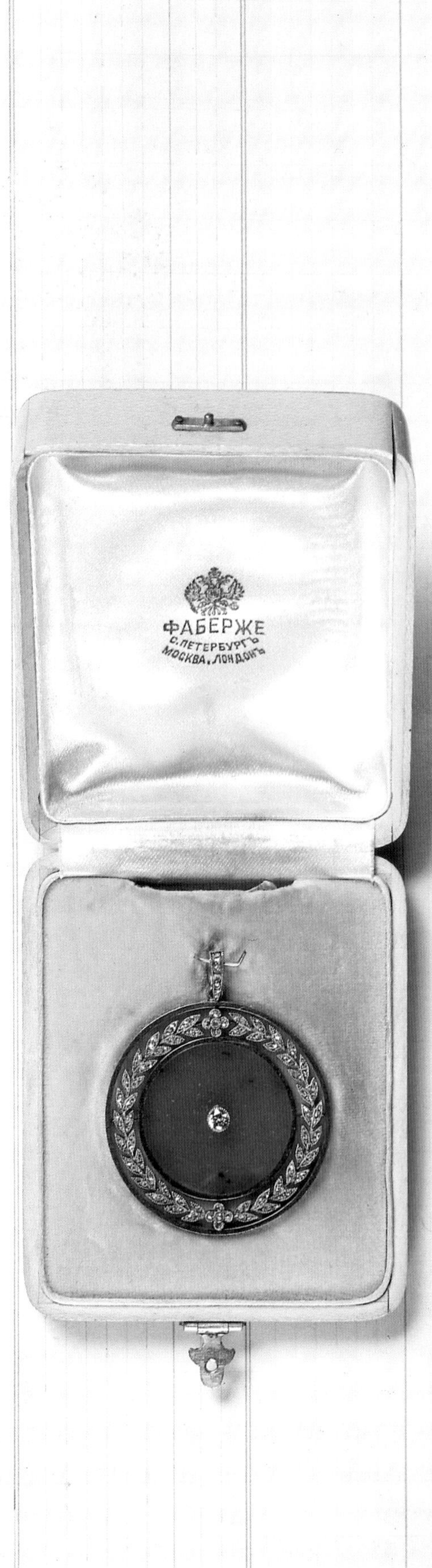

A large brooch forming the initial A composed of 17 rubies and 73 brilliant and 127 rose diamonds, evidently the owner's property, with 101 rose diamonds added by the firm. Dated June 30, 1910.

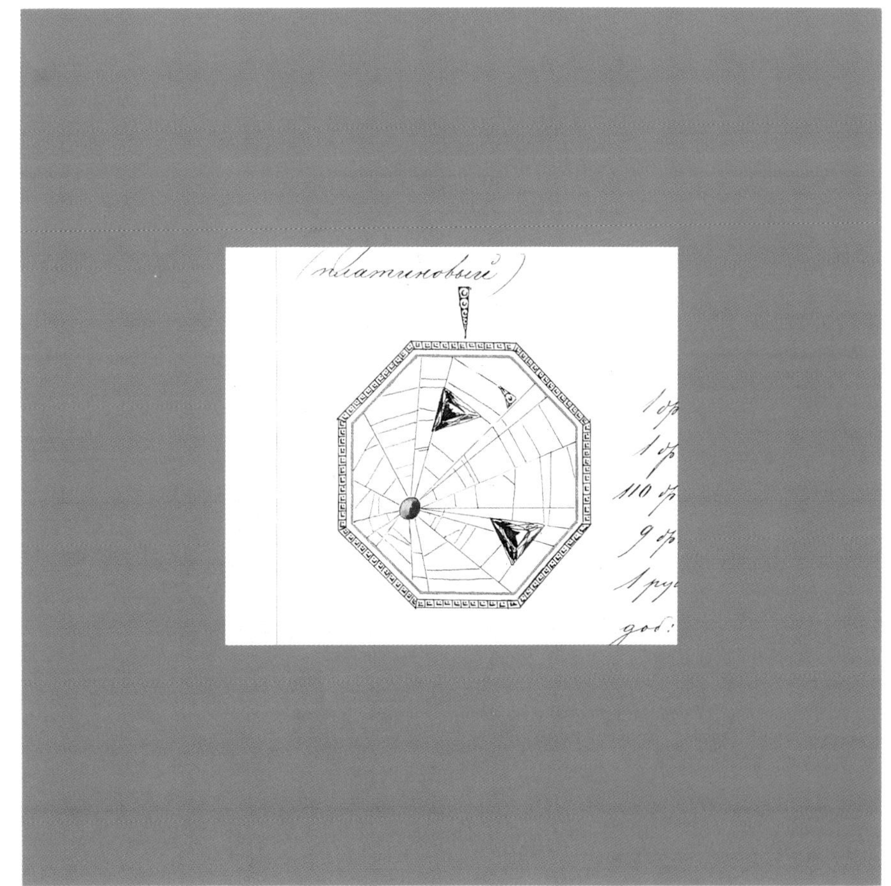

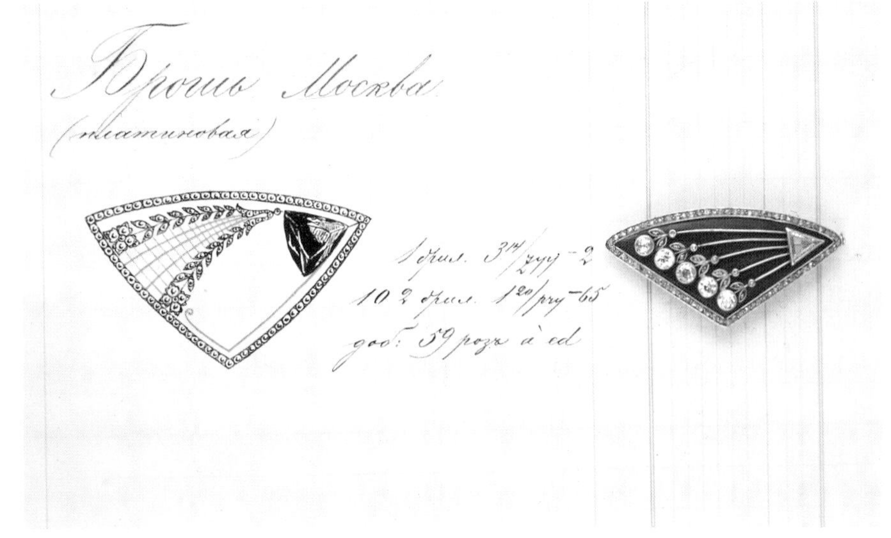

ABOVE:

A platinum pendant of octagonal form bordered by small square-cut diamonds and set with the addition of a small cabochon ruby, possibly suggesting a red spider, and two large triangular diamond raindrops, in the manner of Japanese lacquer. Dated June 30, 1910.

RIGHT:

A design for a platinum-mounted brooch of curved triangular form, featuring a stylized comet represented by a large triangular brilliant diamond with smaller rose and brilliant diamonds depicting the trailing dust and gases emitted in its flight. This design, dated June 30, 1910, was made presumably to commemorate the appearance of Halley's comet seen in Germany on September 12, 1909, and subsequently in other countries until June 1911.

The gold brooch shown on the right, set with brilliant and rose diamonds, is a variation inspired, no doubt, by this drawing, but enameled translucent royal blue over an engraved radiating field. It is stamped with the marks of the Moscow goldsmith Fedor Anatolievitch Lorié (1871–1916). Length of brooch, 2" (5 cm). Wartski, London.

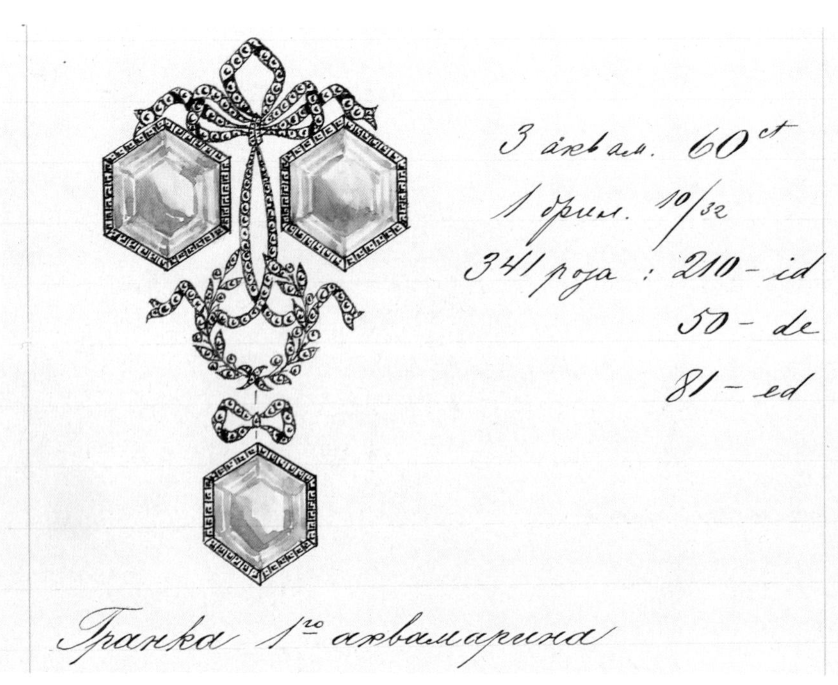

A pendant set with three hexagonal aquamarines within small square-cut diamond borders suspended from a system of rose diamond bows and a laurel wreath. Dated July 16, 1910.

2 Часы № 1819

1) розов. эмаль
2 розы 10/ау
304 розы : 14-
290-

2) бѣл. оп. эма
2 руб. à а
233 розы : 14-
219-

ABOVE:

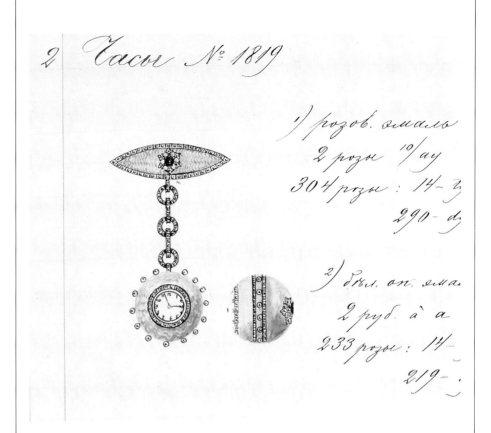

A ball-watch hanging from a shuttle-shaped brooch, enameled translucent pink and set with rose diamonds. The ingenious mechanism of this watch was the discovery of Paul Ditisheim of La Chaux-de-Fonds, who displayed an unfinished example at the Geneva Exhibition of 1896. It is wound by turning one half of the sphere against the other. It was characteristic of Fabergé, always open to new ideas, to incorporate this revolutionary timepiece into his own repertoire. An opalescent white enameled model was also recorded on July 23, 1910.

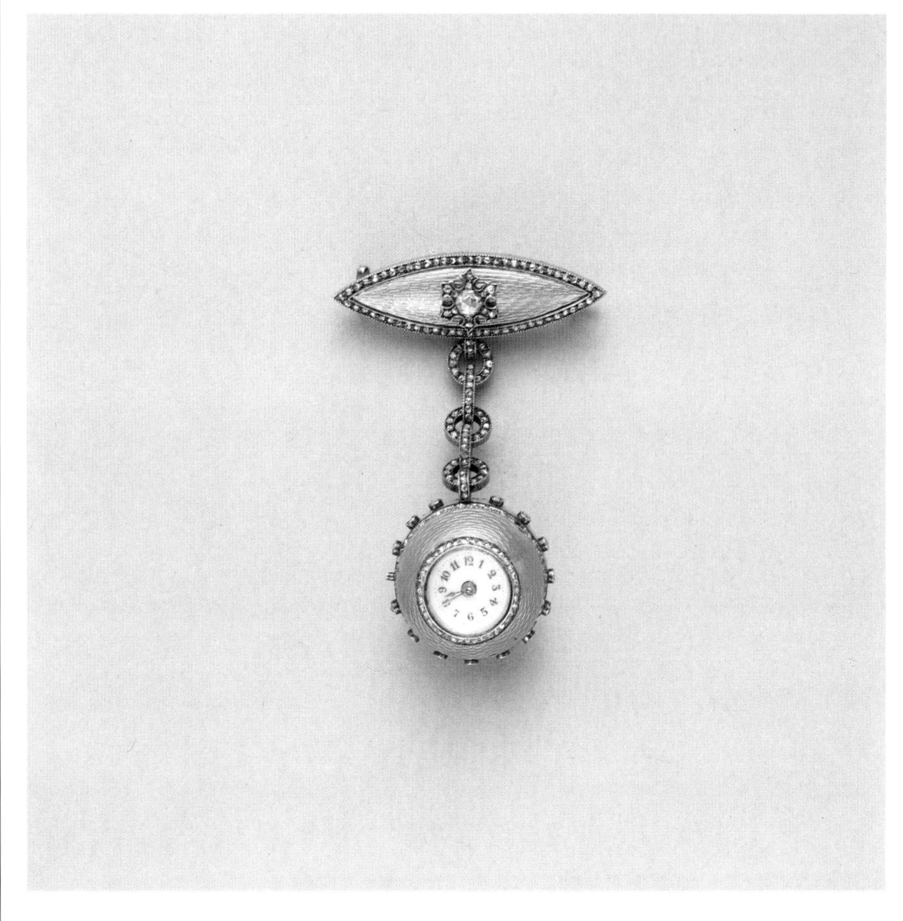

RIGHT:

Gold pendant ball-watch made from the design above, enameled translucent pink over guilloché *fields and set with rose diamonds. Bearing the initials of August Holmström. Height 2" (5.1 cm). A la Vieille Russie, New York.*

ABOVE:

Gold-mounted Siberian nephrite brooch inlaid with rose diamonds forming a Shield of David. Diameter 1 1/16" (2.7 cm). Collection Mrs. Charlotte Robson, London.

LEFT:

A hexagonal ring, enameled opalescent white, set with ten rose diamonds and a central pink sapphire, in the form of a Shield of David. Dated July 29, 1910.

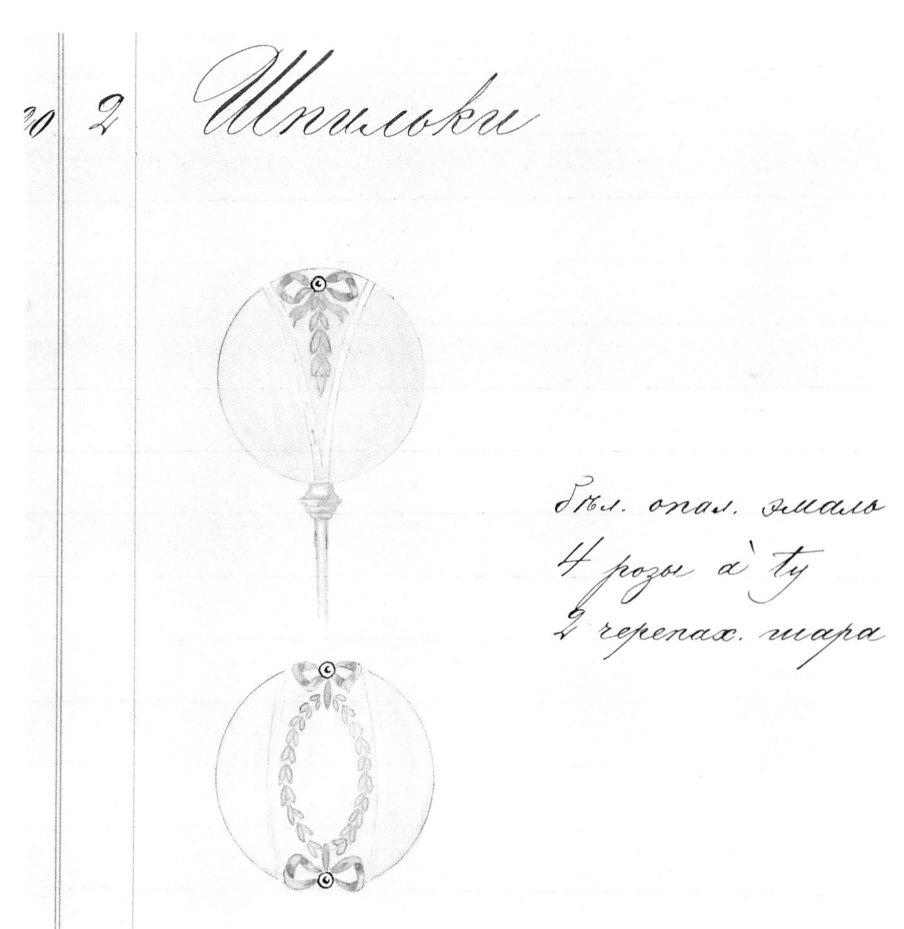

Two blond tortoiseshell hatpins with opalescent enameled bows and borders and rose diamonds. Dated July 20, 1910.

20 Брошь. Москва

1 брил. 20/pmy – 7
11 брил. 11/pzy – 62
22 из. 9/ppy – 15
16 розъ à de

20 Брошь-кулонъ

1 аквам. 39 25/32
56 брил. 1 15/32
251 роза: 60 – id
40 – md
80 – dm
71 – ed

Брошь. Москва

The three striking geometric designs for brooches were intended for the Moscow House, whereas the more conventional aquamarine and diamond pendant (third from top) was made for St. Petersburg. All dated August 20, 1910.

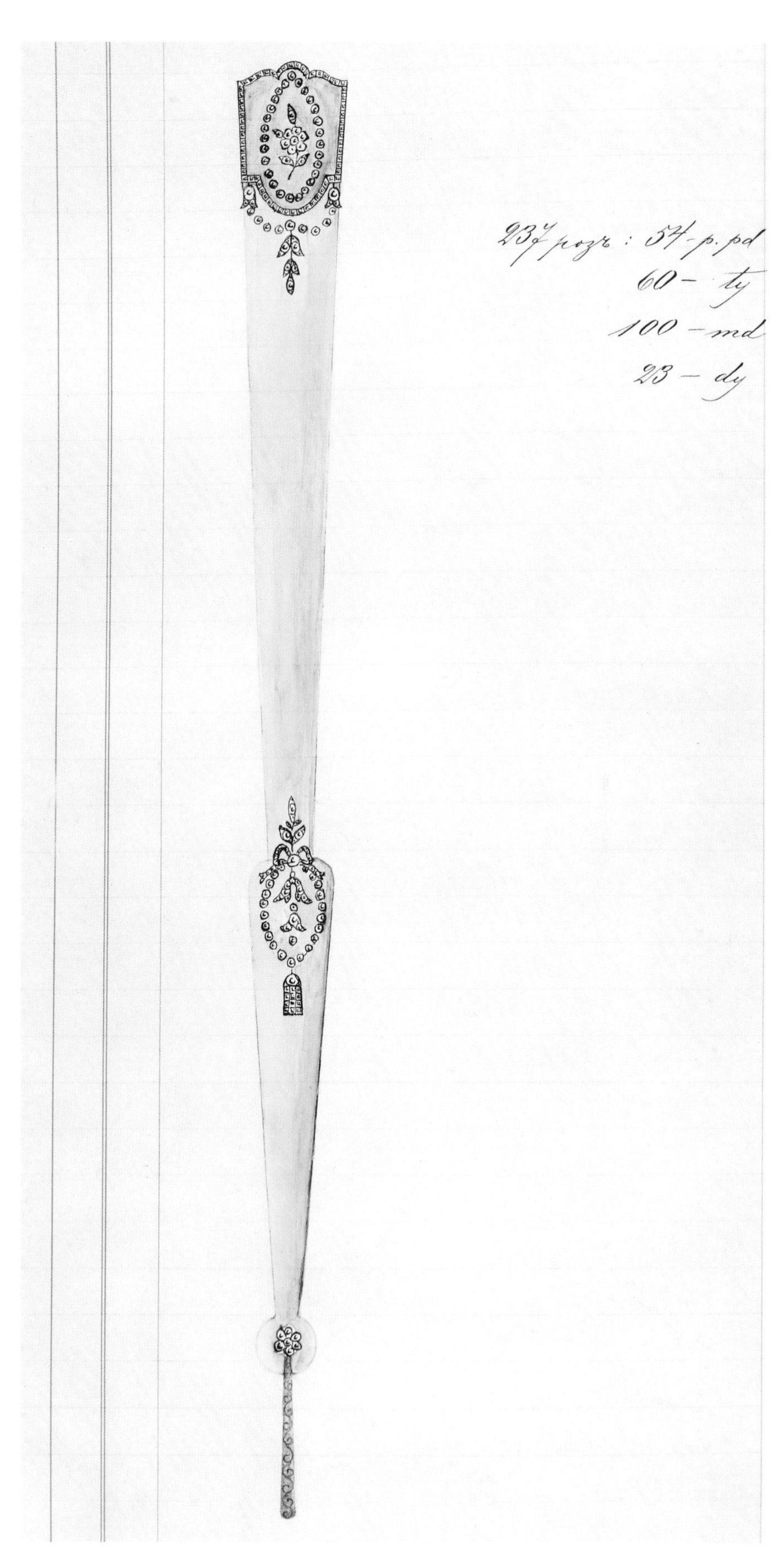

Blond tortoiseshell fan, made for the London branch, set with rose diamonds. Dated August 31, 1910.

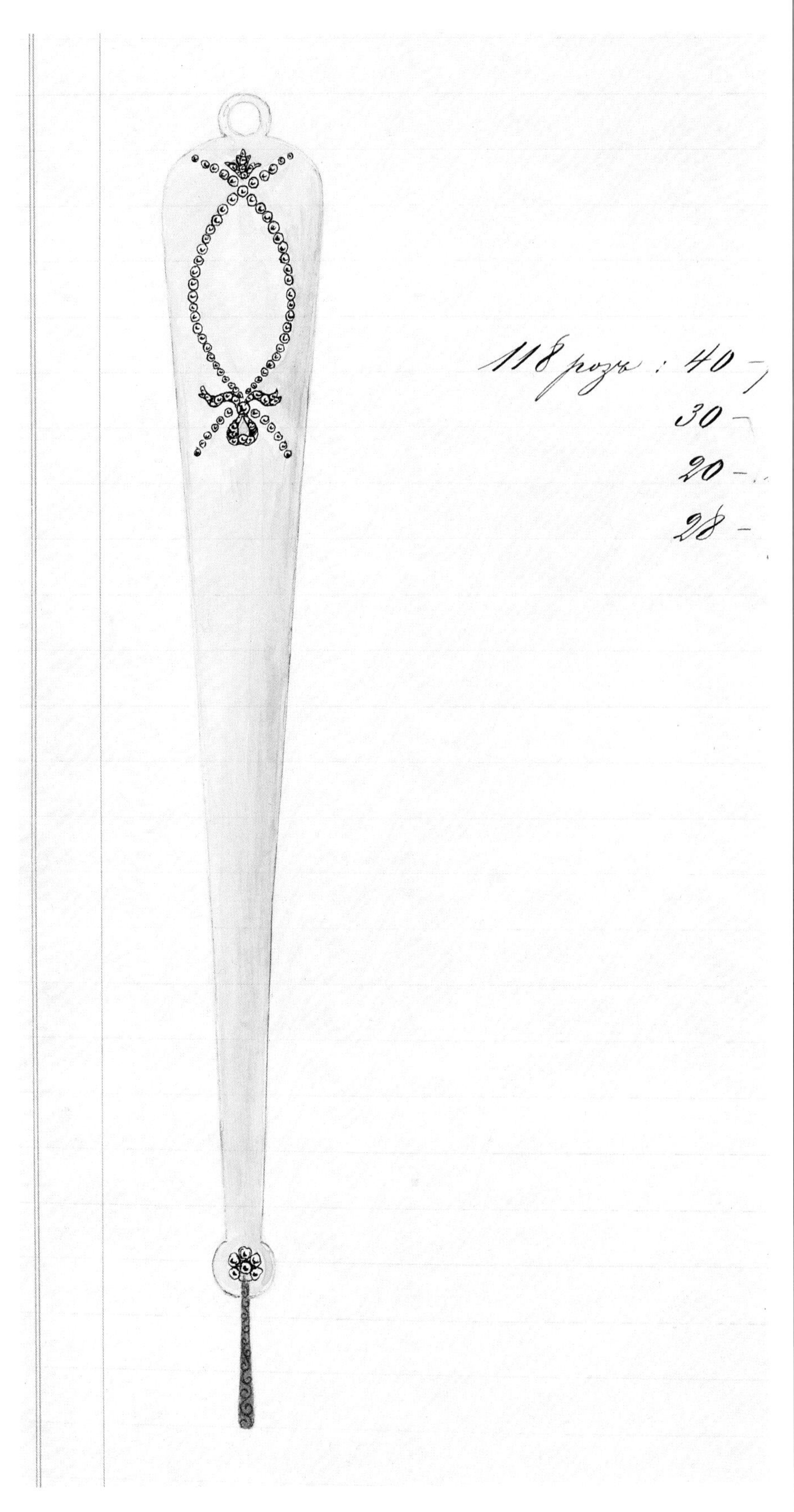

A lorgnette of composition similar to the fan opposite. Dated September 1, 1910.

ABOVE:

A ring formed as a heart composed of a ruby and a sapphire, cut cabochon within a mount, set with brilliant and rose diamonds beneath a bowknot. Dated September 17, 1910.

LEFT:

A brooch in the form of a bunch of grapes expressed in pearls, with vine leaves set with brilliant and rose diamonds. Dated November 12, 1910.

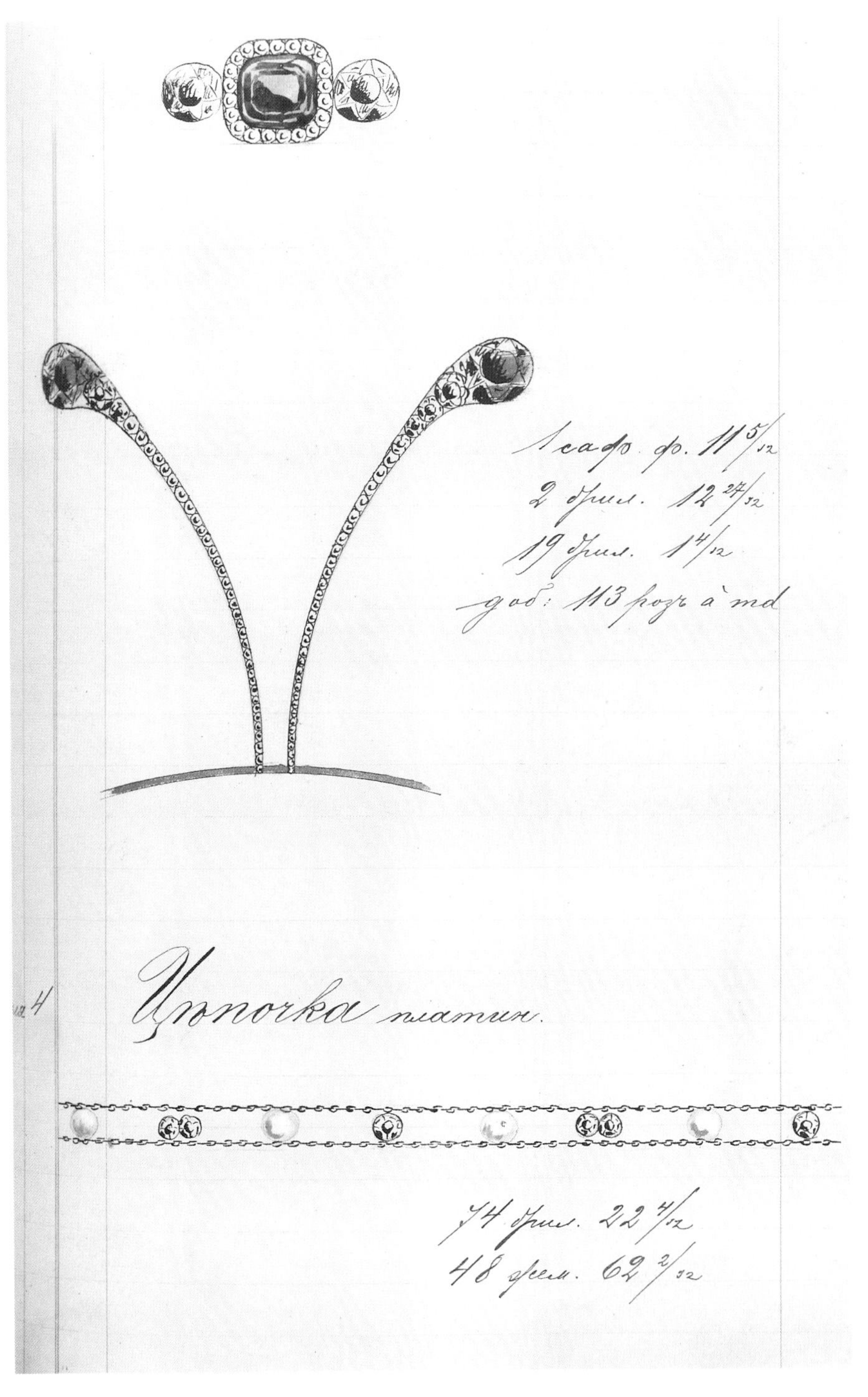

From top, a large sapphire mounted as a bar brooch within a cluster of brilliant diamonds, flanked on either side by a large single stone diamond; a diamond aigrette also set with two large brilliant stones; a chain bracelet with pearls and brilliant diamonds. Dated February 4 and 5, 1911.

OPPOSTE:

An unusually splendid necklet set with an impressive number of brilliant and rose diamonds. Very much a party piece. Dated January 29, 1911.

352 брил. 40 26/
115 брил. 43 30/32
1 брил. 15/
доб. 98 брил. 19 5/12
518 розъ: 100 - aa
200 - iy
218 - dd

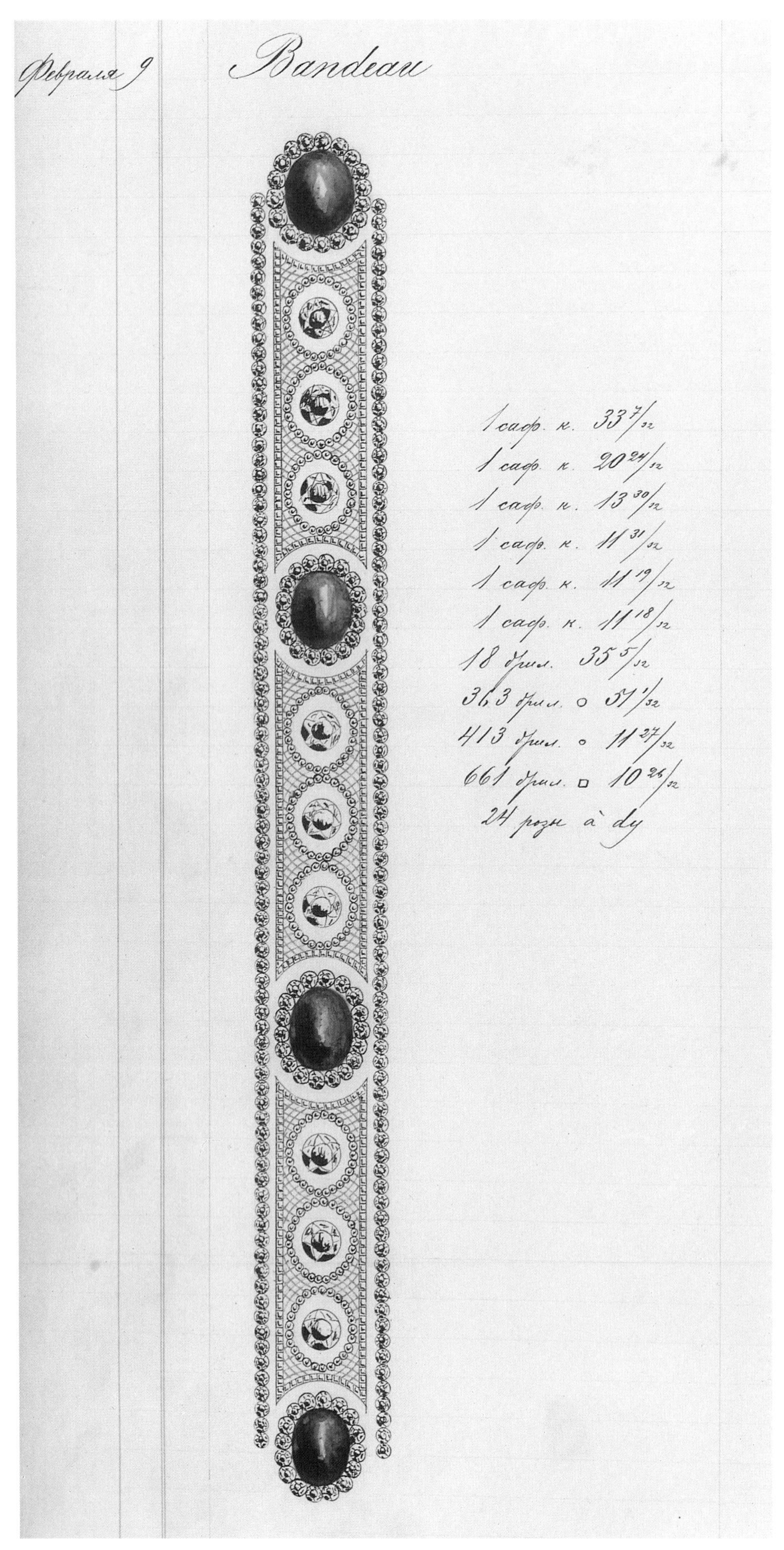

Part of a brilliant and rose diamond bandeau, set with six large cabochon sapphires and eighteen single brilliant diamonds. Dated February 9, 1911.

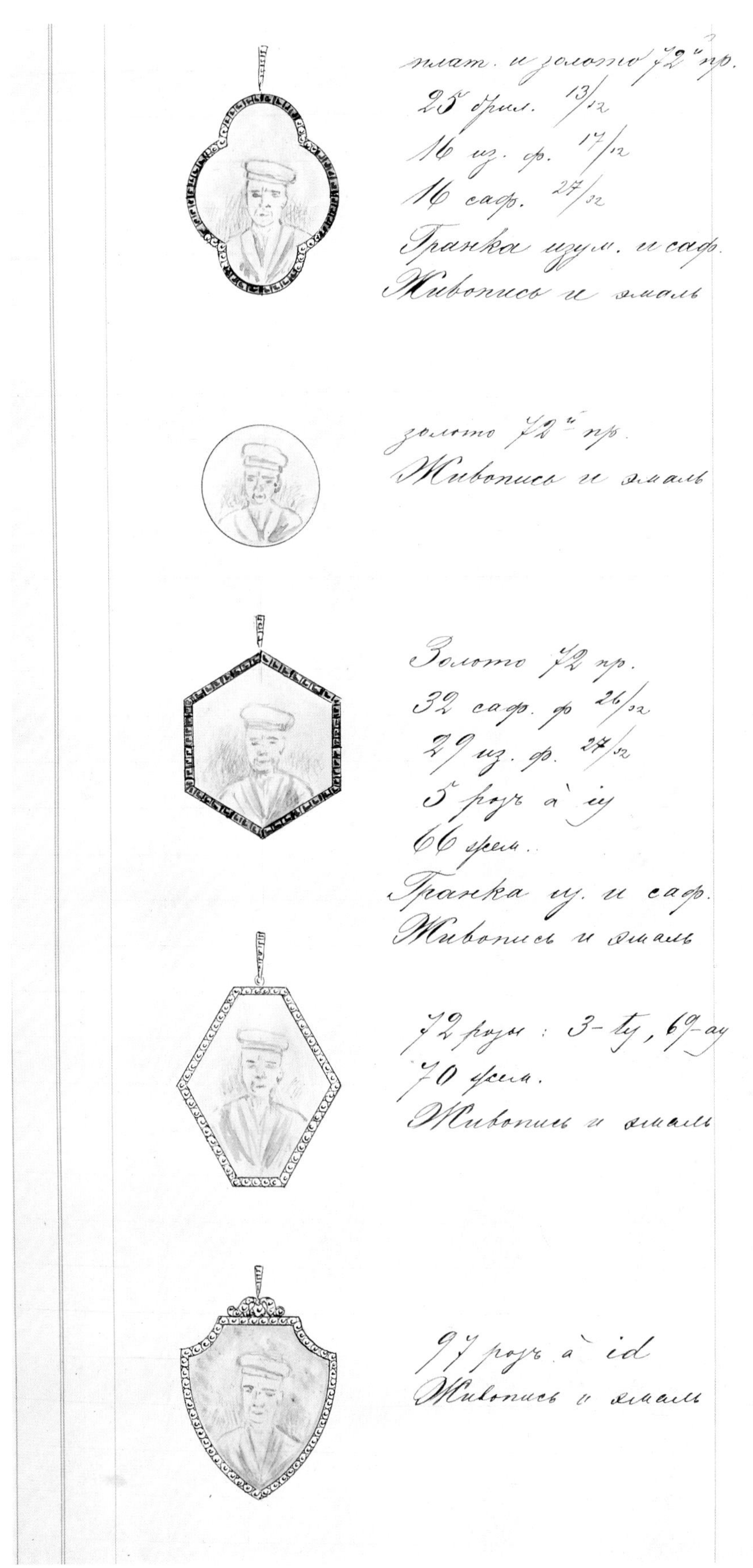

Pendant frames mounted in platinum and set with diamonds, sapphires, and emeralds, the eighteen-carat gold panels to be painted in enamel with portraits of King Chulalongkorn of Siam. Dated March 14, 1911.

23 6 Яйцъ платинов.

1 нефритъ
115 розъ : 4 - id
111 - dp

1 нефритъ
103 розъ à dp

1 нефритъ
54 розы : 6 - ia
48 - d

1 нефритъ
249 розъ : 7 -
242 - a

1 нефритъ
20 розъ à dp
опак. бѣл. эмал

1 нефритъ
2 руб. ф 3/32
24 розы à dp

Six platinum-mounted miniature Easter eggs, carved in nephrite and set with rose diamonds, the last one with rubies also. Dated March 23, 1911. These tiny egg-pendants are generously represented in the record books in countless guises made of silver, gold, or semiprecious stone. We find solemn little stone owls, small portly oviform elephants, and pigs in nephrite or orletz (rhodonite), each one shining with tiny diamond or ruby eyes. Numerous miniature eggs were designed to be enameled entirely in translucent or opaque colors, or striped, quartered, or decorated with stars in the form of gold paillons*, applied with chased colored gold mounts or set with small gemstones. The variety seems as endless as the demand for these gleaming symbols of the Resurrection.*

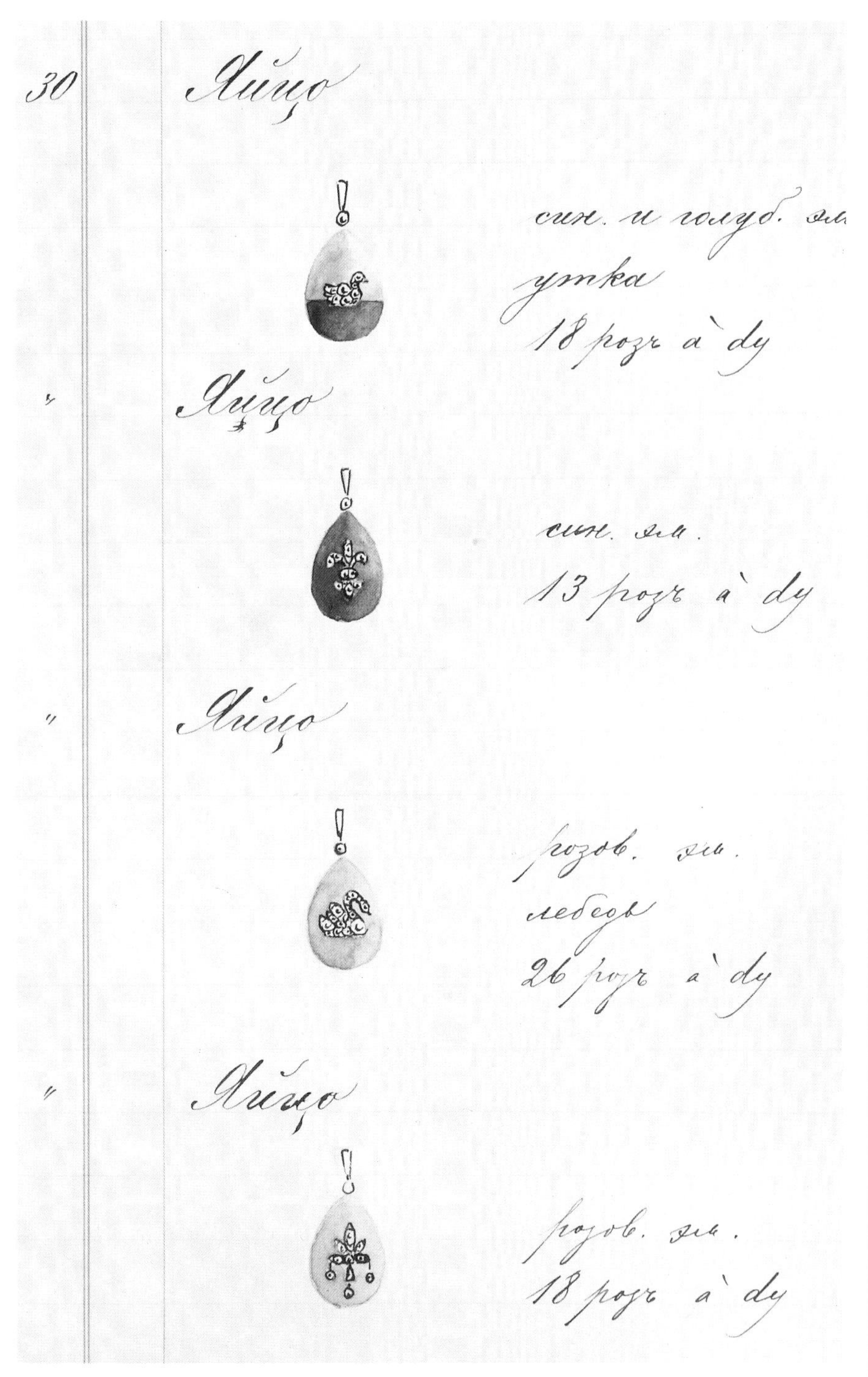

30 Яйцо
син. и голуб. эм.
утка
18 розъ à ду

" Яйцо
син. эм.
13 розъ à ду

" Яйцо
розов. эм.
лебедь
26 розъ à ду

" Яйцо
розов. эм.
18 розъ à ду

Four blue and pink miniature enameled Easter eggs set with a duck, a fleur-de-lis, a swan, and a decorative pendant in rose diamonds. Dated March 30, 1911.

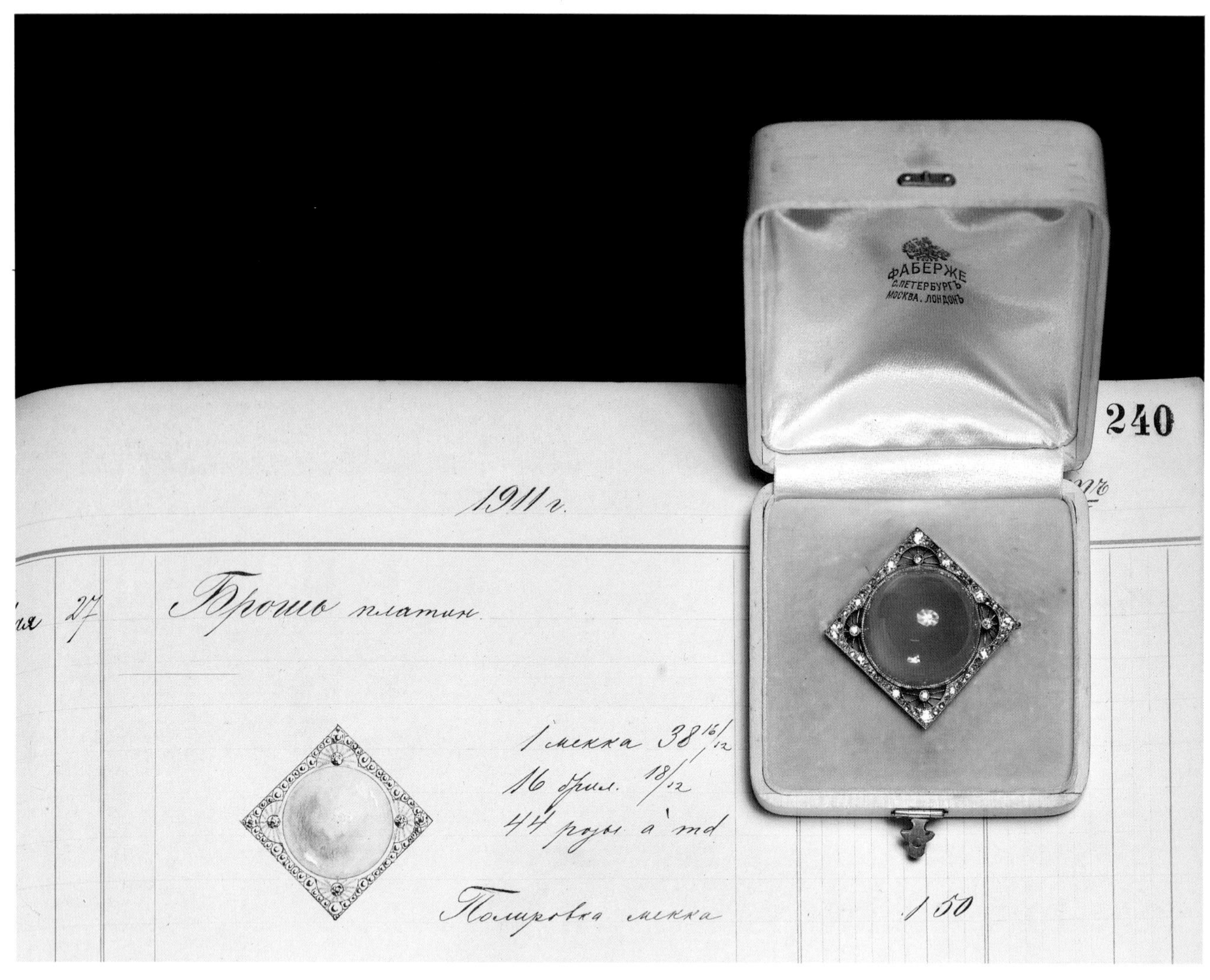
ФАБЕРЖЕ
С.ПЕТЕРБУРГЪ
МОСКВА. ЛОНДОНЪ
240
1911 г.
27
Брошь платин.
1 мекка 38 16/12
16 брил. 18/12
44 розы à md
Полировка мекка
1 50

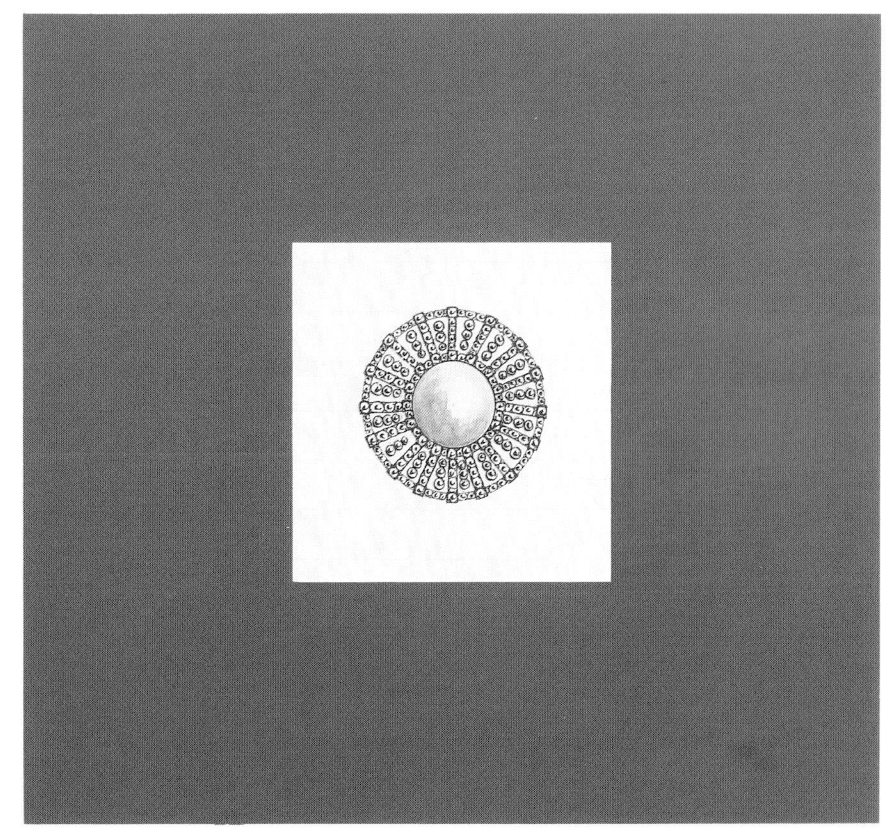

OPPOSITE:

Mecca stone brooch mounted in platinum set with diamonds. The cost of polishing the mecca stone is noted as 1.50 rubles. Dated May 27, 1911. The actual brooch, stamped with the initials A.H., fitted in its holly wood box, is shown in the photograph resting on the page next to the original design. Collection Mr. and Mrs. Maurice Jacobs.

ABOVE:

An unusual pendant composed of swags set with rose diamonds, each hung with a single separate pearl. Dated May 20, 1911.

RIGHT:

A hatpin mounted in platinum with a central mecca stone within a wheel design of spokes set with rose diamonds. Dated May 28, 1911.

Колье № 3328

18 аквам. 23 16/7
73 брил. 28/12
559 розъ : 80 - ty
200 - id
150 - md
129 - dm
Гранка аквам.

Necklet hung with a trellis of single aquamarines, interspersed with floral and foliate motifs set with brilliant and rose diamonds. Dated May 27, 1911.

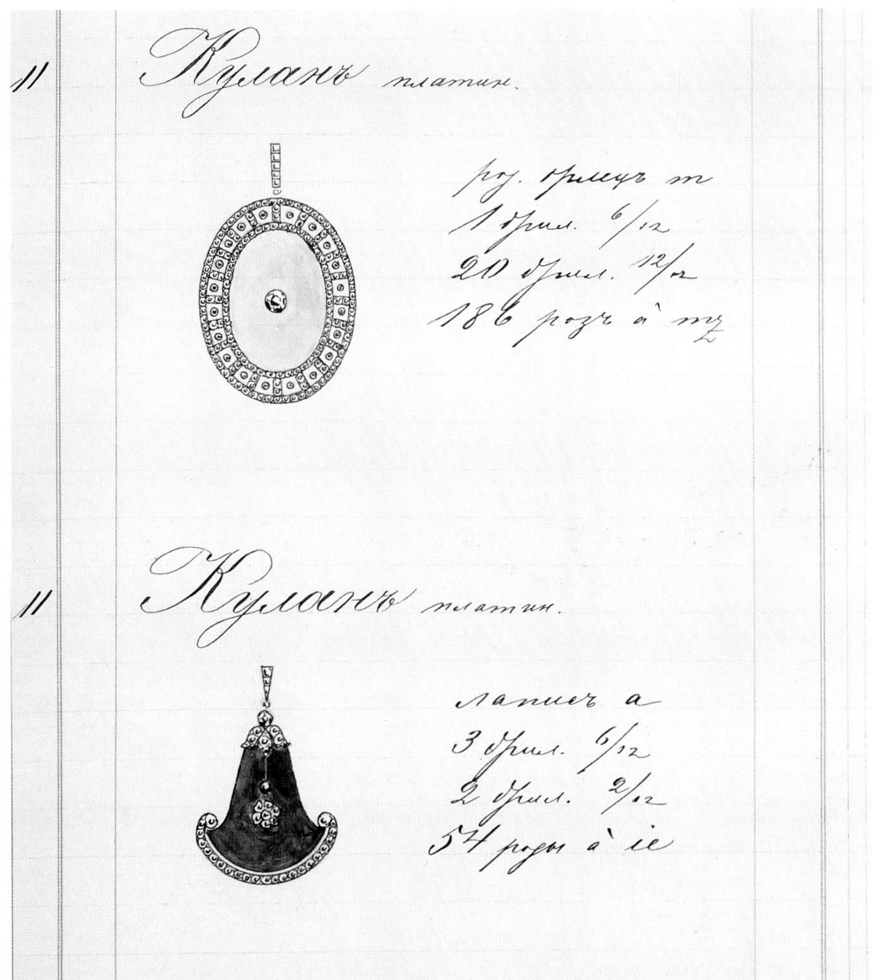

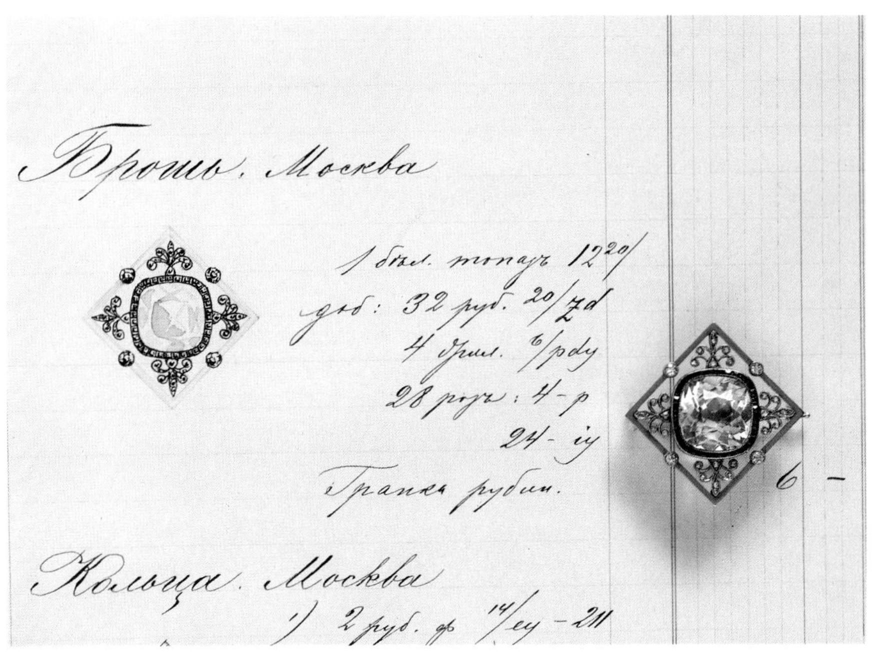

ABOVE:

At top, an oval platinum pendant set with a carved orletz (rhodonite) panel centered with a brilliant diamond within a framework of brilliant and rose diamonds. Below, a carved lapis lazuli platinum pendant in the form of a bell, set with brilliant and rose diamonds. Both dated August 11, 1911.

RIGHT:

The design dated September 6, 1911, for a square framed brooch with a large central white topaz weighing 12.20 carats within a border of thirty-two calibré-cut *rubies and held by four floral motifs set with twenty-eight rose diamonds and four single brilliant diamonds.*

The brooch photographed next to the drawing must be one of the six examples made for the Moscow branch since the details of its composition are precisely those given in the book description. Mounted in a platinized alloy of silver and gold, the pin and clasp in gold. Width 1⁵⁄₁₆" (3.3 cm). Wartski, London.

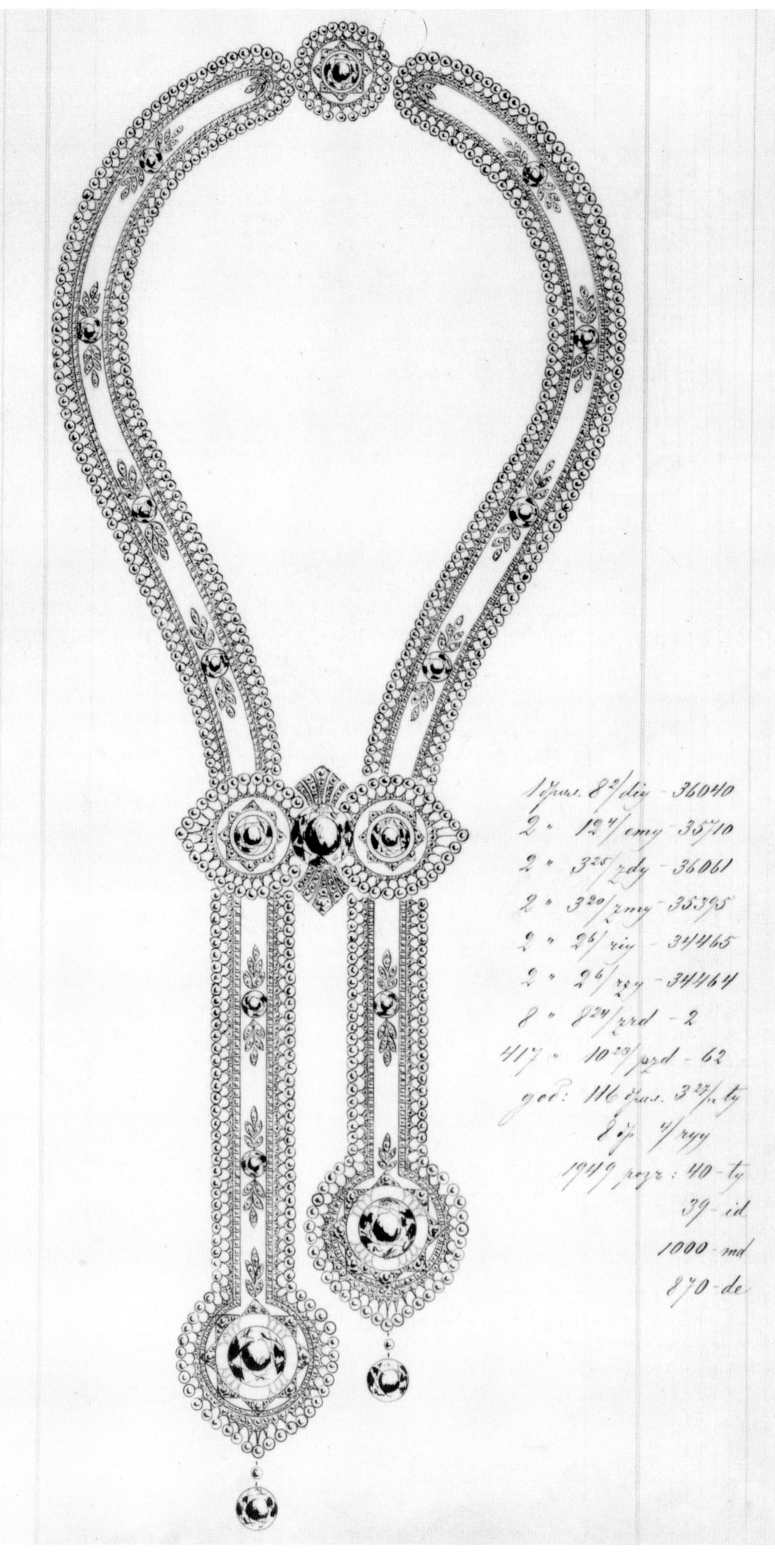

1 брил. 8^2/diy - 36040
2 " 12^4/emy - 35710
2 " 3^25/zdy - 36061
2 " 3^20/zmy - 35395
2 " 2^6/riy - 34465
2 " 2^6/rzy - 34464
8 " 8^24/zrd - 2
417 " 10^23/pzd - 62
ged: 116 бріл. 3^27/n ty
8 ер. 4/ryy
1949 pozr: 40 - ty
39 - id
1000 - md
870 - de

1911 г.

Кулонъ. Москва (платин.

OPPOSITE:

An imposing diamond necklace mounted in platinum and set with brilliant diamonds of substantial weight and a large quantity of smaller brilliant and rose diamonds. Designed for the Moscow House and dated November 10, 1911.

RIGHT:

Platinum pendant of a lace design set with brilliant and rose diamonds. Dated November 30, 1911.

OVERLEAF, LEFT:

A view in section of an aquamarine pendant set with rose diamonds; shown alongside is a brooch-pendant of this character and size, mounted in red gold and set with brilliant and rose diamonds, in the original fitted holly box. The design is a later version since it is dated February 9, 1912, while the jewel shown resting on the page is stamped with the crossed anchors gold mark for St. Petersburg up to 1899. It is signed by Henrik Wigström and measures 1 9/16" (4 cm). Private collection.

OVERLEAF, RIGHT:

A diadem of scrolling leaves mounted in platinum, set with brilliant and rose diamonds and three drop-cut aquamarines. Dated February 18, 1912.

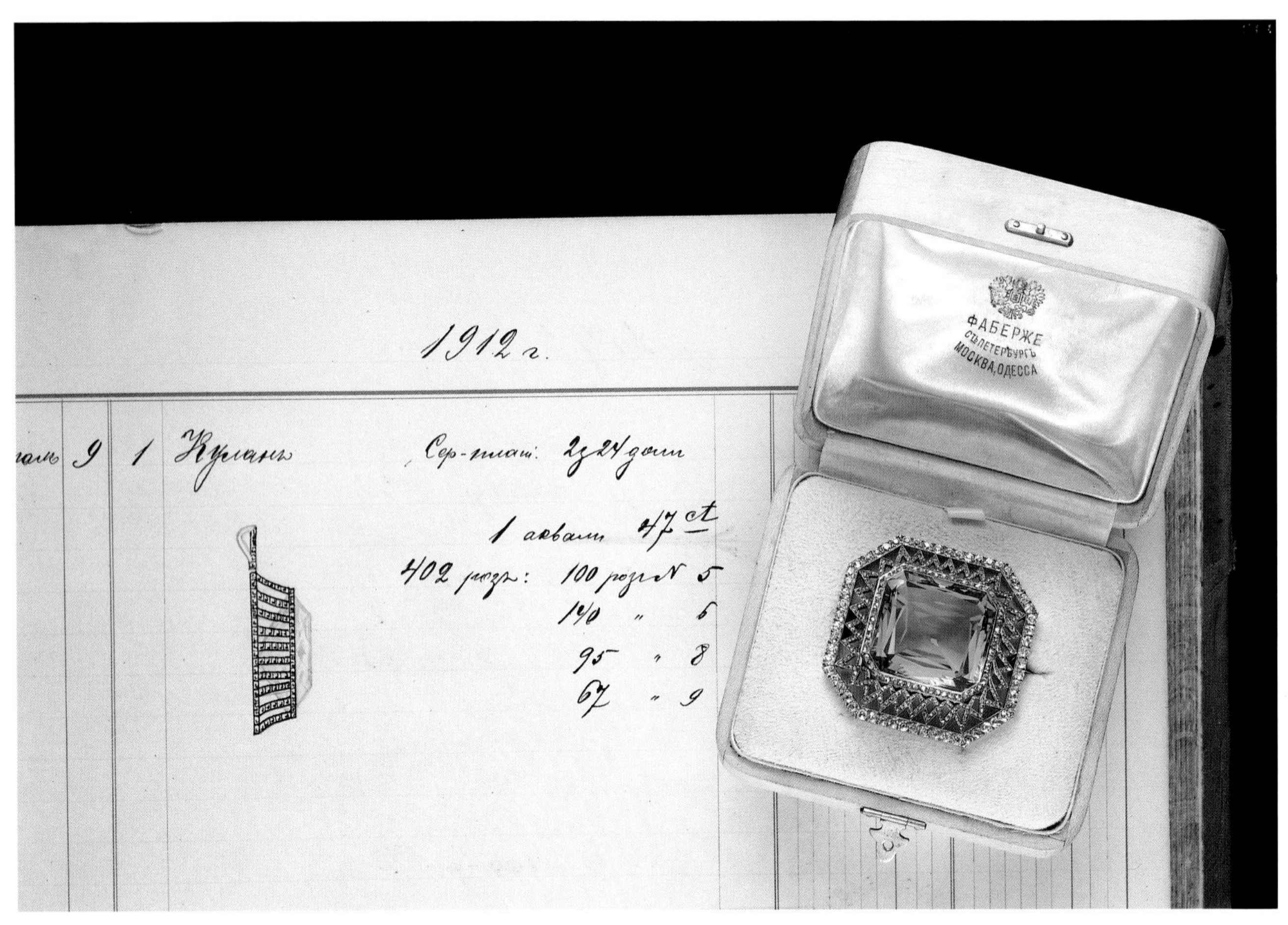
1912 г.
Кулонъ
402 розъ: 100 розъ № 5
140 " 6
95 " 8
67 " 9
ФАБЕРЖЕ
С.ПЕТЕРБУРГЪ
МОСКВА, ОДЕССА

1912 г.

Февраль 18 Діадема Сер. Плат.

1 аквам. 31 47/-

2 " 7 18/-

49 брил. 28/-

632 розы: 351 роза № 6

117 " " 7

163 " " 8

1 " " 9

Мартъ 1 Заяцъ на бюваръ Сер. и Сер-Пл

239 розъ: 104 розы № 5
62 " " 6
67 " " 7
5 " " 10
1 " " 15

" " Кулонъ-брошь Сер-Пл.

1 амет. 6 %-
41 брил. 5 %- } скл.
32 розы
доб. 103 розы: 36 розы № 5
8 " " 6
4 " " 7
51 " " 8
4 " " 9

" 2 Брошь Сер-Пл

1 аквам. 40 с/з
115 розъ: 30 розы № 5
84 " " 7
1 " " 10

" " Кулонъ № 3576

1 аквам. 6 5/- ч
3 брил. 7/-
28 розъ: 20 розы № 7
8 " 5
Плат. цепь ру 1/2

From top: A crowned March Hare in platinum, set with rose diamonds, seated within a wreath of laurel, evidently designed as a decoration to be applied to a desk blotter; dated, significantly, March 1, 1912. A platinum pendant set with a single amethyst and brilliant and rose diamonds; also dated March 1, 1912. A rectangular aquamarine cluster brooch mounted in platinum and framed with rose diamonds and surmounted by a bow. A platinum-mounted brooch-pendant set with brilliant and rose diamonds culminating in a heart-shaped aquamarine. These two designs are dated March 2, 1912.

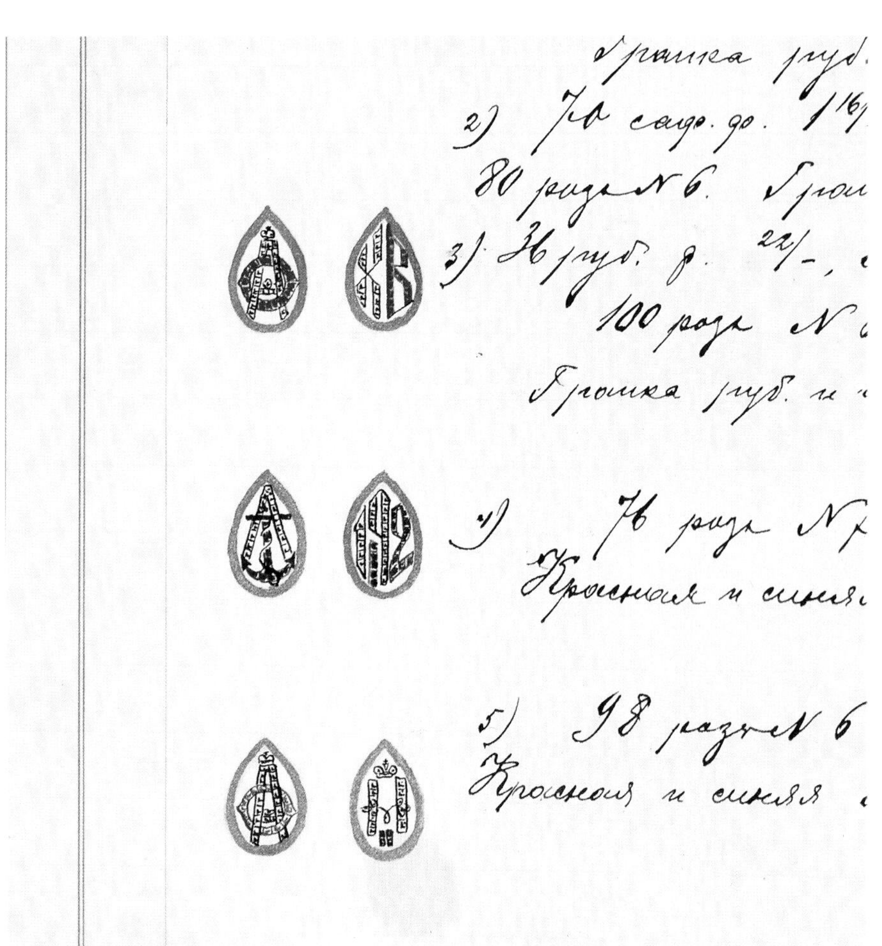

2) 70 ...
80 розъ № 6.
3) 36 руб. ...
100 розъ №
4) 76 розъ №
Красная и синяя
5) 98 розъ № 6
Красная и синяя

Platinum cuff links clearly designed for the Imperial Cabinet as Easter gifts, set with rose diamonds, calibré *rubies and sapphires, or with blue and white enamel. The Russian initials standing for "Christ Is Risen" are set in those on the top, and the crowned initials of Alexandra Feodorovna and Nicholas II are incorporated into the design of the third pair.. Dated March 13, 1912.*

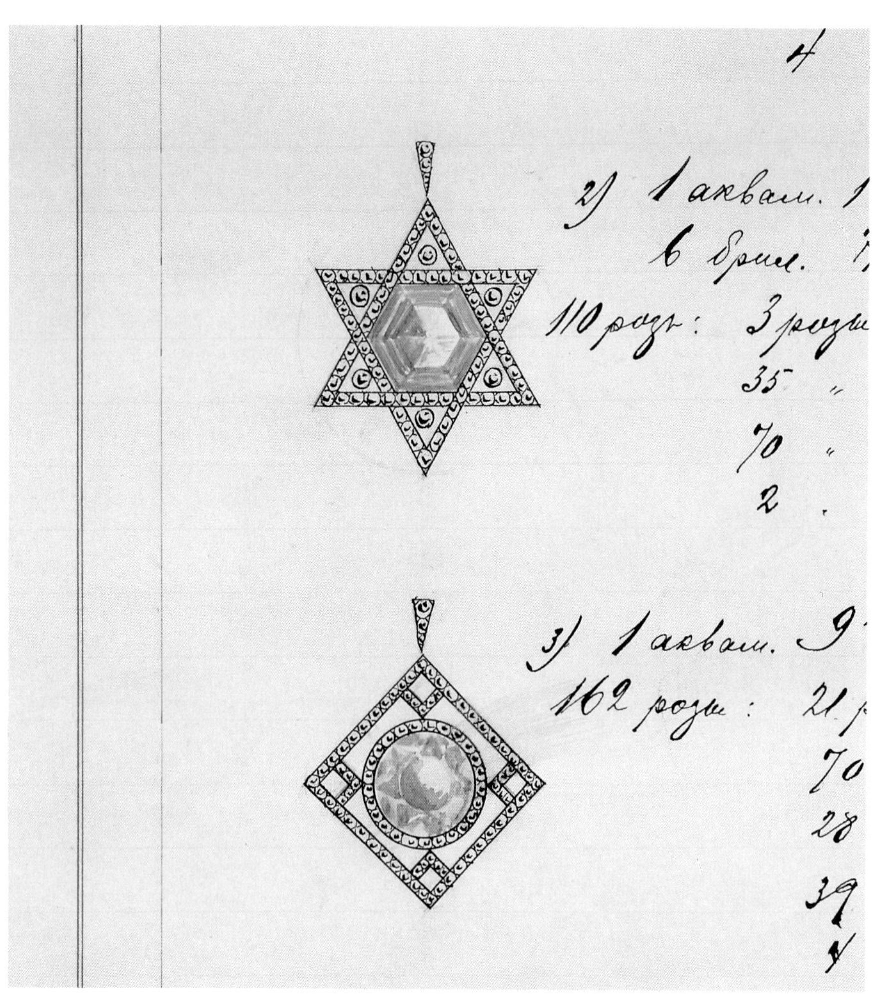

Two pendants, set with brilliant and rose diamonds, one in the form of a Shield of David with a hexagonal aquamarine at its center, the other with a circular aquamarine set within a square latticed frame. Dated March 20, 1912.

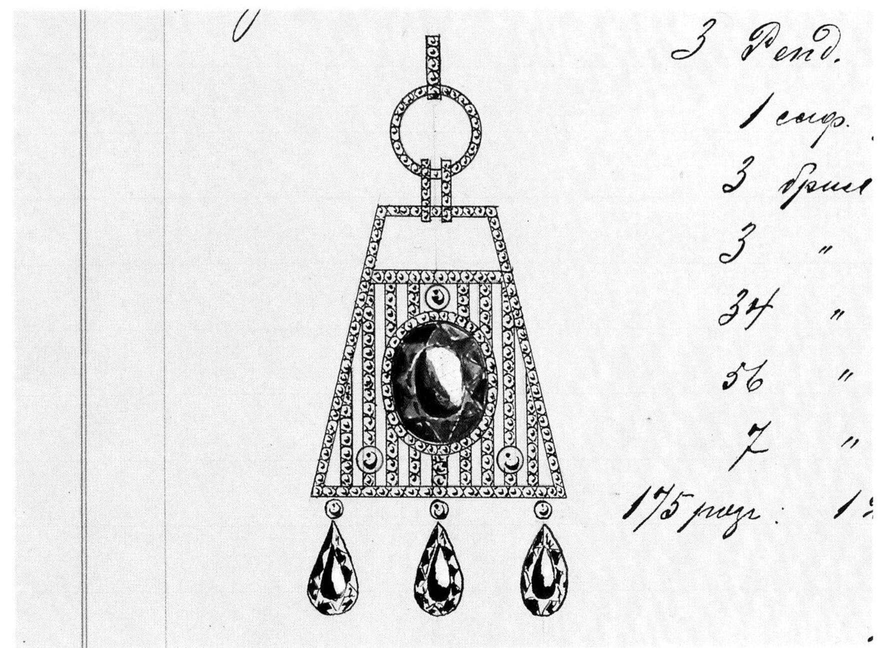

ABOVE:
One of a pair of blond tortoiseshell hair combs, the mount set with brilliant and rose diamonds bordered by pearls. Dated April 11, 1912.

CENTER:
Wedge-shaped pendant set with brilliant and rose diamonds with a large central sapphire and three drop diamonds hanging from the base. Dated April 12, 1912.

RIGHT:
A large circular sapphire set in the center of a brilliant and rose diamond pendant composed of a series of curves and rectangles. Dated April 16, 1912.

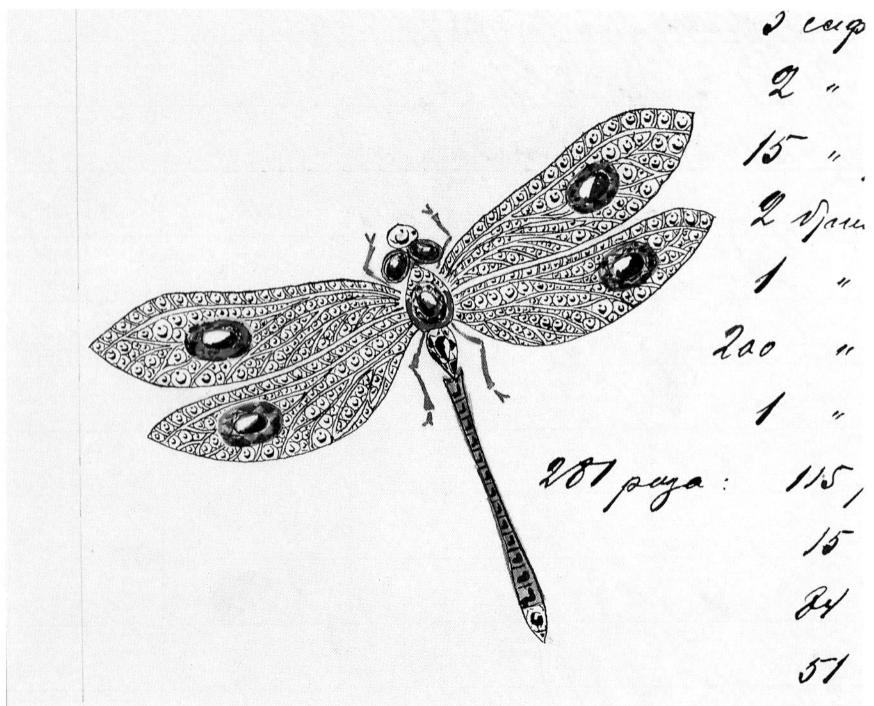

ABOVE:

A necklace and pendant composed of pearls and brilliant diamonds. Dated April 30, 1912.

LEFT:

A naturalistic dragonfly brooch set with faceted oval, cabochon, and square-cut sapphires and brilliant and rose diamonds. Dated May 11, 1912.

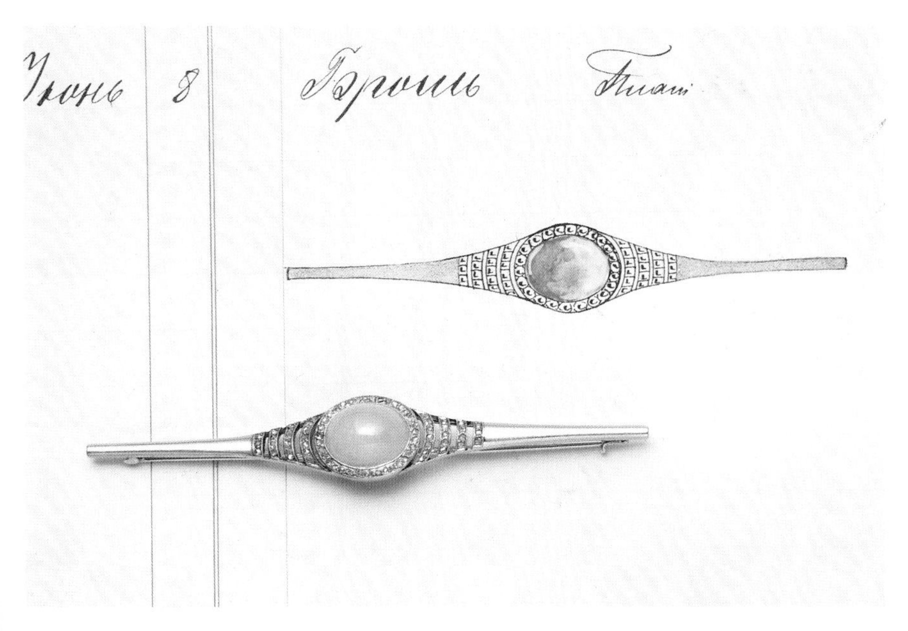

ABOVE:

A platinum bar brooch set with a central mecca stone and rose diamonds. Dated June 8, 1912. A similar brooch composed of the same materials is shown next to this design. Stamped with the initials of August Holmström. Length 3½" (8.8 cm). Wartski, London.

RIGHT:

An unusual platinum pendant in the form of a lace-bordered handkerchief, set with a carved lapis lazuli panel with beveled edges and brilliant and rose diamonds. Dated June 27, 1912.

LEFT:
A spray of forget-me-nots in gold, the flowers in turquoise and rose diamonds, the leaves nephrite, the vase in rock crystal. Dated May 12, 1912.

OPPOSITE:
A spray of forget-me-nots, broadly based on the design at left, with engraved gold stalk, translucent green-enameled gold leaves, and flower heads set with turquoise and rose diamonds, placed in a rock-crystal vase carved to appear to be filled with water. Height 6¼" (15.8 cm). The Wernher Collection, Luton Hoo, England.

LEFT:

Allan Bowe, Fabergé's partner who was born in Springbok Fontaine, South Africa; photographed in Moscow about 1900.

OPPOSITE:

Above, a design for a platinum pendant of marquise form, set with a carved Siberian amethyst panel applied with a floral motif and framed with chased scrolling and set with brilliant and rose diamonds. Below, another design for a platinum pendant, this one composed of a large, single pink sapphire of thirty-two carats and set with brilliant diamonds. Designs dated July 10, 1912. To the left is shown a pendant made from this pattern and of exactly this description. Height 1 9/16" (3.9 cm). Collection Madame Natalie Bourgeois. The pendant is fitted in the original case bearing the name of Allan Bowe, who worked with Fabergé until 1906, when the partnership was dissolved. Bowe later traded from London, as the lining of the box containing the pendant indicates.

ALLAN BOWE
87, GREENCROFT GDNS.
FINCHLEY ROAD,
LONDON, N.W.6.

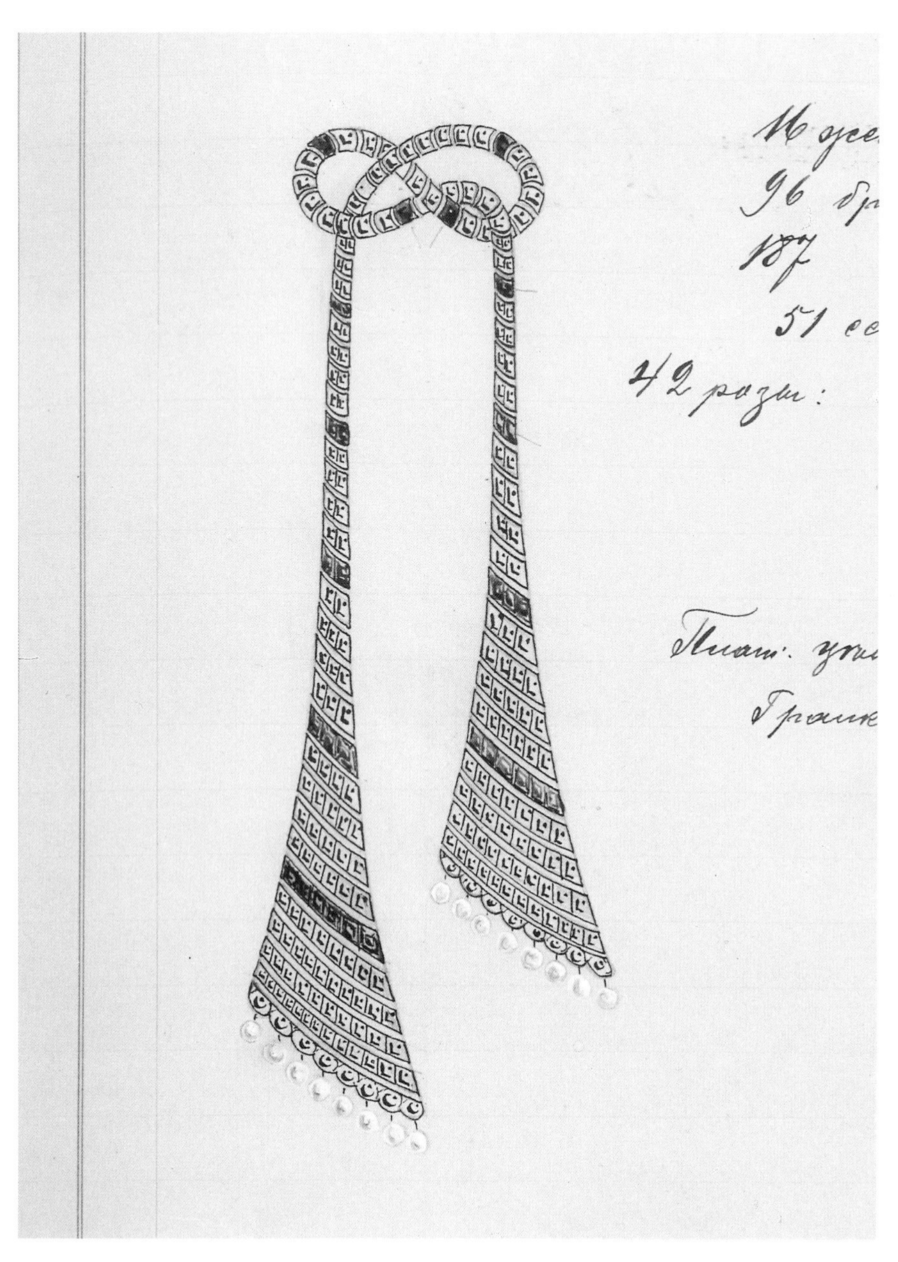

A platinum pendant in the unusual form of a tied jabot in brilliant and rose diamonds and calibré *sapphires, the fringes hung with pearls. Dated July 19, 1912.*

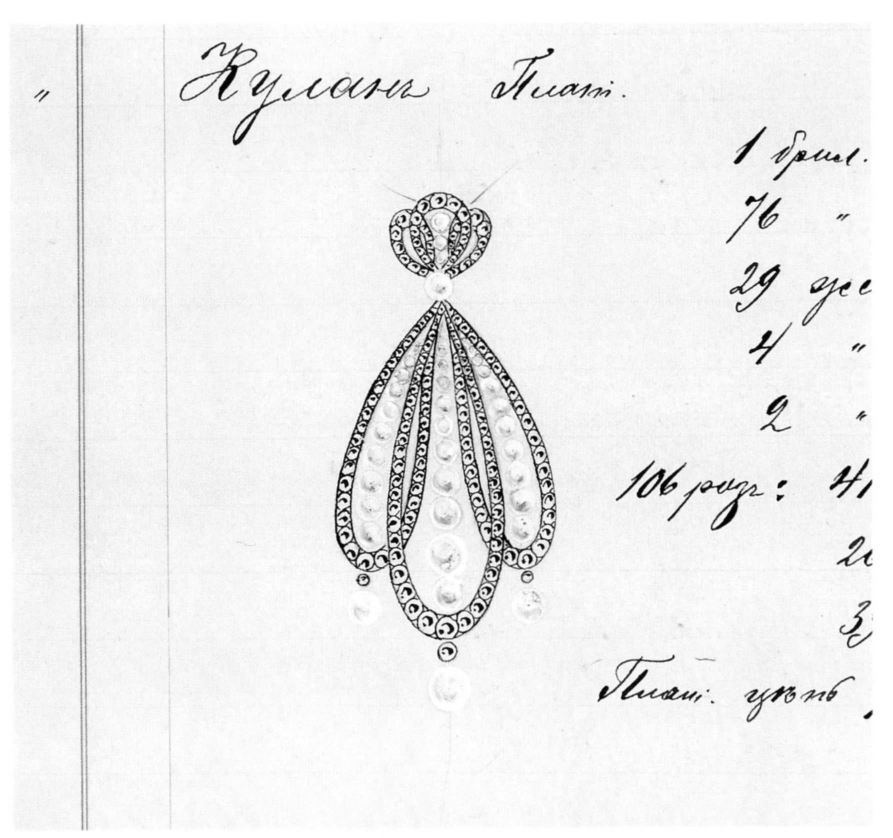

An attractive platinum pendant set with brilliant and rose diamonds and pearls in a pattern of triple loops. Dated August 21, 1912.

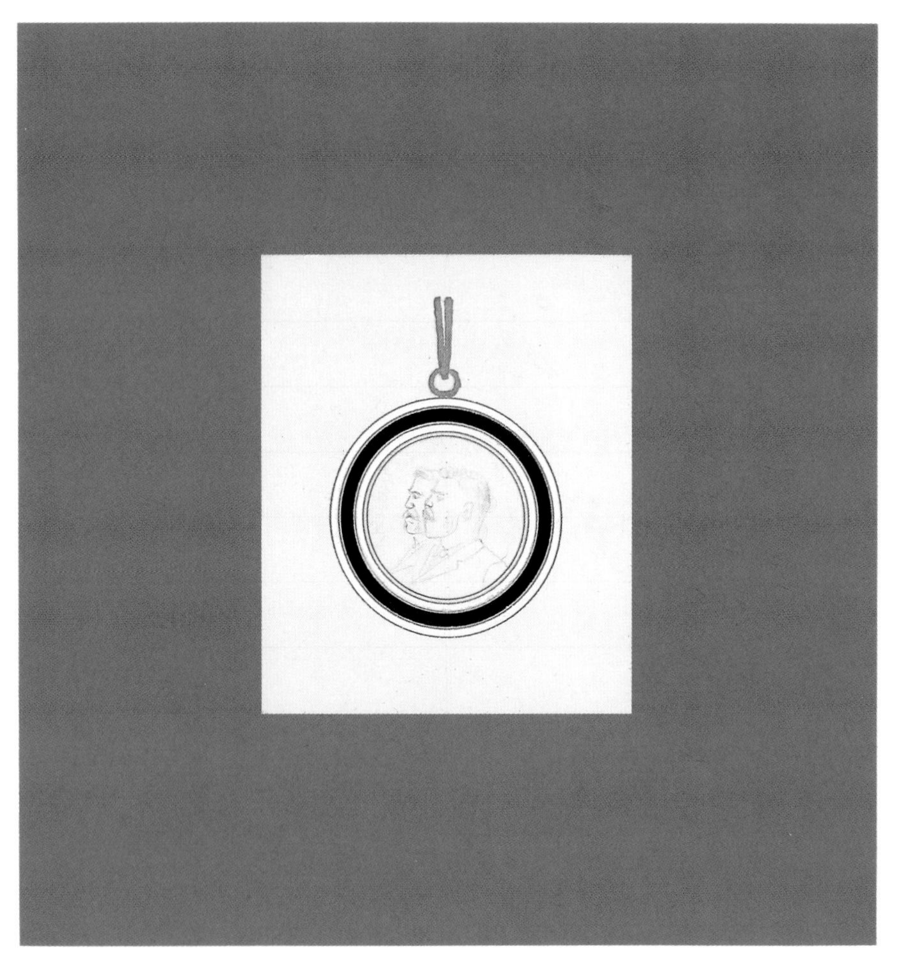

LEFT:

A gold pendant with a circular plaque displaying the painted portraits in profile of Emanuel Nobel and his father, Ludwig. This example is framed with blue enamel, and the notes inform us that two further versions were made, in red and gray enamel. Dated September 29, 1912.

OPPOSITE, ABOVE:

A bracelet comprising seven rectangular framed panels of rock crystal applied with frost flowers set with rose diamonds and to be centered by a circular watch within a cartouche frame, set with brilliant and rose diamonds. This jewel and that shown below were clearly designed for the Nobels. Dated December 3, 1912.

OPPOSITE, BELOW:

A platinum necklace, which may be converted into two bracelets, of fifteen rock-crystal panels framed and applied with snowflake motifs in rose diamonds. The panels are interrupted by a circular diamond-framed platinum medal with relief profile portraits of Emanuel and Ludwig Nobel and the inscriptions "1882–1912 / Mechanical Labor / Nobel." The piece is platinum and therefore unmarked. Length 13⅛" (33.2 cm). Given by Dr. Emanuel Nobel to his wife, Edla Ahlsell-Nobel. Forbes Magazine Collection, New York.

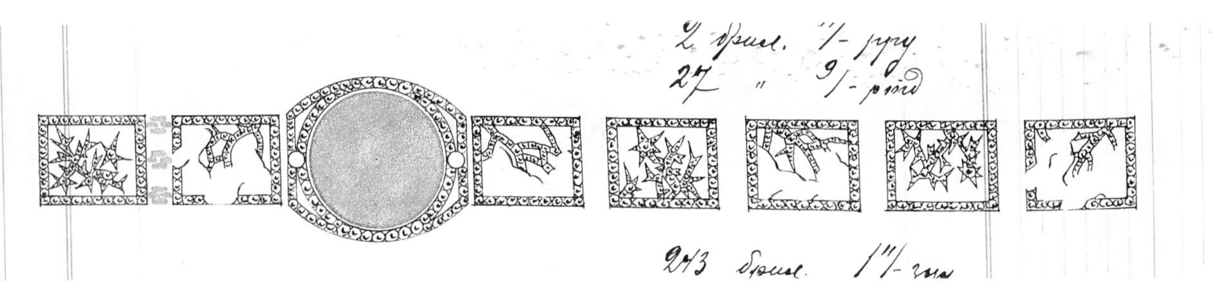

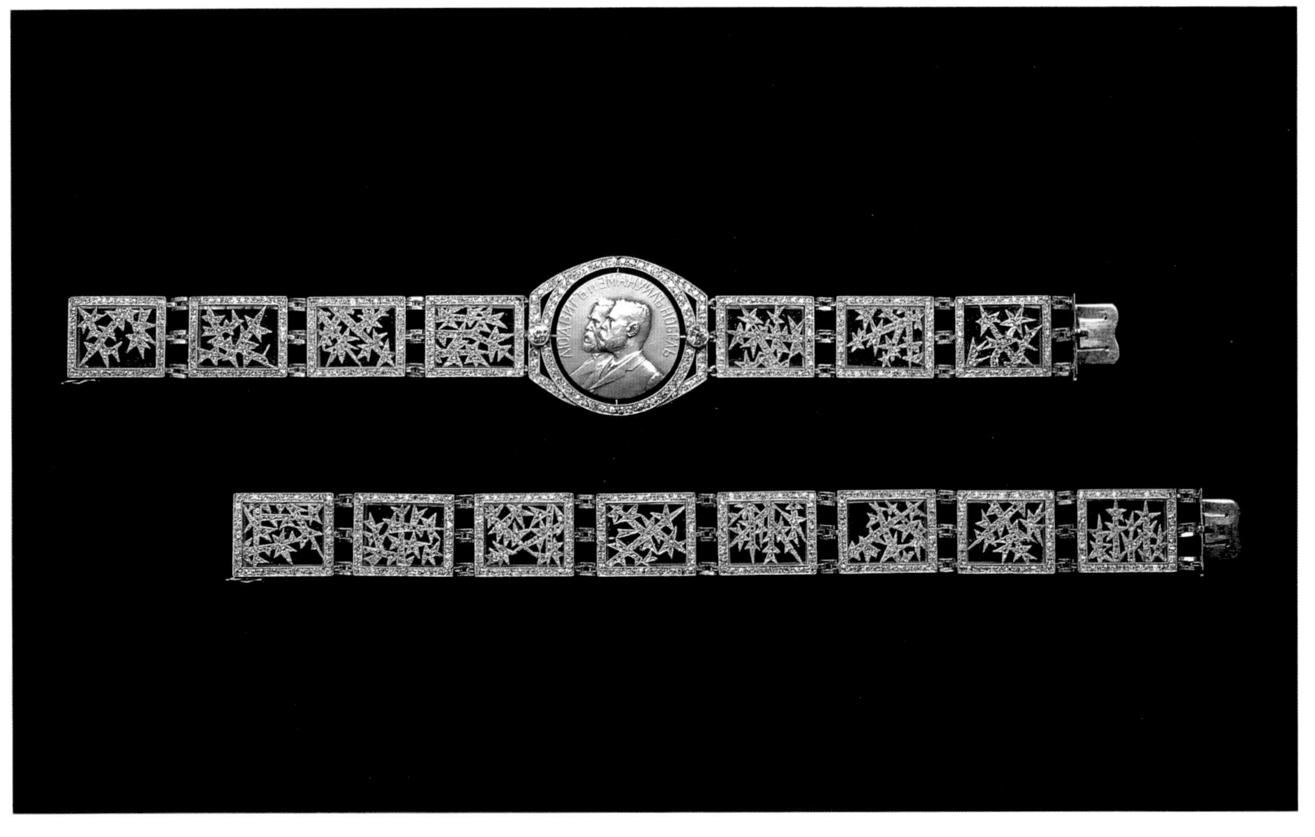

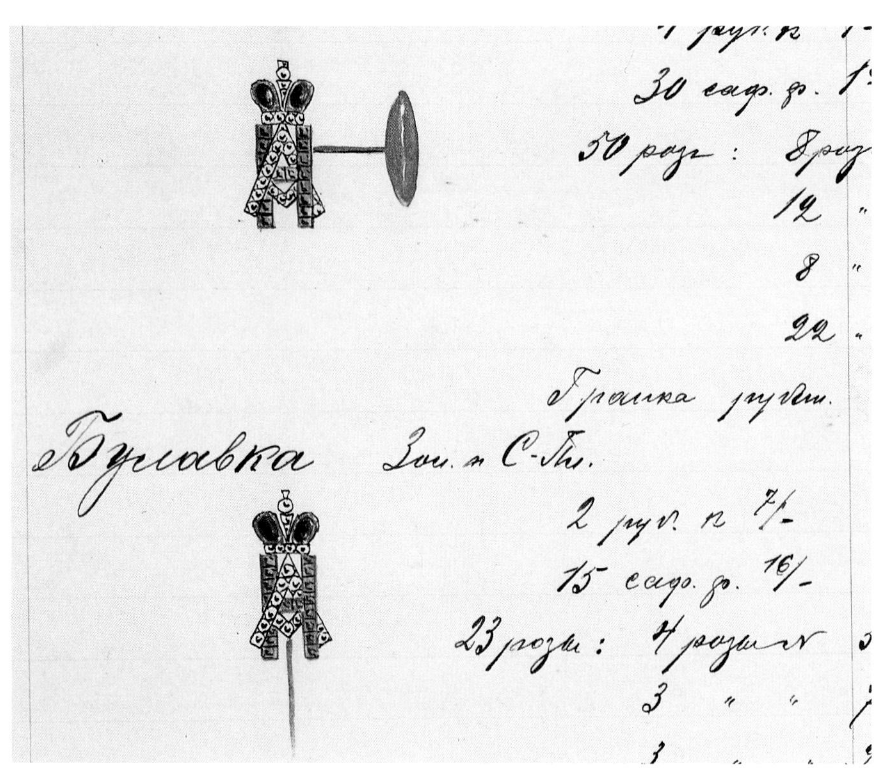

ABOVE:

A pair of cuff links and a tiepin designed from the crowned imperial initials of Nicholas and Alexandra in monogram form in gold and platinum, set with rose diamonds, cabochon rubies, and square-cut sapphires. Dated October 10, 1912.

LEFT:

A pair of diamond-set cuff links composed of the two initials of the Grand Duke Nicolai Nicolaevitch, beneath the Romanoff crown in gold set with cabochon rubies. This tall, spare, and austere man, the grandson of Nicholas I, was Commander in Chief of the Russian army in World War I and was an avowed enemy of Rasputin. Workmaster A. Hollming. Height 7/8" (2.2 cm). Wartski, London.

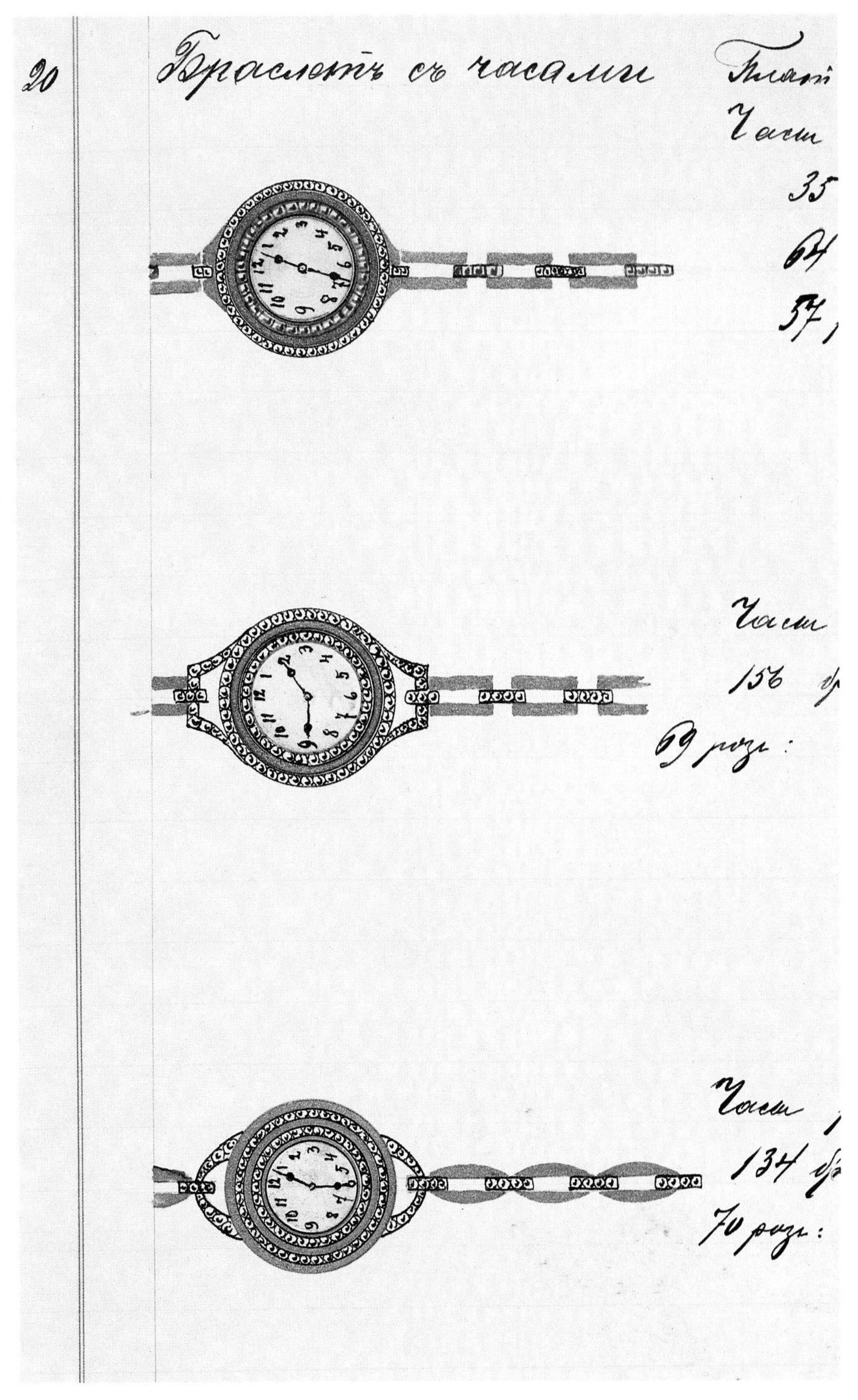

Three designs for watch bracelets to be made in platinum and set with brilliant and rose diamonds, that on the top with the addition of square-cut emeralds. Dated October 20, 1912.

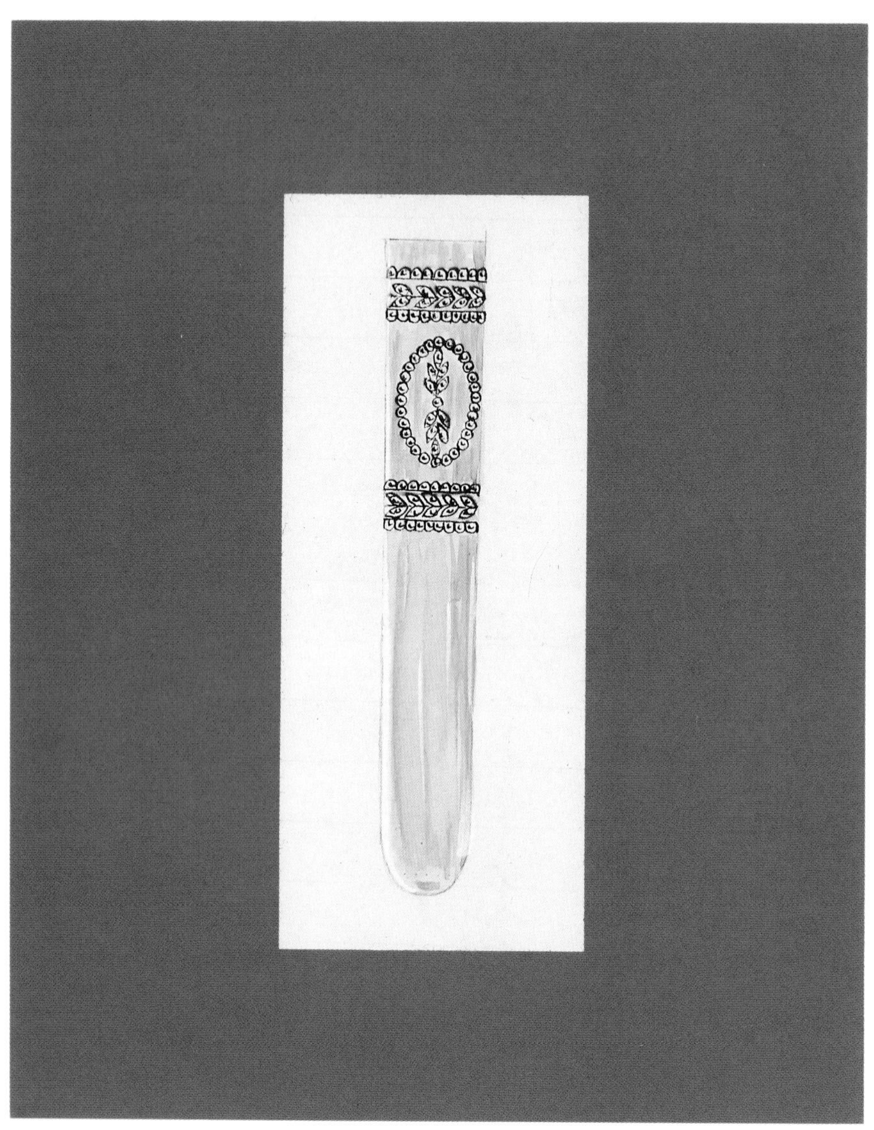

ABOVE, LEFT:

A platinum pendant set with rose diamonds in the form of a birdcage containing a chick, presumably carved from an appropriate stone, such as citrine, and probably set with a rose-diamond eye. Dated October 24, 1912.

ABOVE, RIGHT:

An oval platinum pendant bordered by rose diamonds framing what appears to be a rare example for Fabergé of a reverse intaglio in the English taste depicting a naturalistically painted edelweiss. Dated November 22, 1912.

LEFT:

Amber cigarette holder with a rose diamond-set foliate motif and borders mounted in platinum. Dated October 30, 1912.

A lavish diadem incorporating the client's own pair of large cabochon sapphire drops. It is mounted in platinum and set with large brilliant and rose diamonds. Dated November 16, 1912.

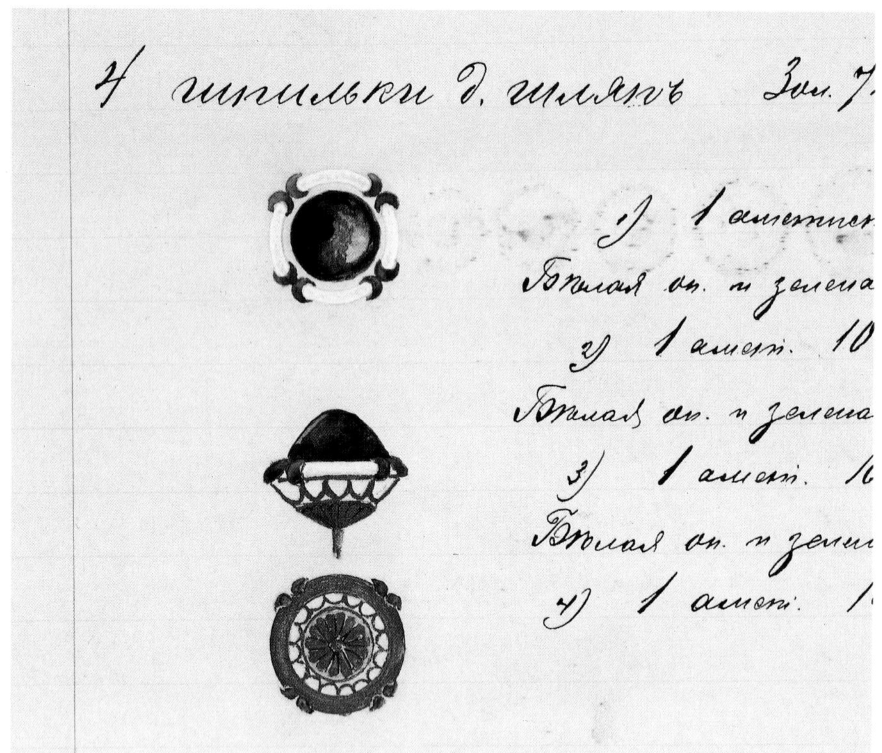

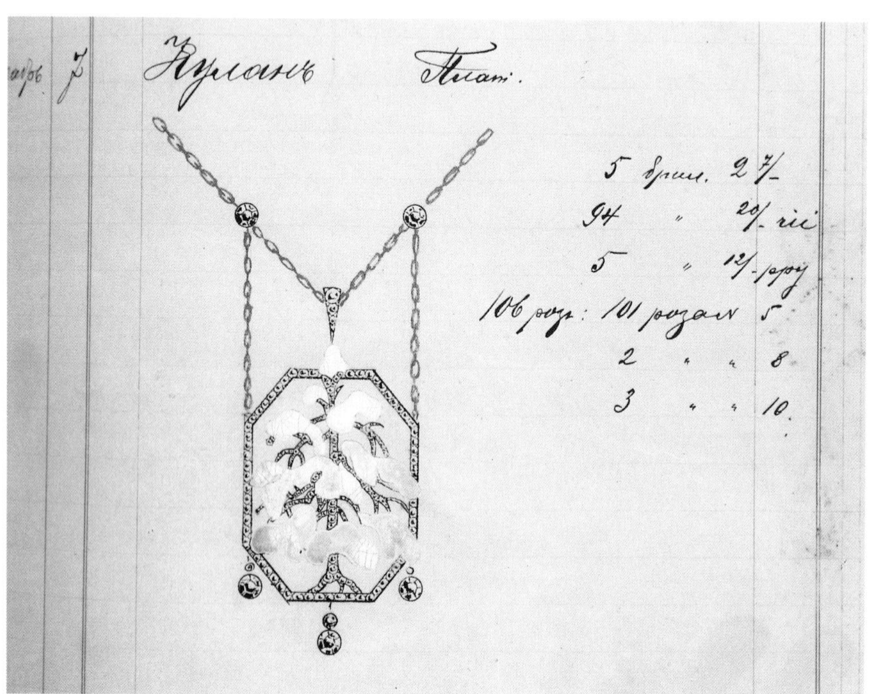

ABOVE:

These drawings show three views of a design for a gold hatpin, of which four were to be set, each with a large cabochon amethyst within an opalescent white enameled border applied with four green-enameled double crescents on mounts. The head is fixed to the pin with an elaborately chased gold mount. Dated December 1, 1912.

LEFT:

Octagonal platinum pendant set with brilliant and rose diamonds framing a snow-covered tree with, presumably, rock crystal carved to represent the snow. Dated December 7, 1912.

OPPOSITE:

Designs for two pairs of blond tortoiseshell hairpins, mounted in platinum and set with brilliant and rose diamonds. Dated December 7, 1912.

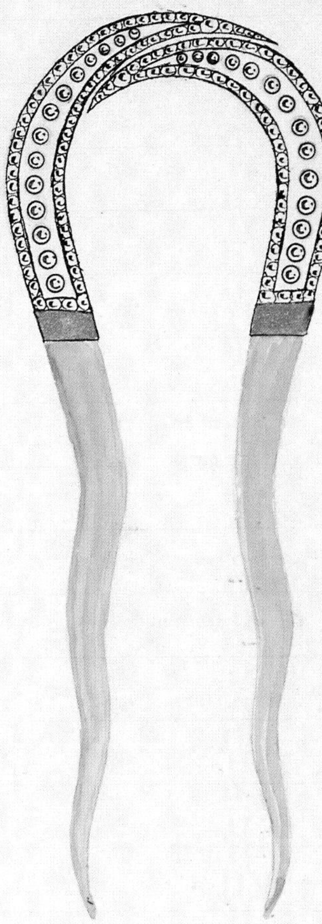

1) 15 брил. 22/- руу
15 " 9/- рощ
194 розы: 45 розы № 5
10 " " 6
75 " " 8
64 " " 9

2) 15 брил. 23/- руу
15 " 9/- рощ
188 роз: 36 розы № 5
54 " " 8
98 " " 9
4 черепах. части рч.

" " 2 шпильки Плат.

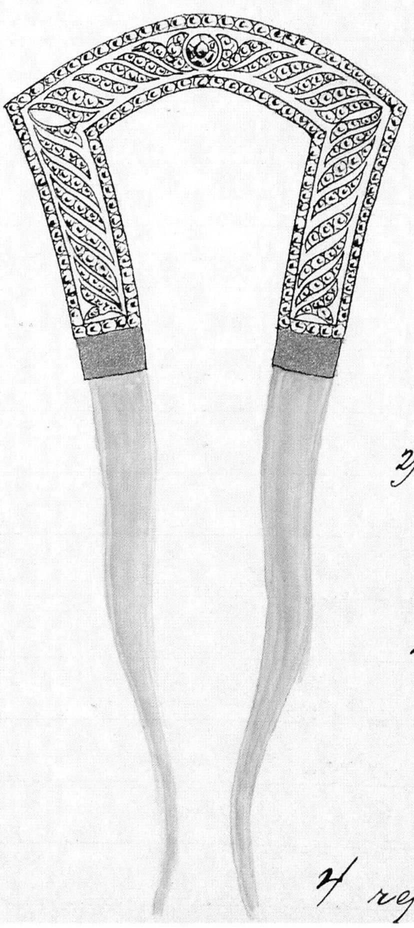

1) 1 брил. 30/-
6 " 7/-
71 " 16/-
259 роз: 25 розы № 5
40 " " 6
25 " " 7
169 " " 9

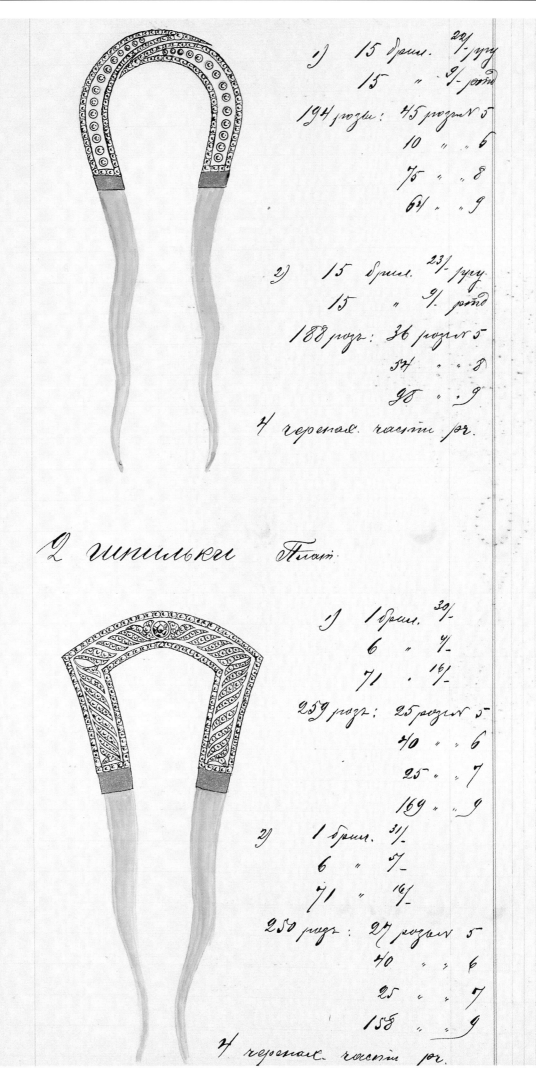

2) 1 брил. 31/-
6 " 7/-
71 " 16/-
250 роз: 27 розы № 5
40 " " 6
25 " " 7
158 " " 9
4 черепах. части рч.

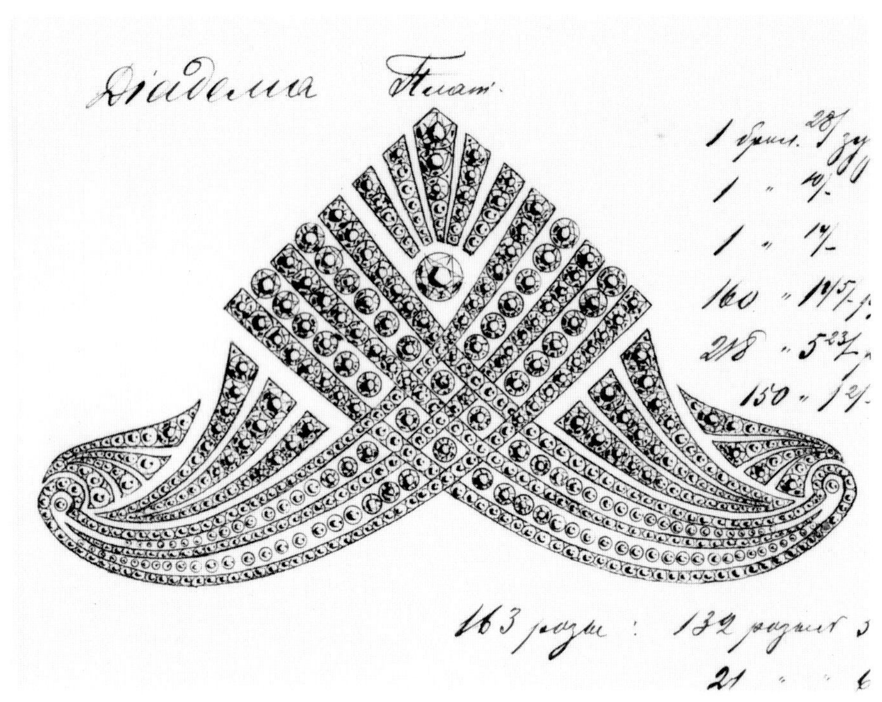

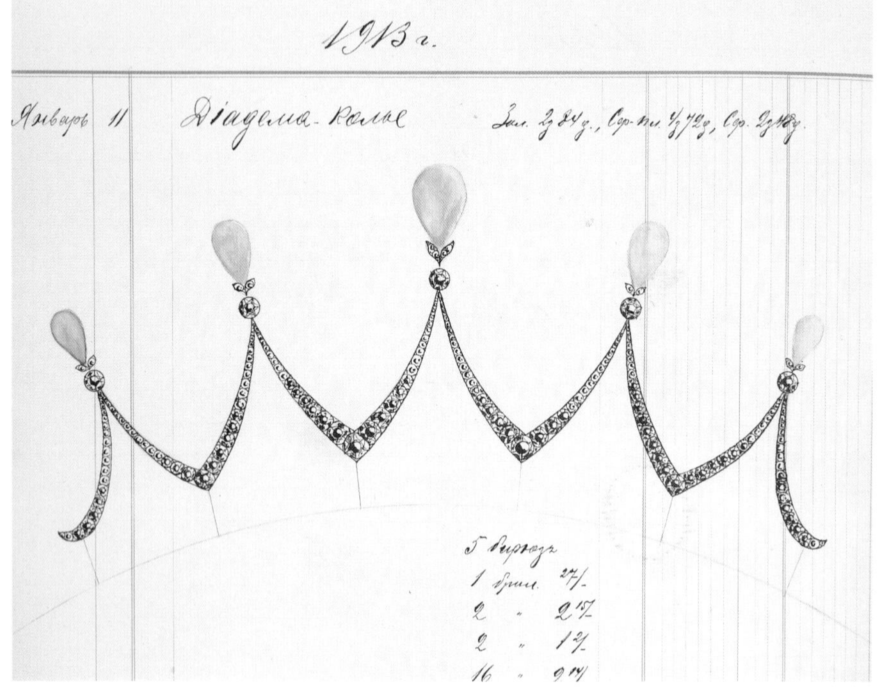

ABOVE:

A boldly conceived diadem mounted in platinum and set with brilliant and rose diamonds. Dated December 17, 1912.

LEFT:

A diamond court tiara set with five carved turquoises mounted in gold and silver. The drawing of the jewel measures $8\frac{1}{4}''$ *(20.9 cm) across. Dated January 11, 1913.*

OPPOSITE:

A lavish and rather conventional necklace in platinum set with four cabochon emeralds and brilliant and rose diamonds with stylized shell motifs, set against a chain-patterned background and finished with five drop diamonds. Dated December 20, 1912.

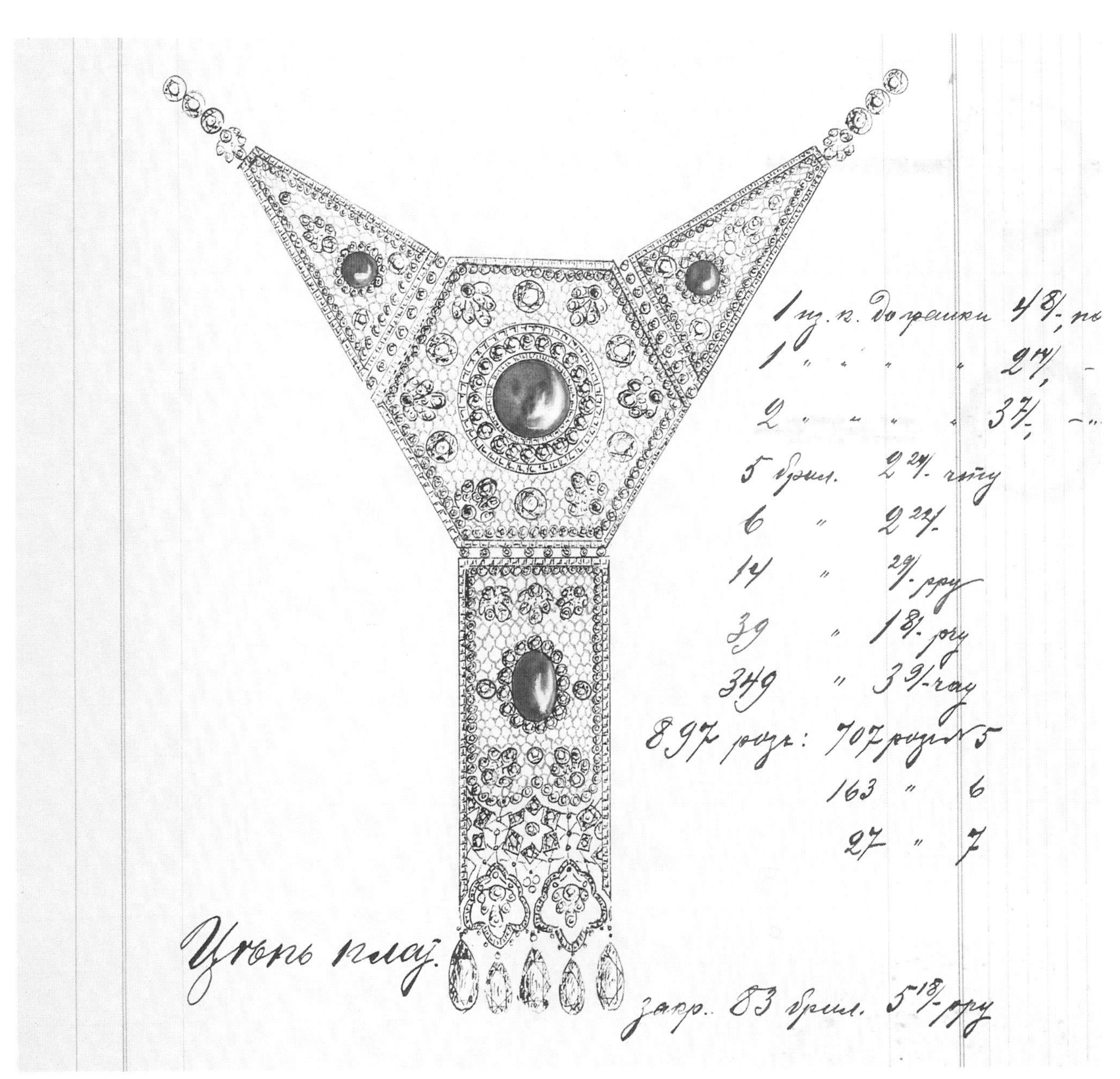
1
1 " " " " 2 7/
2 " " " " 3 7/
5 брил. 2 24/-
6 " 2 24/-
14 " 29/-
39 " 18/-
349 " 39/-
897 розъ: 707 розъ 5
163 " 6
27 " 7
закр. 83 брил. 5 18/-

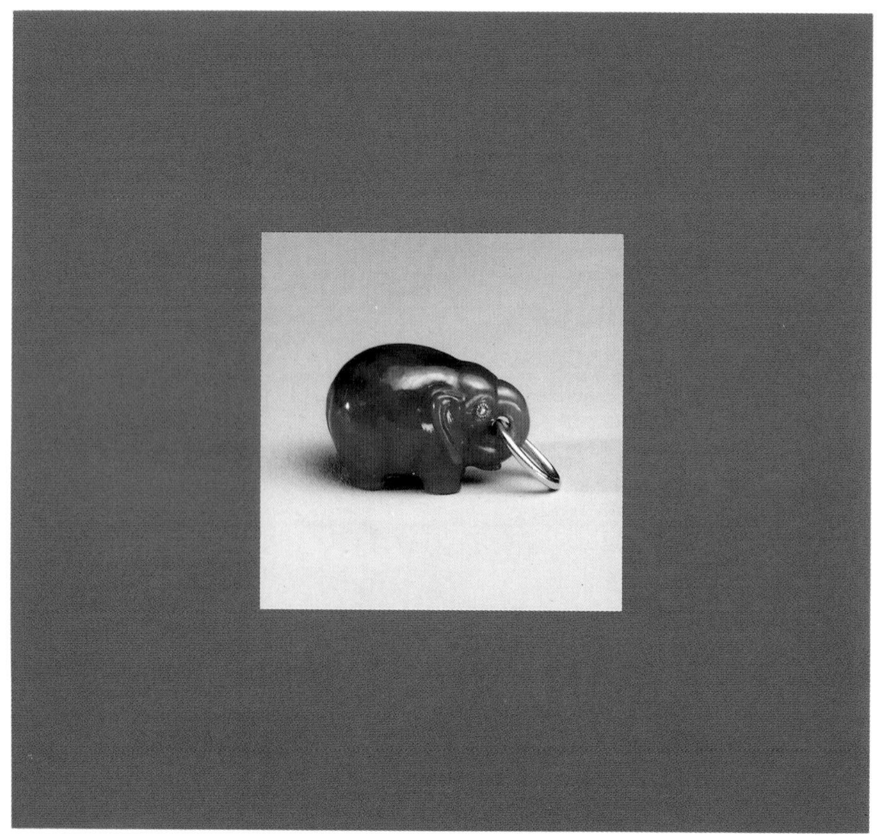

ABOVE:

Cuff links in the form of carved orletz (rhodonite) elephants mounted in platinum and gold and set with sixty-two rose diamonds. Dated January 11, 1913.

LEFT:

A wittily carved elephant in Siberian jade with rose diamond eyes, suspended on a gold ring; the oviform creature serves as a miniature Easter egg pendant. Height 15/16" (2.4 cm). Wartski, London.

ABOVE:

Small breloque in the form of a rotund pig to be carved of nephrite, set with rose diamonds. Dated January 15, 1913.

RIGHT:

An amusing carving of an owl, also designed as a miniature Easter egg pendant, in purpurine with brilliant diamond eyes, suspended on a gold ring. A worker in the Imperial Glass Factory in St. Petersburg, named Petouchov, discovered how to manufacture this attractive crimson material that was much used by Fabergé. Marked **КФ**. *Height* 13/16" *(2.1 cm). Private collection.*

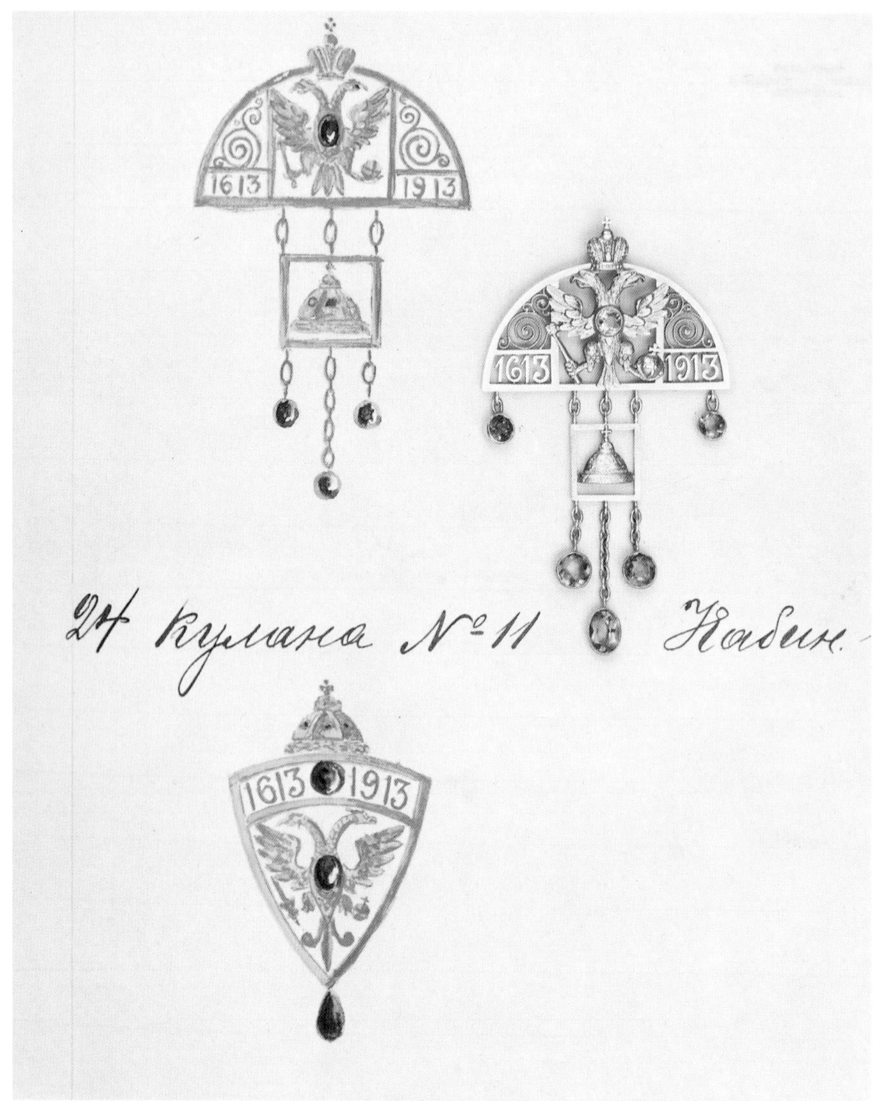

A B O V E :

From His Imperial Majesty's Cabinet; a circular gold pendant with the Romanoff Tercentenary years 1613–1913, surmounted by a faithful replica of Peter the Great's sable-trimmed shapka *set with rubies and emeralds and hung with three single sapphires. Dated February 4, 1913.*

L E F T :

Gold pendants set with amethysts designed for the Imperial Cabinet to commemorate the Tercentenary of Romanoff rule. Dated February 5, 1913. The actual gold pendant placed on the right of the page is set with five amethysts and is signed with the initials of August Holmström. Overall height 2½" (5.7 cm). Wartski, London.

Above, a chased and engraved gold chain incorporating the shapka *to be set with small rubies, sapphires, spinels, and rose diamonds. Below, a chatelaine, similarly fashioned but consisting of three Romanoff double-headed eagles connected by link chains, also to be set with small gems. Three of the chains and two chatelaines were designed for the Cabinet for His Imperial Highness, presumably one of the Grand Dukes. Both dated February 16, 1913.*

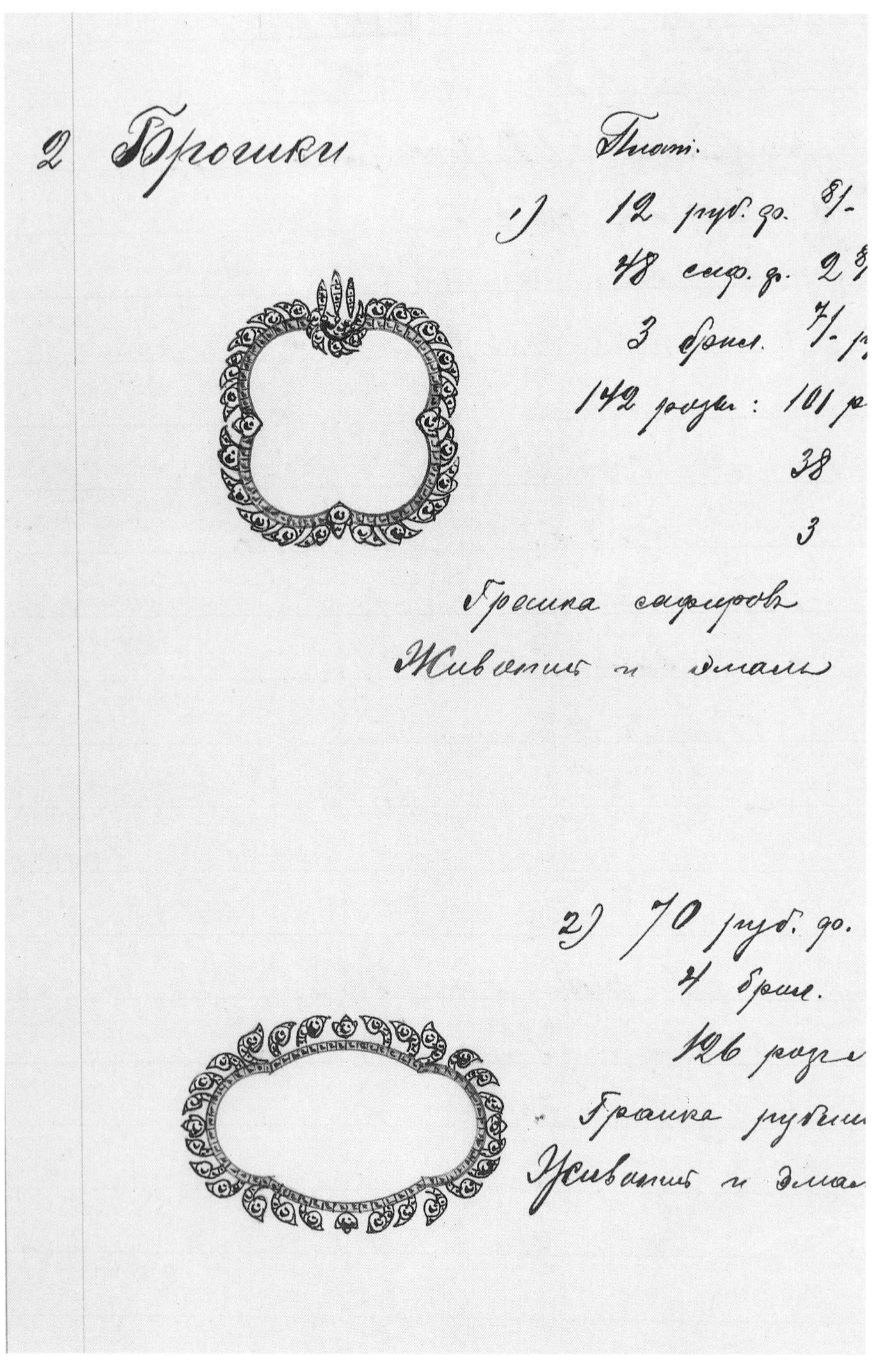

Designs for the platinum brooches intended as frames for the enameled portraits shown opposite, to be set with square-cut sapphires or rubies. Dated March 14, 1913.

ABOVE:

A gold brooch framed with a brilliant and rose diamond foliate border and calibré *sapphires and rubies. It holds a portrait of the Crown Prince Maha Vajirunhis of Siam, who sadly died at the age of only seventeen, painted in sepia enamel against an opalescent oyster background through which a wavy* guillochage *is visible. The brooch is surmounted by a combination of Siamese dynastic weaponry including a three-pronged dagger. 1³⁄₁₆" square (3 cm).*

RIGHT:

A gold brooch similar to the example illustrated above but set with calibré *rubies and framing portraits of the children of King Chulalongkorn, including, in the center, the Crown Prince. Length 1¹¹⁄₁₆" (4.2 cm). Both brooches are stamped with the gold mark 72, the equivalent of eighteen-carat, and the initials of August Holmström.*[9]

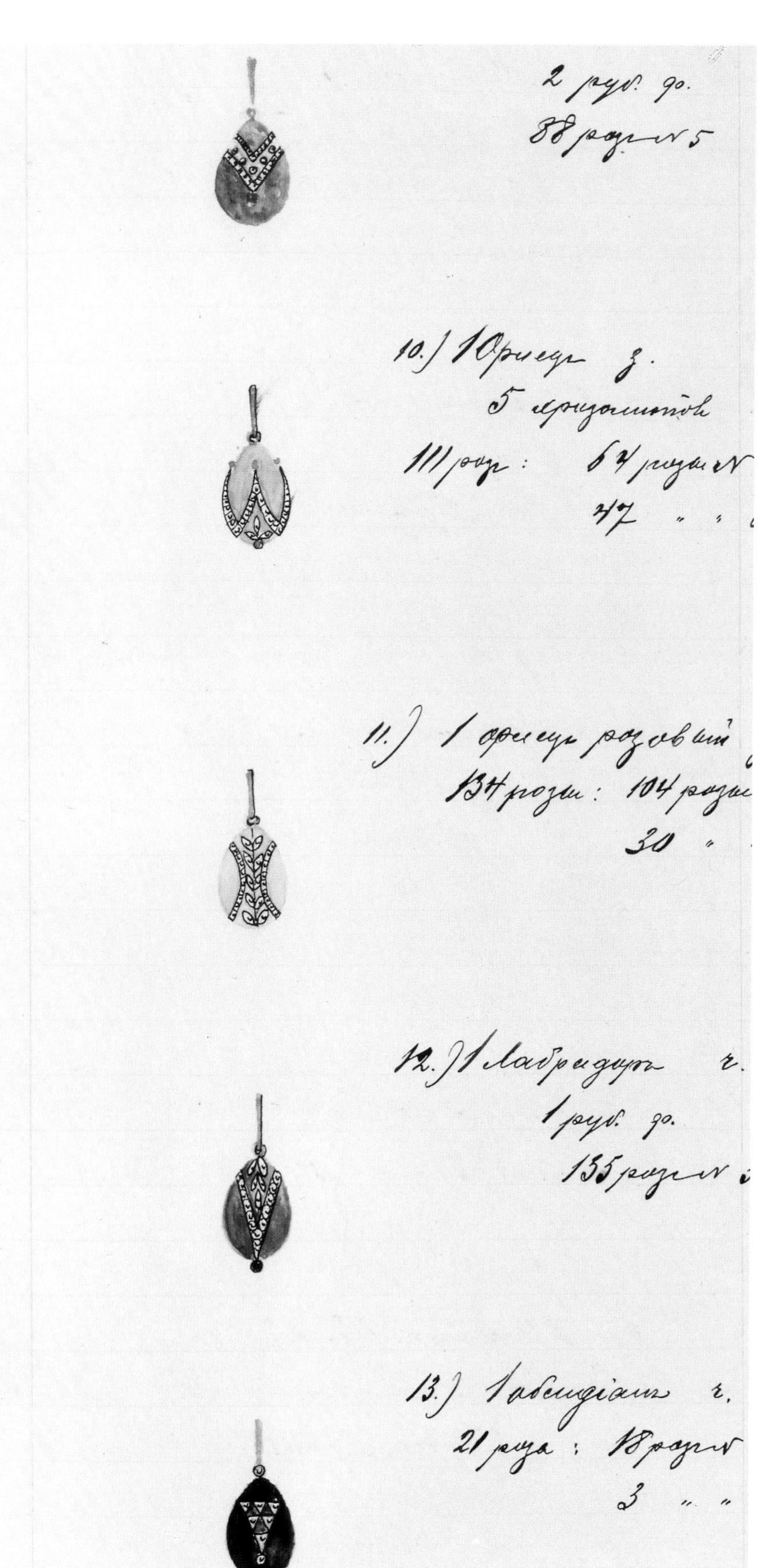

Five miniature Easter eggs carved in various semiprecious stones, the top example evidently in brown Chinese jade, with two orletz (rhodonite) eggs below, then one in labradorite and the last in obsidian. They all are set with rose diamonds; the second egg is set also with five chrysoberyls and the first and fourth with rubies. Dated April 1, 1913.

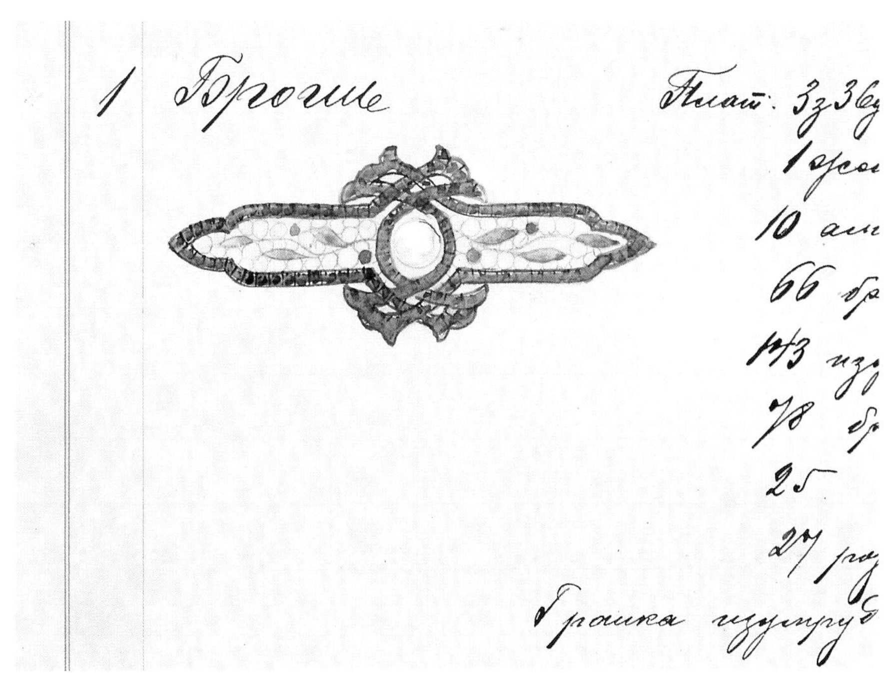

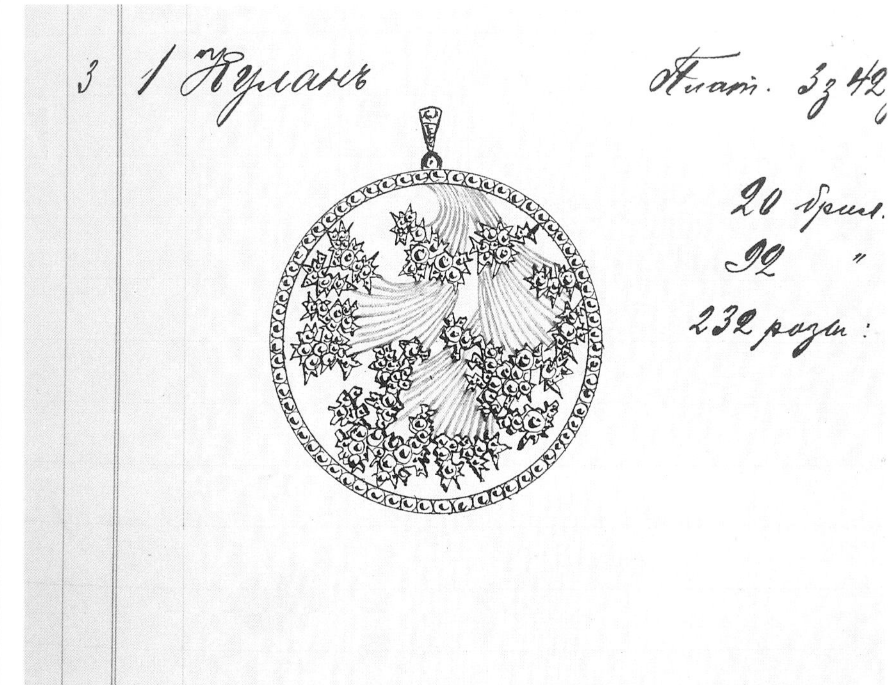

ABOVE:
Platinum brooch with central single pearl with decoration and borders set with square-cut emeralds. The areas flanking the pearl are embellished with leaves and berries carved in amethyst and set against brilliant and rose diamonds. Dated March 23, 1913.

RIGHT:
Platinum pendant set with brilliant and rose diamonds representing bunches of flowers. Dated April 3, 1913.

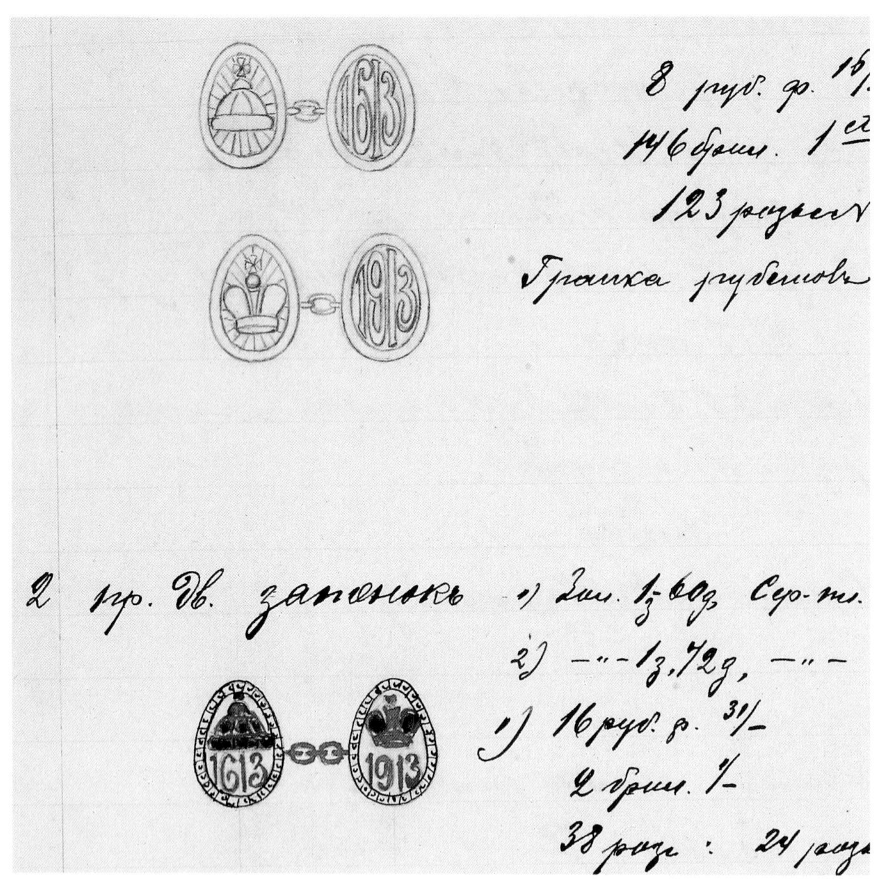

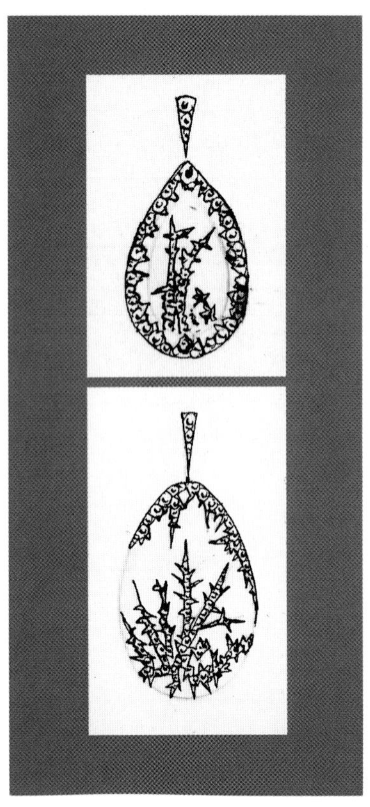

ABOVE:

Gold cuff links designed to be set with rubies or sapphires and brilliant and rose diamonds. They are further examples of jewels specially ordered to commemorate the Romanoff Tercentenary, 1613–1913. Dated April 6, 1913.

FAR LEFT:

Two carved rock-crystal miniature Easter egg pendants, mounted in platinum and set with rose diamonds in frost patterns much favored by the Nobel brothers. The top pendant is designed as a frame within which the stone egg swings, whereas the one below is quite simply a stone pendant. Dated April 10, 1913.

LEFT:

A platinum miniature Easter egg pendant composed of a large cabochon sapphire, rose diamonds, and opaque white enamel applied in imitation of snow. Dated April 11, 1913.

Alma Theresia Pihl, a leading designer in the Holmström workshop, photographed possibly about the time of her marriage in 1912.

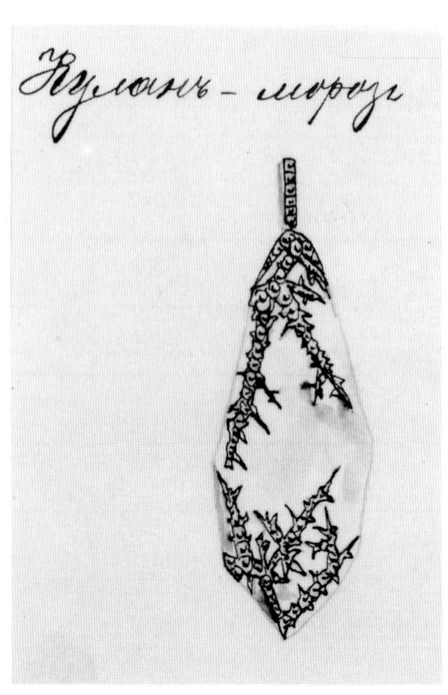

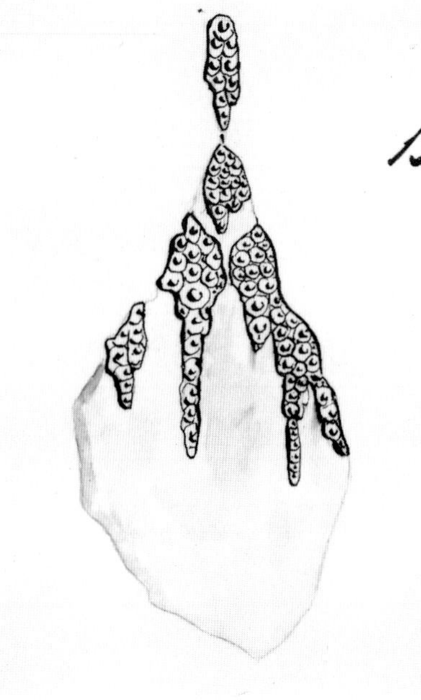

ABOVE:

Carved rock-crystal frost pendant mounted in platinum and set with 30 brilliant and 131 rose diamonds. Dated April 30, 1913.

CENTER:

A rock-crystal pendant based on the design above, with platinum mounts set with rose diamonds in imitation of frost. This pendant was acquired from Fabergé's London branch by a Mr. Oppenheim on December 23, 1913, for £60. Unmarked. Height 1³⁄₈" (3.5 cm). Forbes Magazine Collection, New York.

FAR LEFT:

Carved rock-crystal frost pendant mounted in platinum and set with fifteen brilliant and ninety-two rose diamonds. Dated May 2, 1913.

LEFT:

Carved rock-crystal frost brooch mounted in platinum and set with rose diamonds. Dated May 2, 1913.

Winter Egg, presented to the Dowager Empress Marie Feodorovna by Nicholas II in 1913. This enchanting composition consists of an egg carved from a block of rock crystal with frost flowers engraved on the inside and carried out in diamonds outside. Each half of the egg, which opens on a hinge, is rimmed with brilliant diamonds; it is surmounted by a moonstone covering the date, and is set throughout in platinum. Within the egg, a rose diamond and platinum basket of snowdrops hangs by the handle from a hook; the flowers are executed in white quartz with gold-set olivine centers, the leaves in pale nephrite, stalks in gold, and the earth in spun gold. The egg, which is removable, rests on a rock-crystal block of ice set with brilliant and rose diamonds; it is held firmly in position by a projecting pin that fits into the bottom of the egg. Sacheverell Sitwell has described this piece as a "Winter Egg," and the surprise it contains is particularly felicitous with its promise of spring. This is one of the best examples of Fabergé's use of gems to express his composition as opposed to their introduction merely as enrichment. The egg itself bears no marks, but the bottom of the basket of flowers is engraved "Fabergé 1913." Height of egg, 4" (10.2 cm); height of basket, 3¼" (8.3 cm). Formerly in the collection of the late Bryan Ledbrook, London.

LEFT:

Circular gold brooch designed to commemorate three hundred years of Romanoff rule, incorporating the dates 1613 and 1913 and a replica of Peter the Great's shapka. *Set with brilliant and rose diamonds, aquamarines, and a ruby. Stamped with Holmström's initials. Diameter 1 3/16" (3 cm). Hillwood Museum, Washington, D.C.*

OPPOSITE:

From top: a pendant mounted in platinum and set with a beveled Siberian jade (nephrite) panel framed by rose diamonds with brilliant diamond drops; a platinum pendant set with rose diamonds and hung with nephrite beads; a circular gold brooch incorporating the Romanoff Tercentenary dates and set with rubies and rose diamonds. Commissioned by the Imperial Cabinet. All dated May 22, 1913.

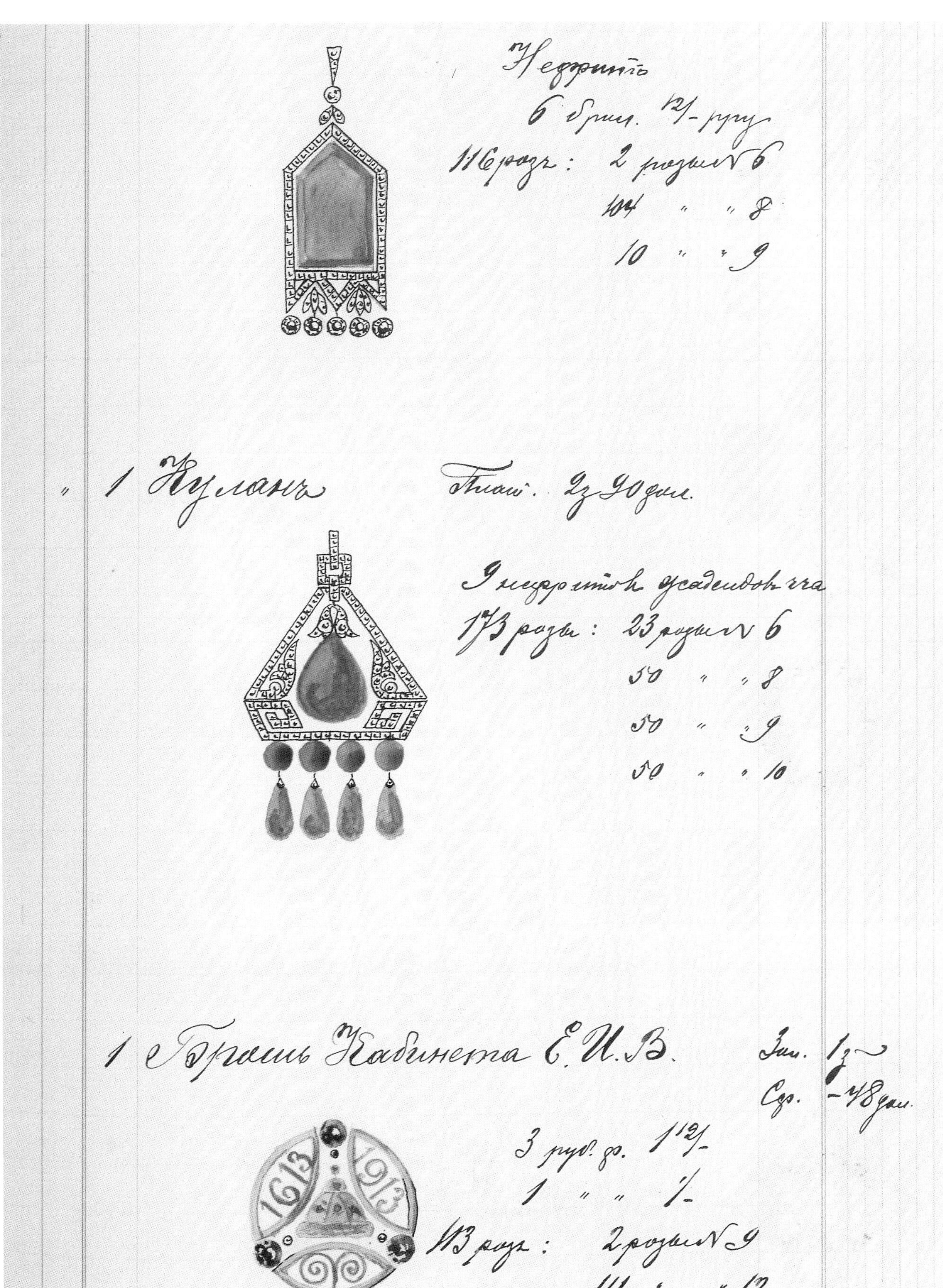

Нефритъ
6 брил. 12/- руб
116 розъ: 2 розы № 6
104 " " 8
10 " " 9

1 Кулонъ   Плат. 2з 90 дол.

9 нефритовъ усадебовъ
173 розы: 23 розы № 6
50 " " 8
50 " " 9
50 " " 10

1 Брошь Кабинета Е.И.В.   Зол. 1з
Сер. –48 дол.

3 руб. гр. 1²/-
1 " " ¹/-
113 розъ: 2 розы № 9
111 " " 12

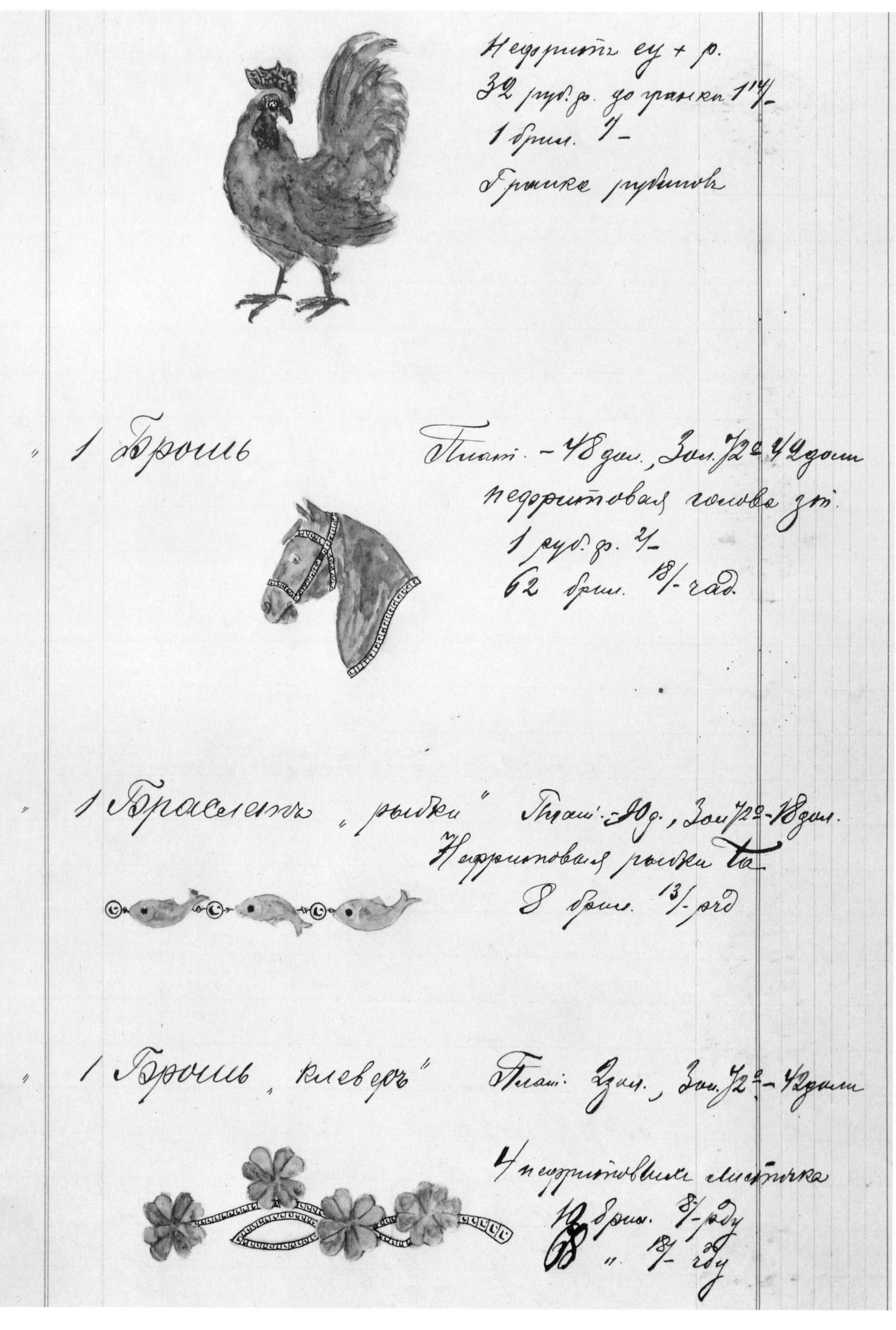
Нефритъ су + р.
32 руб. р. до гранка 1¼-
1 брил. ¼-
Глазки рубиновъ

1 Брошь Плат. – 48 дол., Зол. 72° – 42 дол.
нефритовая голова зт.
1 руб. р. ¼-
62 брил. ⅛-чад.

1 Браслетъ „рыбки" Плат. – 30 д., Зол. 72° – 18 дол.
Нефритовыя рыбки 6а
8 брил. ⅓-р

1 Брошь „клеверъ" Плат. 2 зол., Зол. 72° – 42 дол.
4 нефритовыхъ листочка
12 брил. ⅛-р
8 " ⅛-

OPPOSITE:

From top: Brooch designed as a hen, carved in nephrite and presumably mounted in gold, set with thirty-two rubies and a brilliant diamond. Brooch formed as a horse's head, carved in nephrite, mounted in gold and platinum, and set with sixty-two brilliant diamonds and a ruby. Bracelet of small nephrite fish, mounted in gold and platinum and set with eight brilliant diamonds. Brooch mounted in gold and platinum, composed of four heads of clover carved in nephrite, the stalks set with seventy-eight brilliant diamonds. All dated June 1, 1913.

RIGHT:

From top: Cuff links of lapis lazuli mounted in platinum, the principal panel carved bas-relief with a bear within rose diamond borders, the other lapis link set with a brilliant diamond. A cuff link with a freestanding lapis carving of an elephant in the same platinum and rose diamond setting. A pendant cross carved in orletz (rhodonite) mounted in platinum and bordered with rose diamonds with one brilliant diamond at the top. A pair of cuff links in the form of four-leaf clovers carved in nephrite and mounted in platinum, set with rose diamonds. All the designs on this page are dated August 31, 1913.

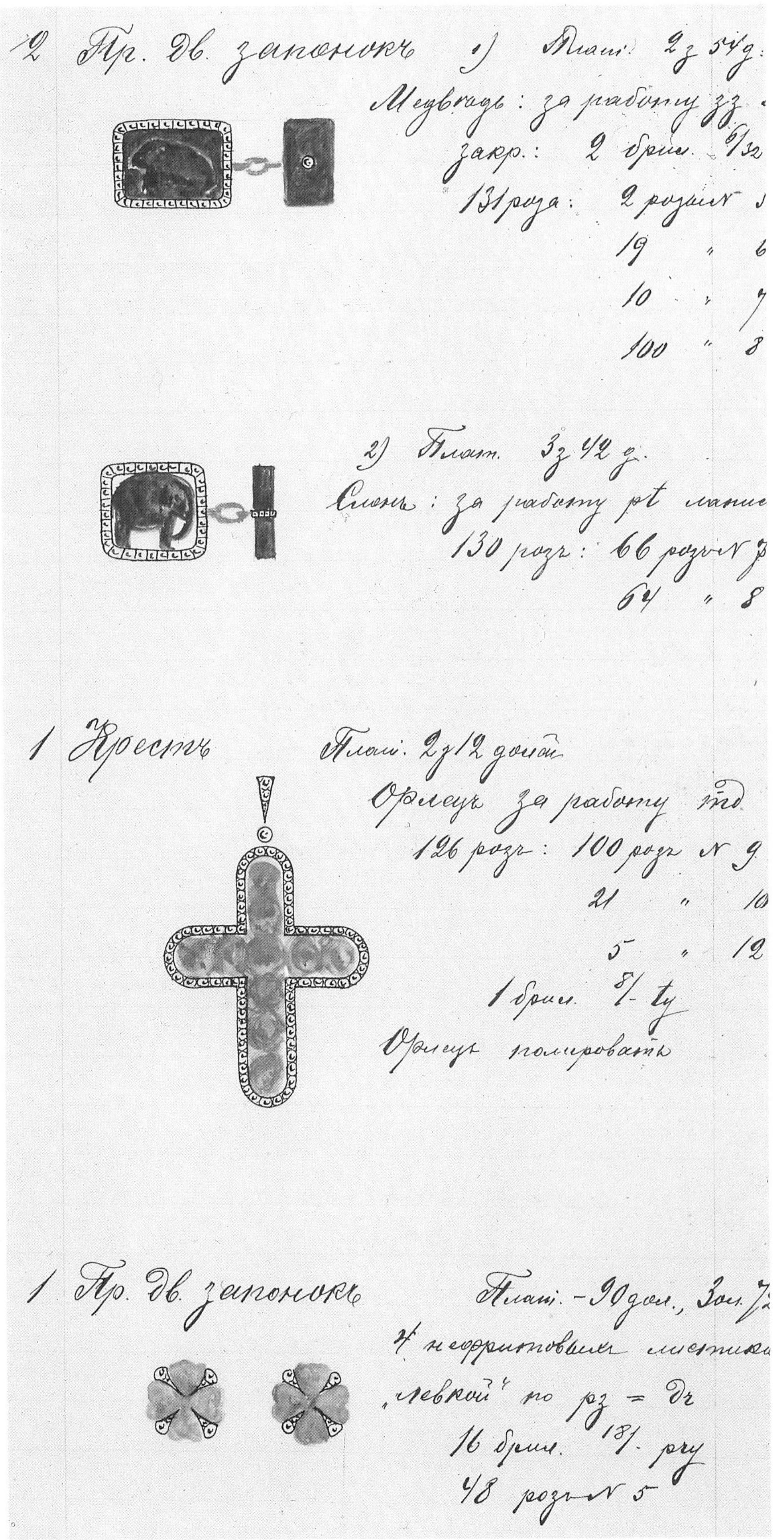
2 Пр. дв. запонокъ 1) Плат. 2 з 54 д.
Медвѣдь: за работу
закр.: 2 брил. 6/32
131 роза: 2 розы
19 " 6
10 " 7
100 " 8
2) Плат. 3 з 42 д.
Слонъ: за работу pt
130 роз.: 66 роз. №
64 " 8
1 Крестъ Плат: 2 з 12 долей
Орлецъ за работу
126 роз.: 100 роз. № 9
21 "
5 " 12
1 брил. 8/-
Орлецъ полировать
1 Пр. дв. запонокъ Плат: - 90 дол., 3 ол.
4 нефритовыхъ листика
„левкой" по рз =
16 брил. 18/-
48 роз № 5

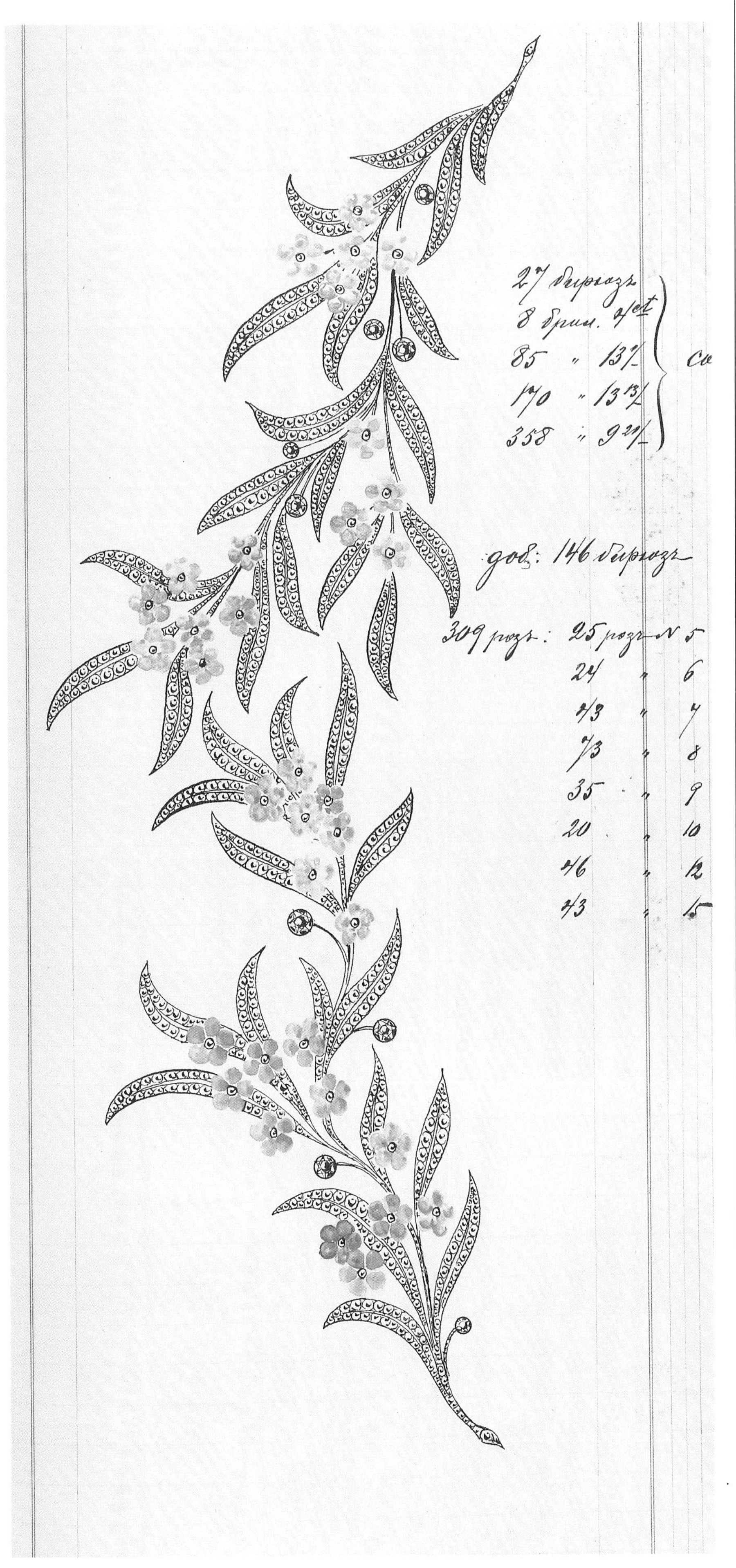

Described here as a diadème-bandeau, *this magnificent jewel is mounted in gold and silver and is made up of twin sprays of forget-me-nots set with brilliant and rose diamonds, the flower heads set with turquoise. Dated August 1, 1913.*

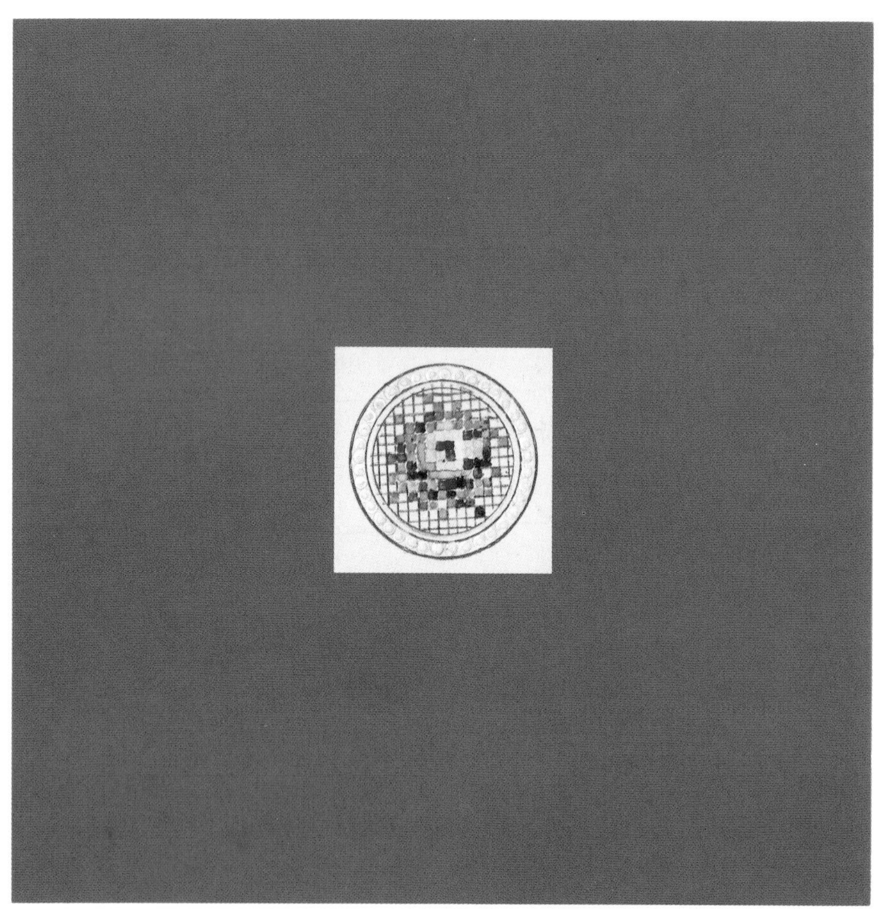

LEFT:

Gold brooch, set with colored stones and with a border of half-pearls and another of opaque white enamel. This design by Alma Theresia Pihl provided the mosaic motif for her Imperial Egg of 1914, now in the collection of Her Majesty Queen Elizabeth II. Dated July 24, 1913.

OPPOSITE:

The Mosaic Egg, presented to Tsarina Alexandra Feodorovna by Nicholas II on Easter Day, 1914, is shown resting on the page of the Fabergé design book next to the original watercolor drawing by Alma Theresia Pihl, dated July 24, 1913, from which the Imperial Egg derives. The egg's skeleton consists of a system of yellow gold belts to which is applied a platinum network partially pavé*-set with diamonds and colored gems, including sapphires, rubies, emeralds, topaz-quartz, and green (demantoid) garnets in flower patterns. The egg is divided into five oval panels by these gold belts, which are set with half-pearls within lines of opaque white enamel, and five brilliant diamonds are set at each intersection. It is further decorated by grills of rose diamond scrolls and one end is set with a moonstone beneath which may be seen the gold initials of the Tsarina in*

Russian characters inlaid in an opaque pink enameled plaque serving as a foil.

The surprise concealed inside, and held in place with two gold clips, consists of a gold, pearl, and translucent green and opaque white enameled pedestal, set with diamonds and green garnets and surmounted by a diamond Imperial Crown, supporting an oval plaque. On one side of the plaque the profiles of the five imperial children are painted in pale sepia grisaille *enamel against a background of engraved vertical parallel lines enameled opalescent* rose Pompadour. *The reverse is enameled with a pale sepia basket of flowers against a pale green background, around which the year 1914 and the names of the children are painted in sepia on the opaque ivory enameled border. Designed as a jewel, this beautiful egg was made in Holmström's workshop and is engraved with the name "*К. ФАБЕРЖЕ,*" but underneath the pedestal, in addition to the sun-in-splendor design, the words "G. FABERGE, 1914" have been engraved, presumably by a later misguided hand. Height of egg, $3\frac{5}{8}$" (4.8 cm); height of pedestal, 3" (7.6 cm). From Queen Mary's collection. Her Majesty the Queen. Reproduced by gracious permission of Her Majesty Queen Elizabeth II.*

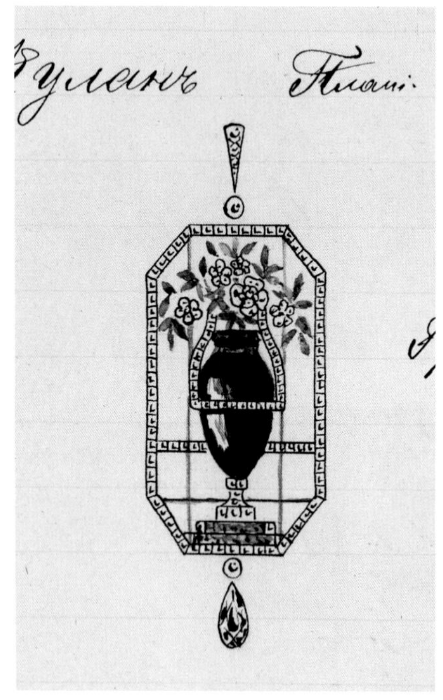

ABOVE:
A platinum and gold pendant of uncharacteristically suburban Art Nouveau taste, possibly a particular client's special commission, depicting a swallow flying over a choppy sea, both enameled blue, with a glimpse of sandy shore in gold set with pearl pebbles and a gold setting sun on the horizon. The circular frame is set with brilliant diamonds, as is the platinum chain necklace to which it is attached. Dated September 5, 1913.

CENTER:
Pendant mounted in platinum with a vase of flowers within an octagonal frame, set with a carved almandine vase, and flowers in chrysoberyls and diamonds. Dated September 6, 1913.

LEFT:
Vase of flowers pendant mounted in platinum and eighteen-carat gold, the vase carved in cornelian and chrysoberyls, set with emeralds and rose diamonds within an opaque white enameled frame. Dated September 6, 1913.

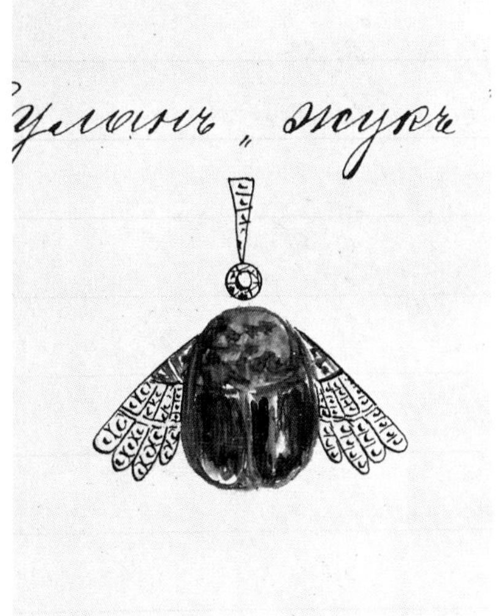

ABOVE:
A brooch of simplified cartouche form, mounted in platinum and gold and set with borders of rose diamonds and, in the center, a carved oval moss-agate panel, the natural dendritic inclusions giving the impression of shrubbery. This panel is bracketed on either side by a sapphire specifically shaped and polished for the purpose. Dated September 17, 1913.

CENTER:
Pendant designed as a winged scarab, carved from a large emerald of nineteen carats, mounted in platinum and set with a brilliant diamond, forty-five roses, and four sapphires. Dated September 20, 1913.

RIGHT:
Brooch mounted in platinum, set with diamonds and three sapphires of different colors. Dated September 27, 1913.

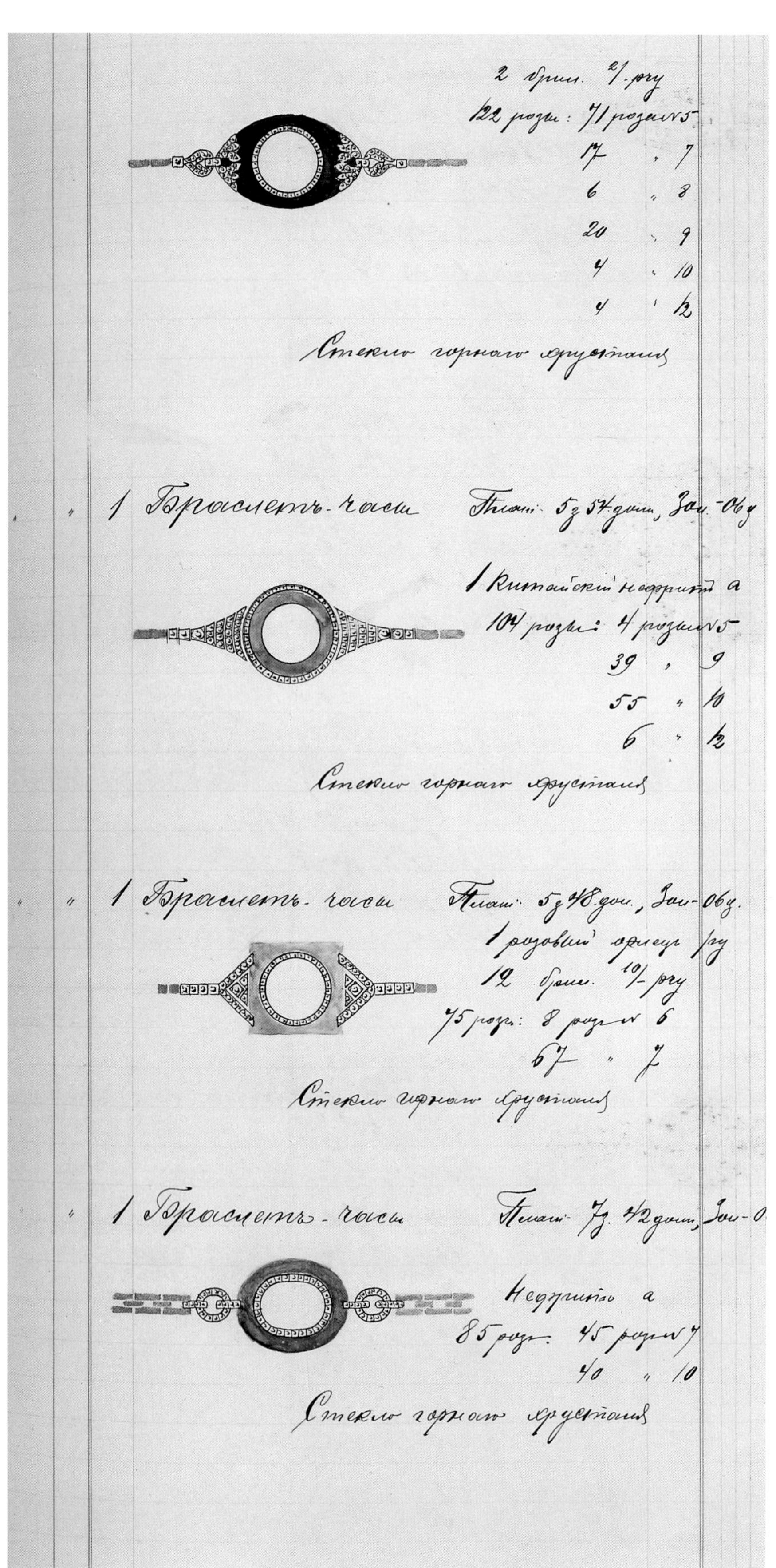

Designs for watch bracelets, mounted in platinum and gold, set with brilliant and rose diamonds, and incorporating the use of stones of color (from top): lapis lazuli, Chinese jade, orletz (rhodonite), and Siberian jade (nephrite). Dated September 25, 1913.

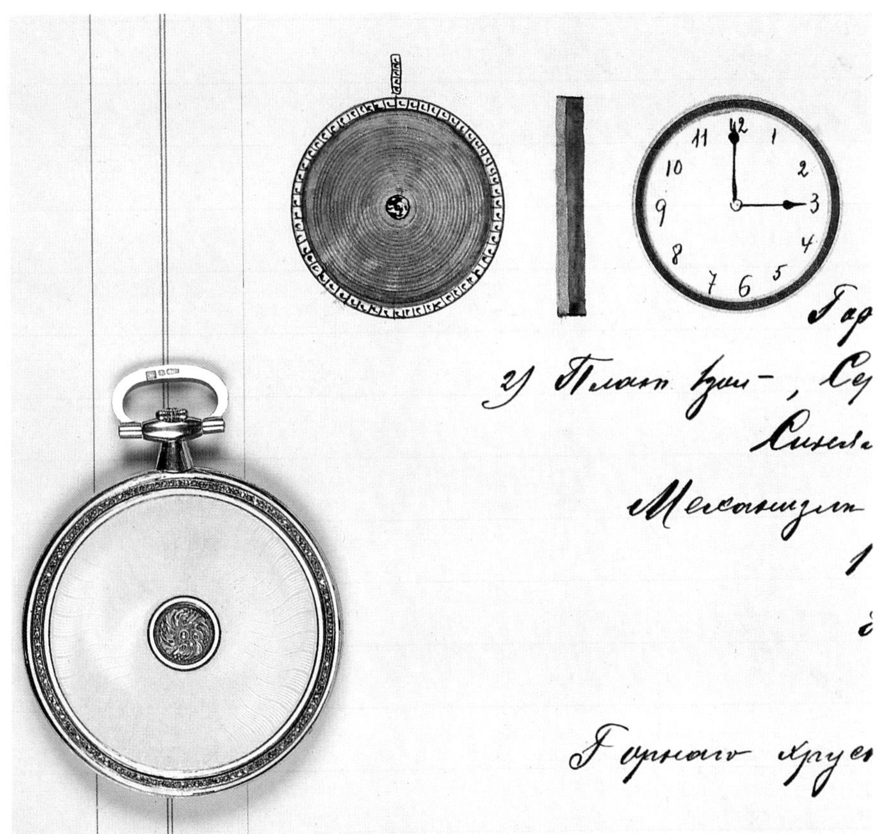

A design for a gentleman's circular gold dress-watch set with a central brilliant diamond and a border of rose diamonds, enameled translucent blue over an engine-turned pattern of concentric circles. The white enameled dial is covered by a rock-crystal panel. A second example was to be made enameled opalescent white, usually refered to as "oyster." Dated November 7, 1913. A watch made in yellow and green gold answering this description, deriving from this design, is shown on the page. Stamped with the initials of Henrik Wigström and the gold mark 72. Diameter 1¾" (4.5 cm). Private collection.

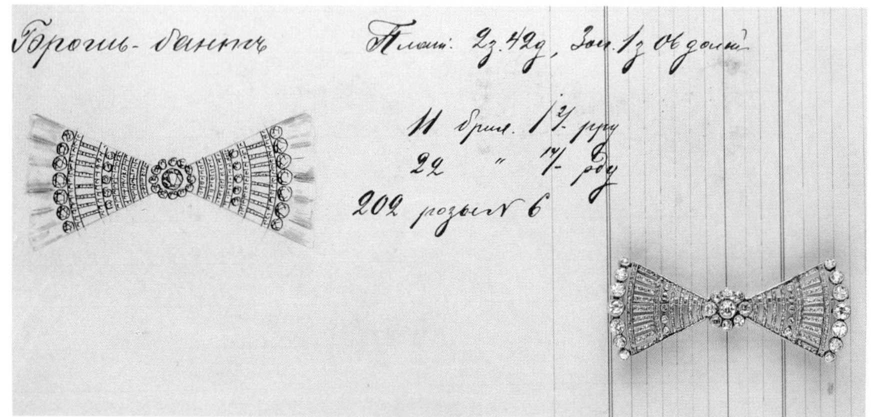

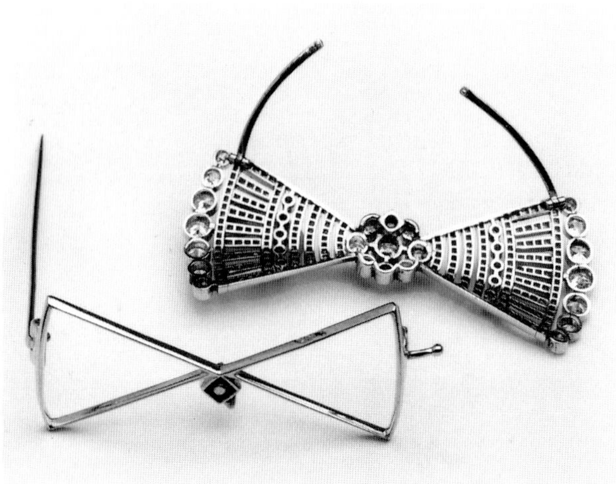

FROM TOP:

Bow brooch mounted in platinum, gold, and silver, set with brilliant and rose diamonds and the trellis forming the body of the jewel, enameled probably translucent blue. The shade of blue for the ribbon on which the bow was intended to be pinned is indicated in the design. Dated October 25, 1913.

A bow brooch also mounted in platinum and gold and set with brilliant and rose diamonds with the addition of rubies. The suggested color for the ribbon is, in this case, emerald green. Dated October 31, 1913.

Design for a bow brooch dated November 22, 1913, very similar to those shown above, to be mounted in platinum and gold and set with brilliant and rose diamonds with the proposed ribbon color expressed in watercolor. On the right is the actual brooch that is clearly based on this design and composed in exactly the same way. It is signed by August Holmström and measures 2″ (5 cm) in length. Wartski, London.

The brooch above seen from the back with the fitting detached; the curved hinged clips, which are intended to secure any ribbon that might be chosen, are shown open.

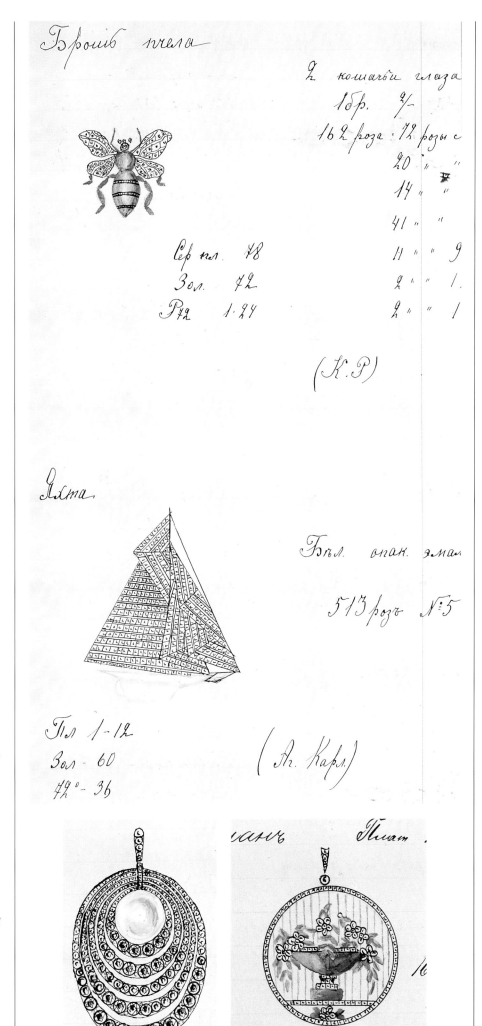

RIGHT:

At the top, a gold- and silver-mounted naturalistic bee brooch, set with one brilliant diamond, rose diamonds, and two cat's-eyes. The Russian initials KP in brackets indicate the unidentified maker. Below this is a brooch designed as a yacht, mounted in platinum and gold and set with rose diamonds, the keel enameled opaque pale blue. The initials bracketed here are those of Agathon Karlovitch, Fabergé's second son. Both designs dated December 7, 1913.

BELOW, LEFT:

An oval platinum pendant set with brilliant and rose diamonds and a single pearl at the center of a system of five interlocking swags. Dated February 18, 1914.

BELOW, RIGHT:

Circular pendant mounted in platinum and gold, featuring a carved lapis lazuli bowl with flowers of rose diamonds with jade leaves. The pendant is bordered with rose diamonds, and the bowl of flowers is applied to a background of vertical platinum bars. Dated February 21, 1914.

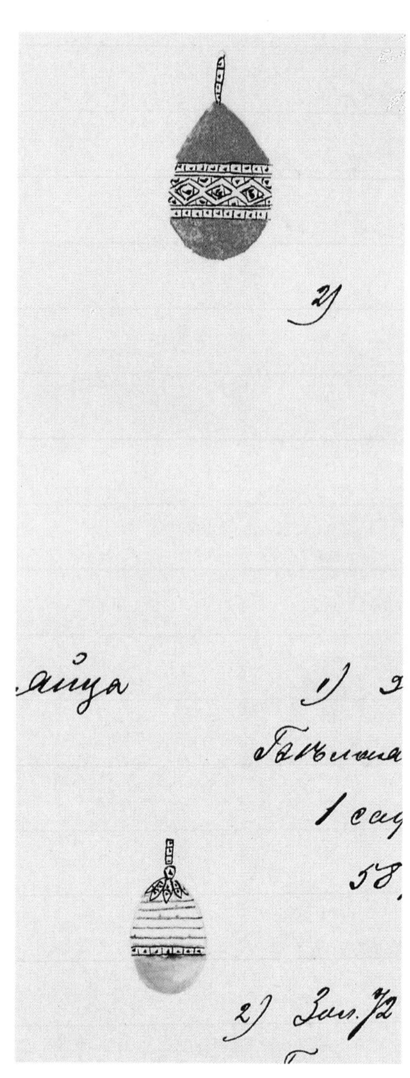

FAR LEFT:

Two ice pendant eggs mounted in platinum, the one shown above set with brilliant and rose diamonds and a panel of rock crystal; the example below is set with rose diamonds, and the rock-crystal Easter egg hangs within a diamond border. Both dated March 13, 1914.

LEFT:

Two miniature Easter egg pendants, above in platinum, set with brilliant and rose diamonds, below a smaller egg set with rose diamonds and mounted in eighteen-carat gold and platinum, decorated with opaque white enamel bands and set with a cabochon sapphire base. Dated March 19 and 20, 1914.

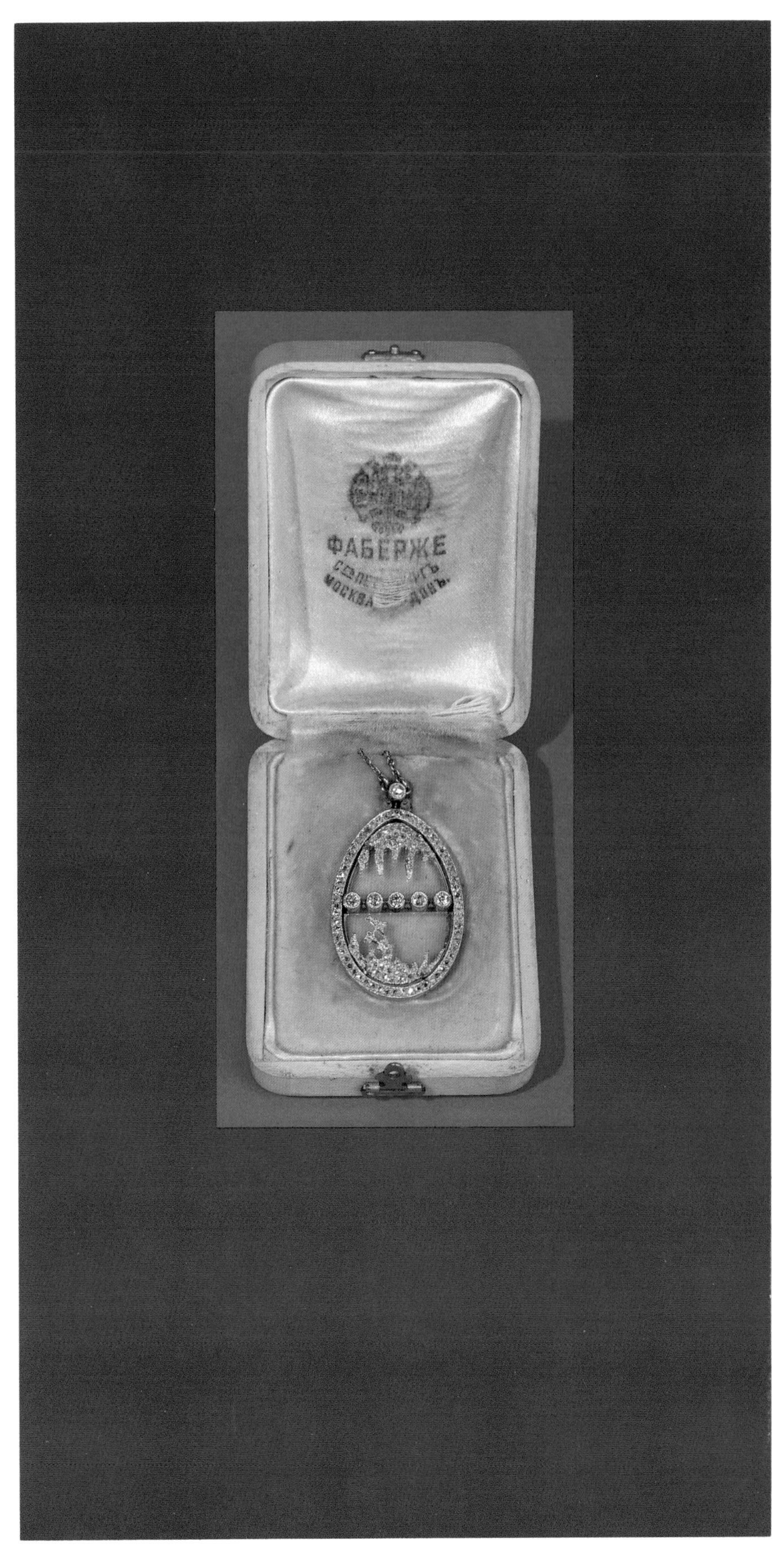

A pendant exactly as shown in the top design on the far left, opposite, in its original holly box. Height 1⅛" (2.8 cm). A la Vieille Russie, New York.

Miniature Easter egg pendants. The design at top is for a stone pendant, mounted in platinum and set with rose diamonds, of which six examples were made: two of orletz (rhodonite), as shown, and two each in obsidian and nephrite. It is noted that the stones came from Sverdlov. The center design is for a platinum egg set with a brilliant diamond and three rose diamond bands; a version of this pendant was carried out in rubies. Dated March 22, 1914. At the foot of the page is a design for another platinum egg, set with a rose diamond grill. Dated March 24, 1914. Two miniature Easter egg pendants in platinum have been photographed on the page next to the designs from which they were made. Since they are of platinum, neither egg bears any mark. Height of both, excluding the loop, 13/16" (2 cm). Private collection.

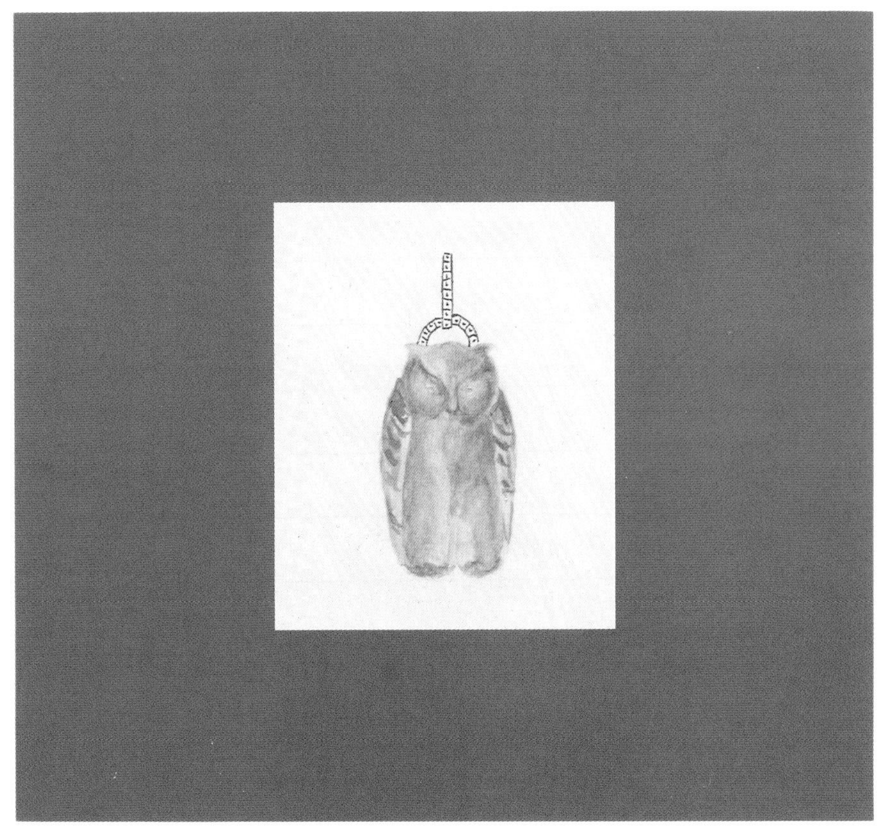

ABOVE:

A convoluted Chinese jade carving in the style of a netsuke, mounted as a pendant in platinum and set with brilliant and rose diamond leaves. Dated April 21, 1914.

RIGHT:

An orletz (rhodonite) carving of an owl mounted in platinum as a pendant, set with rose diamonds. Dated April 21, 1914.

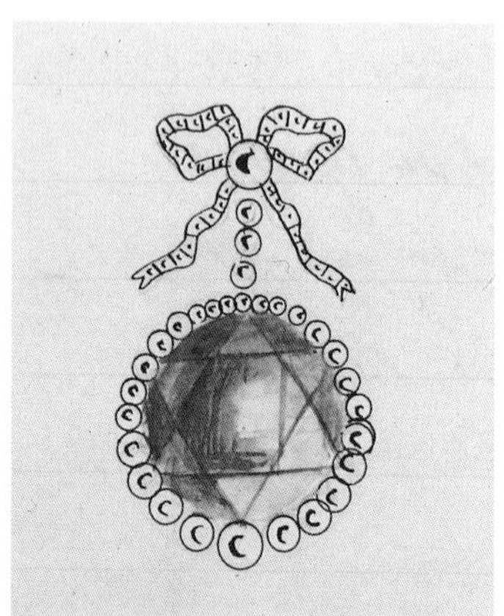

ABOVE:

Carved orletz (rhodonite) pendant, mounted in platinum and set with rose diamonds and two brilliants. Dated May 12, 1914. A finished example is shown resting on the page with the original design. Overall height $2\frac{1}{8}$" (5.4 cm). Private collection.

CENTER:

A design incorporating a large sapphire of 32.25 carats to be mounted in platinum with brilliant and rose diamonds as a pendant surmounted by a bowknot. Dated April 16, 1914.

LEFT:

Sapphire and diamond pendant set in platinum with no marks, based on the design above. Length $1\frac{3}{4}$" (4.4 cm). Private collection.

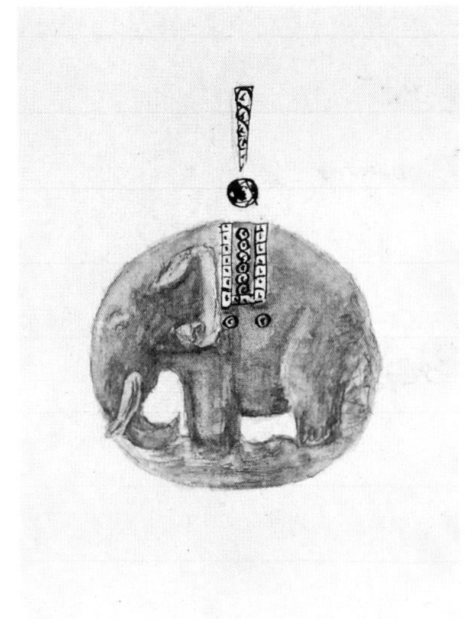

ABOVE, LEFT:

Carved nephrite pendant designed as an elephant; the howdah and pendant fitting mounted in platinized silver and set with a brilliant diamond and eighty-two rose diamonds. Dated May 20, 1914.

ABOVE, RIGHT:

Carved nephrite head after an ancient Egyptian model, mounted as a pendant in platinum and set with a brilliant diamond, twenty-three rose diamonds, and a ruby. The initials **ФБ** *(F.B.) for François Birbaum, Fabergé's chief designer, appear next to this watercolor drawing. Dated August 8, 1914.*

RIGHT:

A photograph taken of François Birbaum, Fabergé's head designer, in Aigle in 1935. He was a gifted artist also fascinated by the crafts of the goldsmith, the enameler, the lapidary, and the jeweler. When the House was closed down by the Bolsheviks, he returned to Switzerland, his homeland, and settled down as a painter and pastelist until his death in 1947.

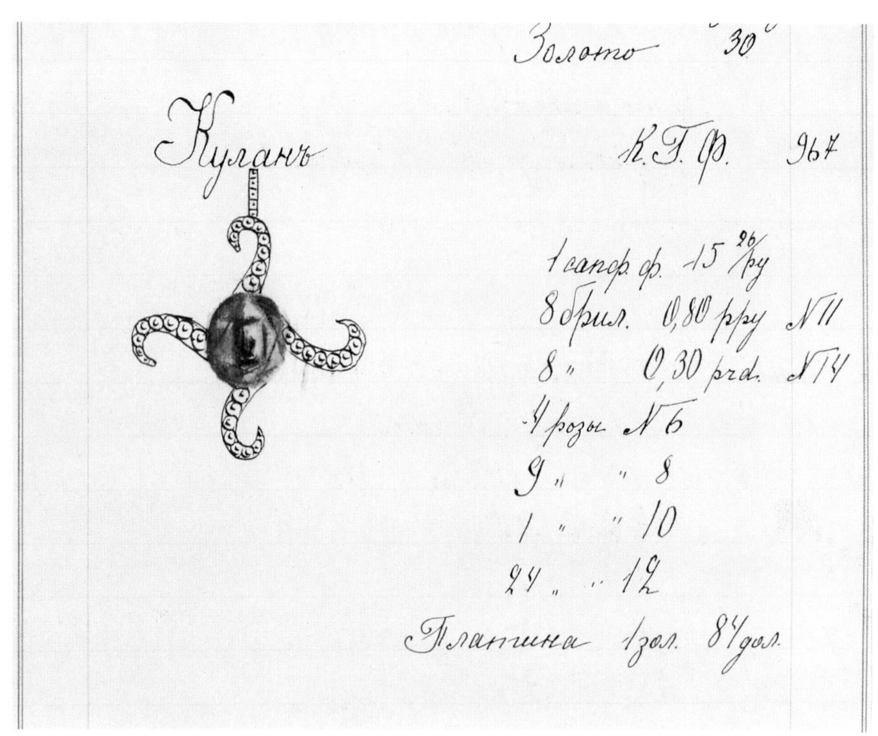

ABOVE:

Large single sapphire mounted in platinum as a pendant, with four scrolls set with brilliant and rose diamonds. This design and seventeen others in the two record books are accompanied by the Russian characters **КГФ** *in brackets—the initials of Karl Gustavovitch Fabergé himself. Dated June 21, 1914.*

LEFT:

Aquamarine of forty-three carats, mounted in platinum and gold and set as a brooch with brilliant and rose diamonds. Signed with the initials **КГФ** *for Carl Fabergé and dated July 15, 1914.*

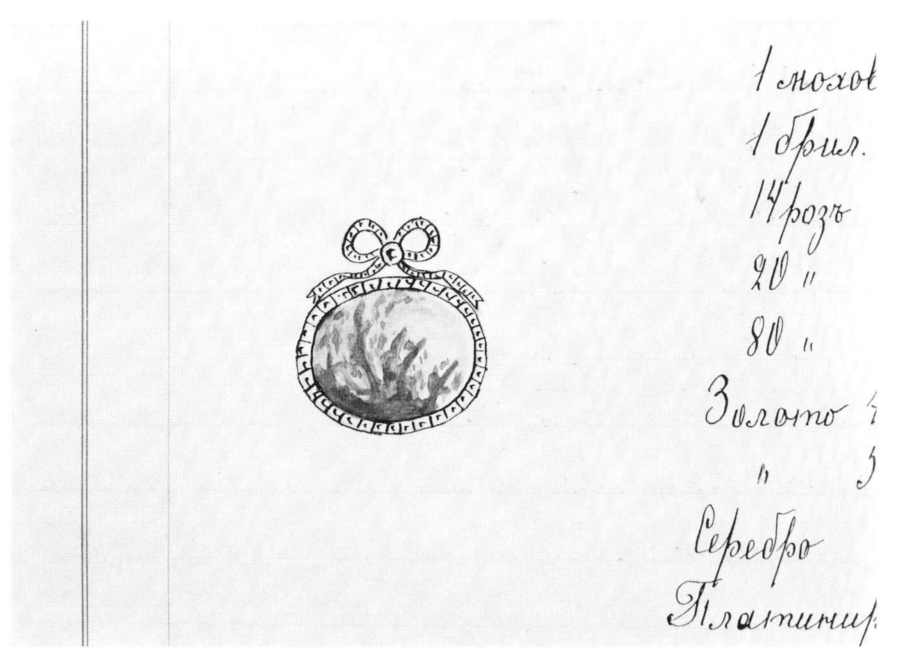

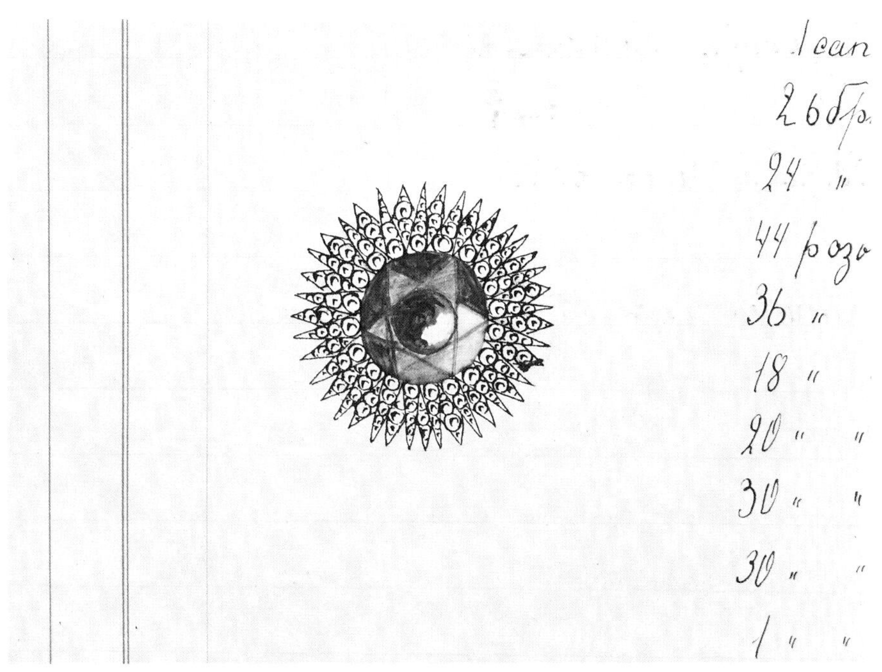

ABOVE:

A carved oval moss-agate panel with natural inclusions suggesting trees, mounted in gold and silver as a brooch and set with a rose diamond border surmounted by a bow set with one brilliant diamond. Signed with the initials **КГФ** *for Carl Fabergé. Dated August 1, 1914.*

CENTER:

A brooch as described in the drawing above, except that a cabochon ruby is set in place of the brilliant diamond. Stamped with the initials of August Hollming. Width 1 5/16" (3.3 cm). Wartski, London.

LEFT:

A brooch-pendant of sunburst design, mounted in gold and platinum with a large central sapphire of twenty-five carats and set with brilliant and rose diamonds. Signed with the initials **КГФ** *for Carl Fabergé and dated August 16, 1914.*

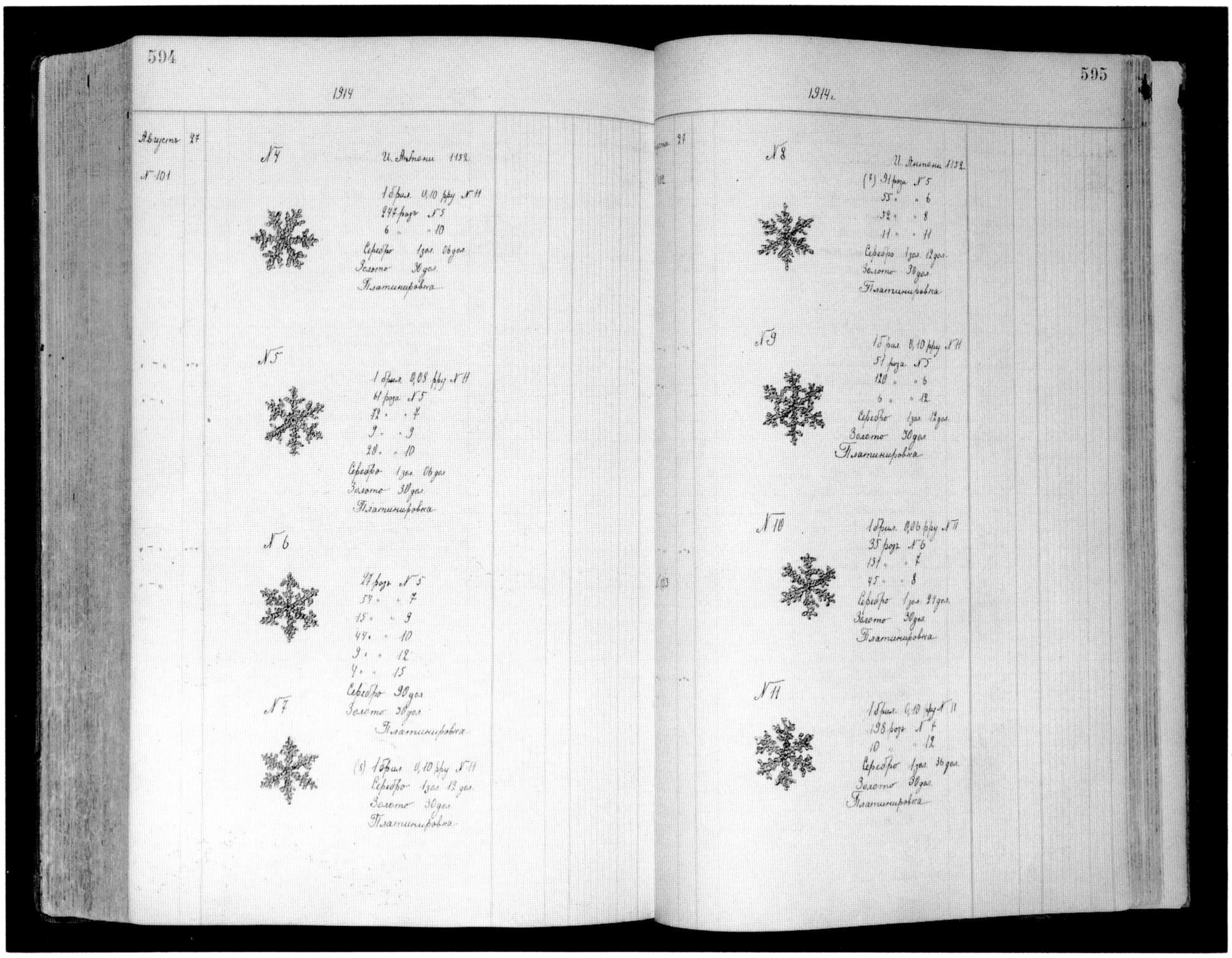

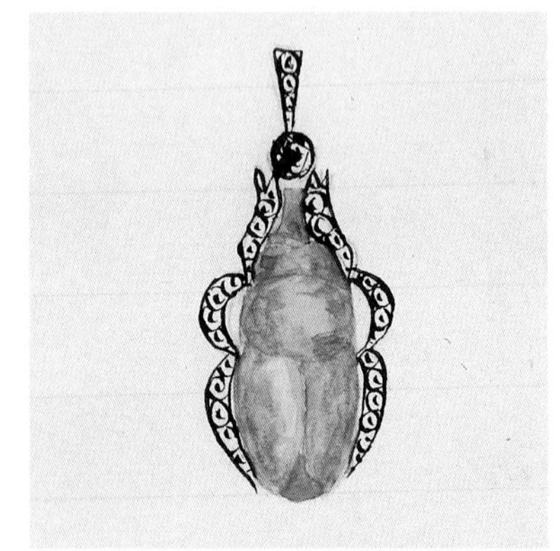

OPPOSITE, ABOVE:

A photograph of pages 594 and 595 of the second volume of the Fabergé record books, dated August 27, 1914, showing designs numbers 4 to 11, each a slightly varied form of a frost flower to be set with rose diamonds and occasionally a central brilliant stone. The mounts to be composed of a platinized alloy of gold and silver; this highly unusual technique is discussed in the text on pages 14–16. Average diameter, 1¼″ (3.2 cm).

OPPOSITE, BELOW, LEFT TO RIGHT:

Carved emerald scarab, mounted in platinum and silver as a pendant, set with brilliant and rose diamonds. Design signed "F. Birbaum" in Cyrillic. Dated September 4, 1914.

Brooch-pendant mounted in gold and platinized silver, set with a large mecca stone within a frame decorated with scrolling, set with brilliant and rose diamonds. Signed with the initials **КГФ** *for Carl Fabergé and dated September 10, 1914.*

A large faceted emerald bead mounted in platinum and silver as a pendant, set with brilliant and rose diamonds. Signed "F. Birbaum" in Cyrillic. Dated September 9, 1914.

RIGHT:

An elaborate evening bag decorated with frost motifs mounted in platinum and set with brilliant and rose diamonds. There is no indication as to the material of the bag itself. The name I. Antony appears above this design. Dated September 3, 1914.

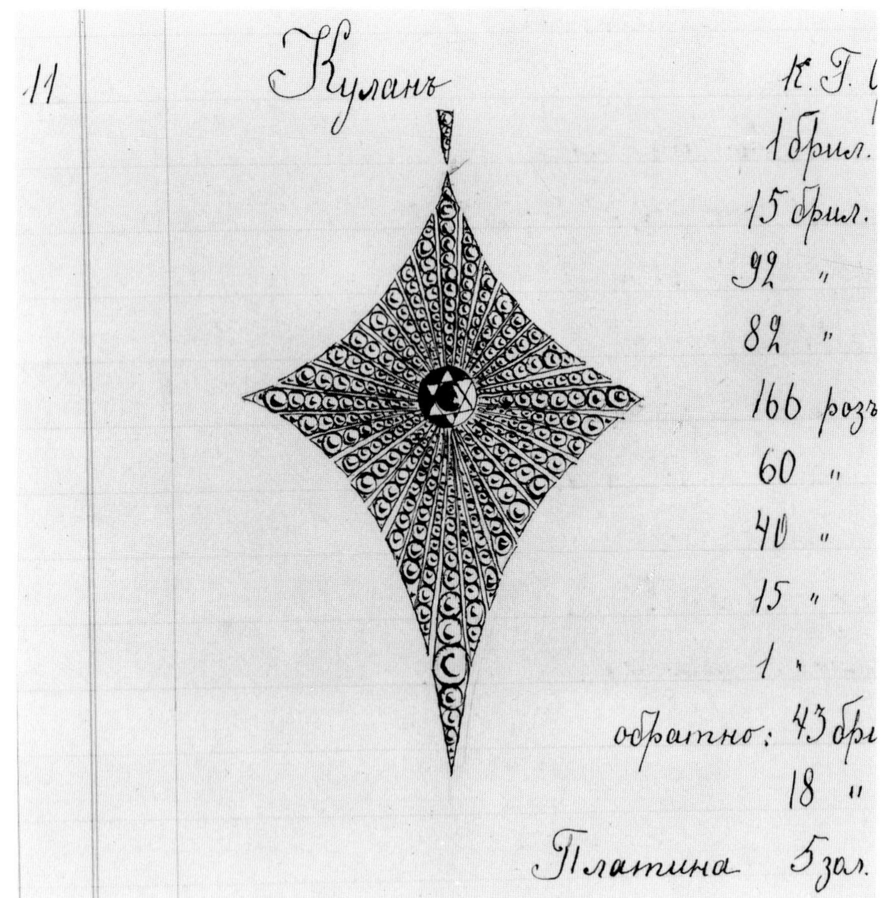

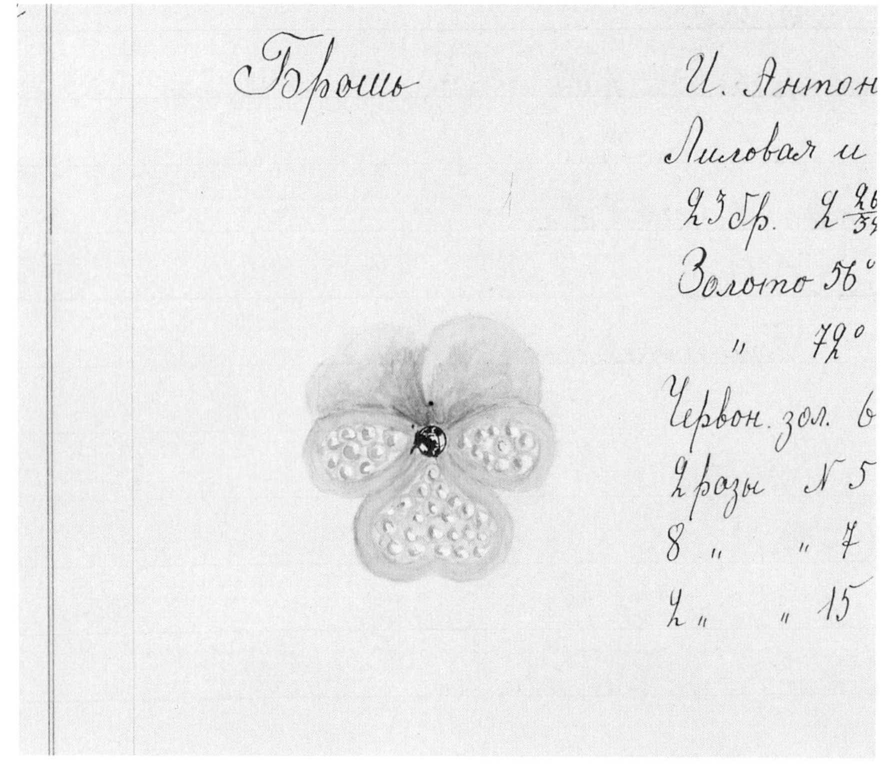

ABOVE:

Platinum pendant set with brilliant and rose diamonds; the initials of Carl Fabergé (КГФ) appear next to this drawing. Dated September 11, 1914.

LEFT:

Gold-mounted brooch designed as a pansy, set with brilliant and rose diamonds, the petals enameled pale yellow and lilac. The name I. Antony appears above this design. Dated November 17, 1914.

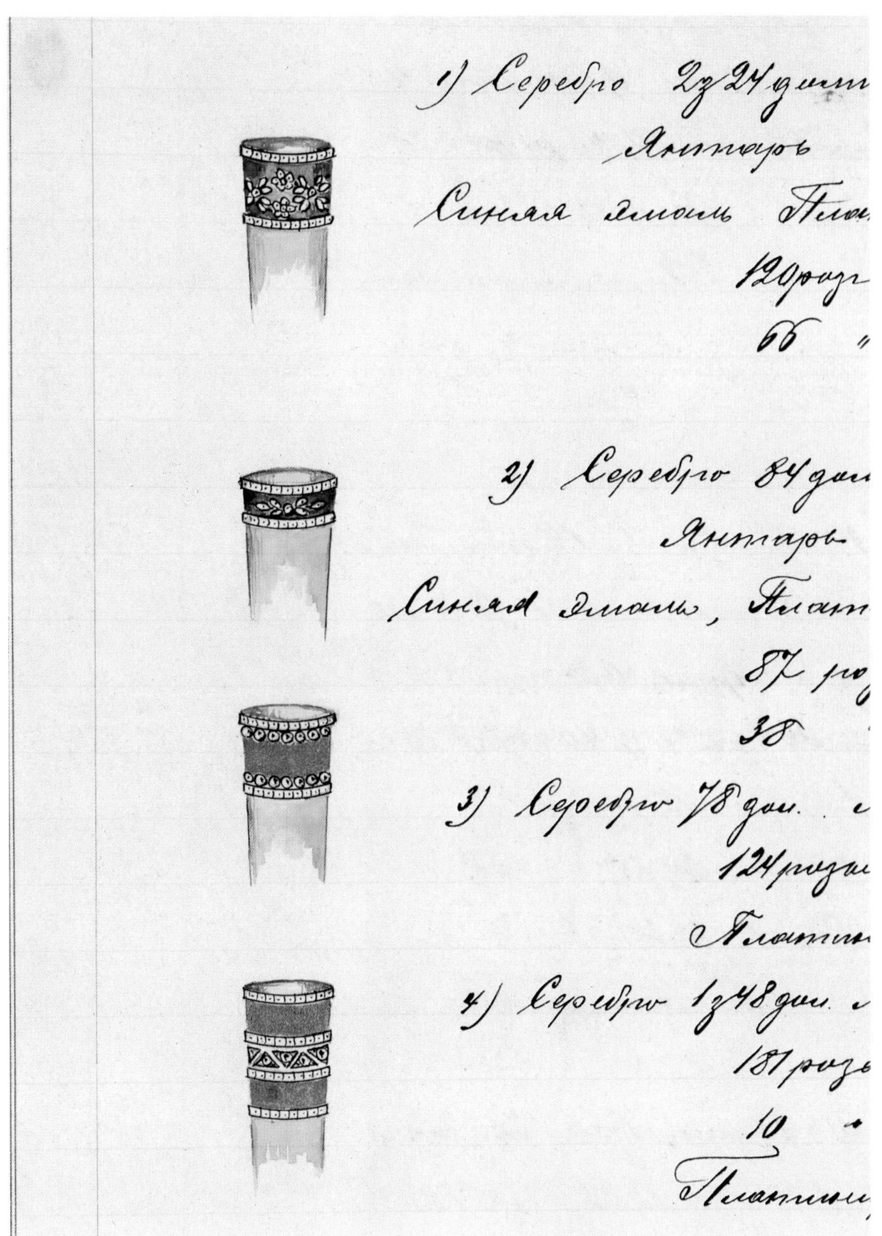

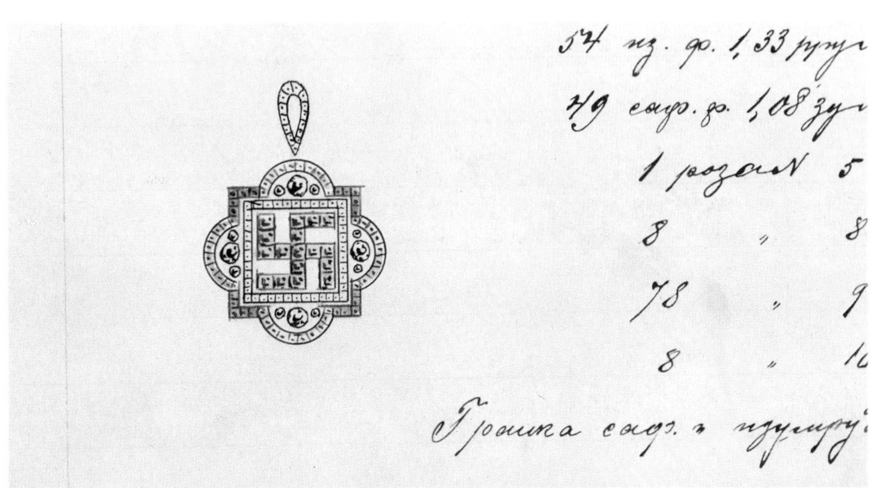

ABOVE:

Four amber cigarette holders with silver and platinum mounts, the top two enameled translucent blue, the lower two finished in matt silver; all are set with rose diamonds. Dated January 7, 1915.

RIGHT:

A platinum pendant in the form of a swastika, a primitive symbol of well-being or luck, set with square emeralds and sapphires and brilliant and rose diamonds. Dated January 29, 1915. Nobody at the time could possibly have predicted how this harmless talisman was to be explôited and debased by Adolf Hitler and his loathsome followers.

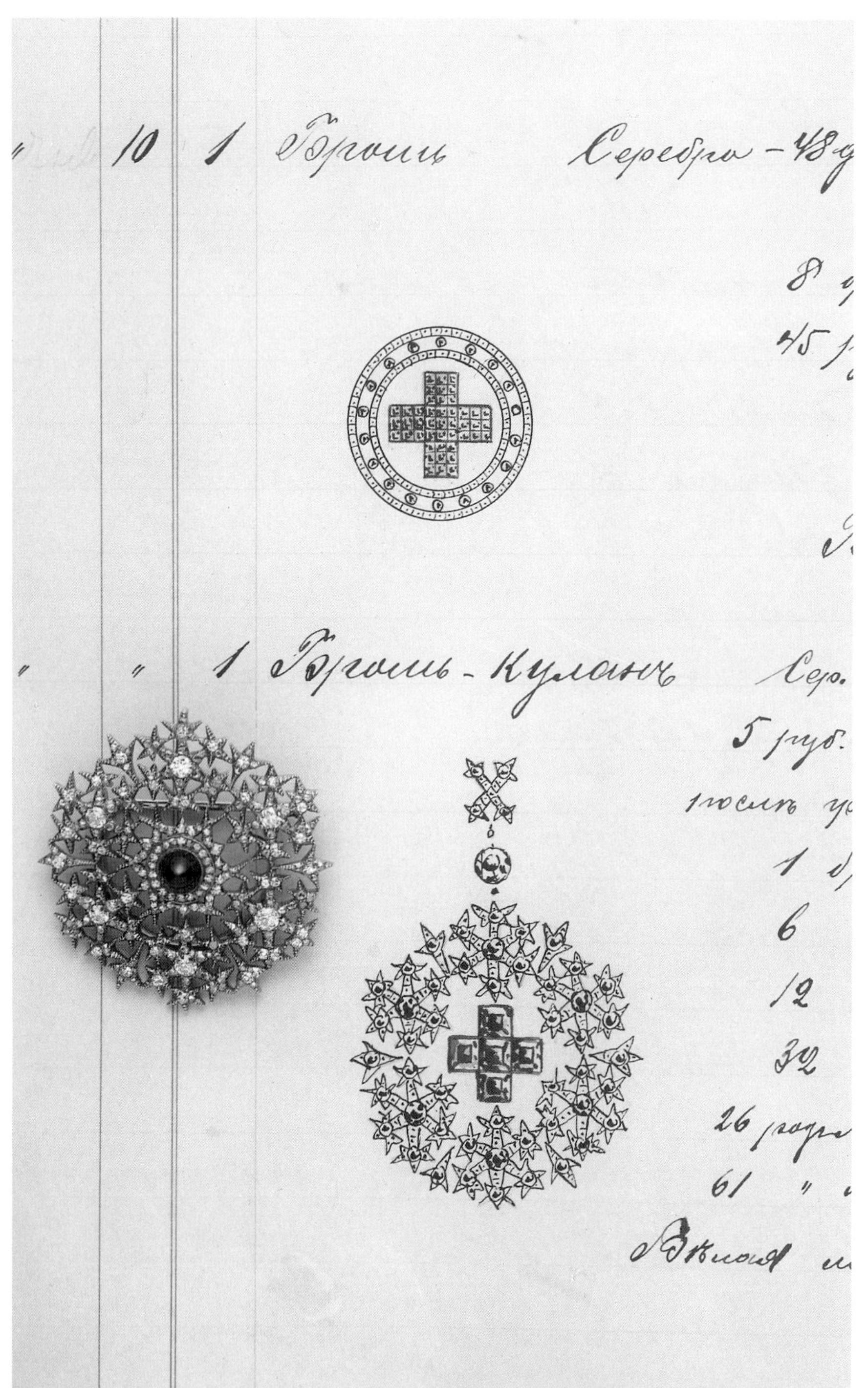

Above, a simply designed circular brooch with a ruby-set Red Cross within a border of rose diamonds, and below, a Red Cross brooch-pendant mounted in platinum and eighteen-carat gold, set with five large rubies and brilliant and rose diamonds formed as tiny stars of frost, the Red Cross applied to an opaque white enameled panel. Dated January 10, 1915. A circular cluster brooch set with a central cabochon ruby surrounded by very similar brilliant and rose diamond frost flowers mounted in platinum is shown on the page. Height 1½" (3.8 cm). Wartski, London.

When World War I broke out, a favorite theme became a Red Cross boldly expressed on a small oyster-enameled egg, a reference to the Tsarina's dedication to and patronage of that eponymous organization. Other jewels using the motif proliferated.

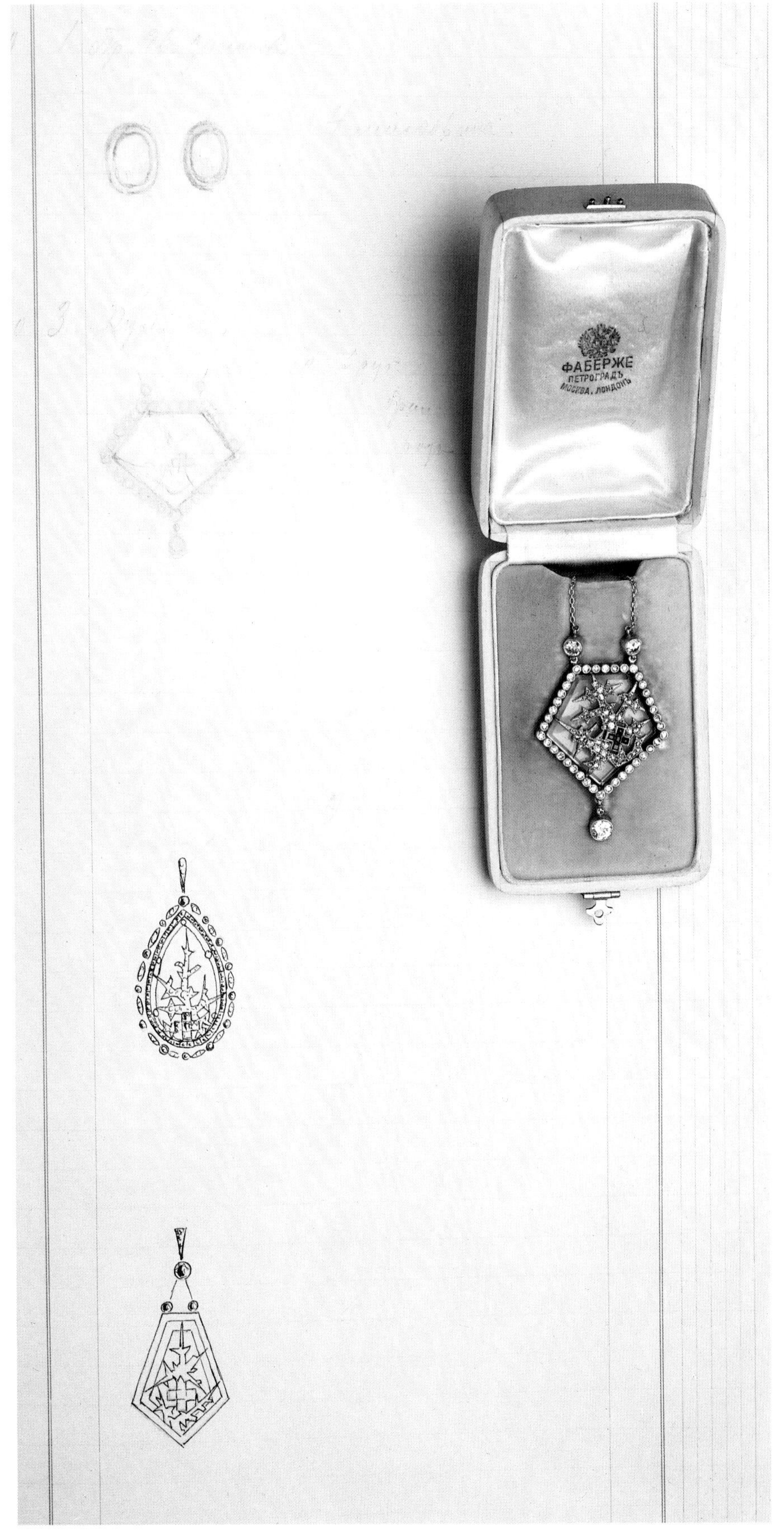

These wartime designs are drawn on the very last page of the books—the top two in pencil are in the nature of jottings and not at all highly finished. The first drawings are for a pair of oval moss-agate cuff links to be framed by what appear to be gold snakes. Below is a five-sided pendant (one of three ordered) to be set with brilliant and rose diamonds. The Red Cross symbol in our drawing appears to have been a clumsily added afterthought, but nevertheless provision is made for it in the scribbled note, where mention is made of five rubies being required for one of the pendants. The jewel which was made from this tentative drawing has been found and is photographed next to it, in its original case: a platinum and rock-crystal pendant of asymmetrical shape in the form of a tablet of ice. A small Red Cross set with rubies can be seen among the diamond-set ice flowers. Height 1⅝″ (4 cm.) Her Grace the Duchess of Westminster. The last two designs in the books offer further essays on the familiar themes of Easter eggs and winter. Dated March 20, 1915.

ФАБЕРЖЕ
МОСКВА, ОДЕССА

OPPOSITE:

A diamond-set court tiara, called a kokoshnik, *here photographed in its original fitted case.* $2\frac{1}{8} \times 4\frac{11}{16}''$ *(5.3 × 11.9 cm). Wartski, London.*

ABOVE:

This design painted on card was one of many pasted in the album of working drawings acquired with the record books. It depicts a tiara to be set with brilliant and rose diamonds and hung with oriental pearl drops. It measures $7\frac{1}{16}''$ *(17.9 cm) across.*

RIGHT:

Included in the book of working drawings accompanying the two principal record books is this design for a lavish tiara in pearls and diamonds including a number of large brilliant stones. Unusually, it bears the bold signature of the House. The tiara measures $8\frac{1}{2}''$ *(21.6 cm) across in the drawing.*

LEFT:

Working drawing, faintly washed with watercolor, showing the model of the royal yacht Standart *from three different angles. c. 1908. 6½ × 5½" (16.4 × 13.9 cm). Private collection. This is a preparatory design for the imperial* Standart *Egg of 1909 (opposite page). Photographed in front of the drawing is the finished model of the yacht from the imperial egg.*

OPPOSITE:

The Standart *Egg, presented to Alexandra Feodorovna by Nicholas II in 1909. This rock-crystal egg is mounted in gold richly enameled and set with gems; it is supported on a rock-crystal pedestal similarly decorated, two intertwined lapis lazuli dolphins forming the shaft. The Renaissance-style egg opens to reveal a faithful replica in gold of the nineteeth-century yacht* Standart, *set on a large piece of aquamarine to give the impression of the sea. Derived from Jürg Ruel's sixteenth-century masterpiece in the Dresden collection, the* Standart *Egg is one of the most interesting of the series. Eugène Fabergé put the date of this egg at about 1908, and it may well have been made to commemorate the part played by the Tsarina when, on September 11, 1907, the yacht struck a rock and appeared to be sinking fast and, as Baroness Buxhoeveden tells us in her* Life and Tragedy of Alexandra Feodorovna: *"The Empress arranged that the children and the ladies' maids should be first lowered into the boats. Then she rushed into the cabins, tore the sheets off the beds and tossed all the valuables into them, making huge bundles of the most necessary and precious things. It was all done in about a quarter of an hour. The Empress was the last woman to leave the yacht." The egg is signed "HW." Height 6⅛" (15.5 cm). Armory Museum of the Kremlin, Moscow.*

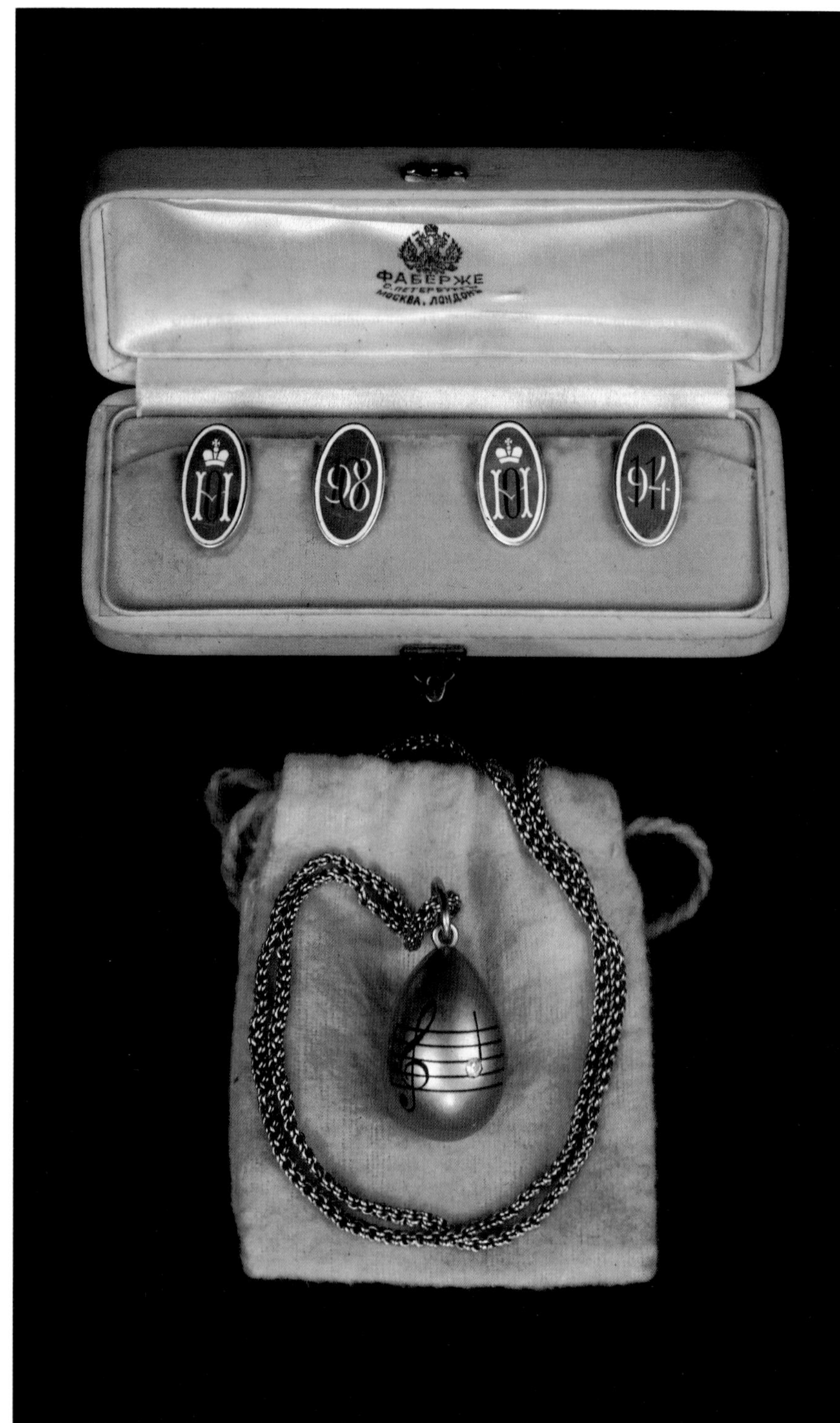

These Fabergé objects were in the collection of Charles Sydney Gibbes, who first went to Russia in 1901 to become the tutor to the children of noble Russian families. Edward VII had told his sister-in-law Tsarina Alexandra that her children spoke abominable English and should be taught by a Cambridge graduate. It subsequently became known that Gibbes was in Russia at the time, and in 1908 he was summoned to the Court to teach the four Grand Duchesses English. In 1912 he became tutor to the Tsarevitch.

One of the items in Gibbes' collection, at top, is a pair of gold cuff links by Fabergé with the crowned monogram of the Grand Duchess Olga and the dates 1908–1914, the period during which he taught her. Below, the little gold Easter egg with its necklet is decorated with a musical clef, with a single diamond for the musical note A for Anastasia, the Tsar's youngest daughter, to whom this miniature Easter egg belonged. The egg opens, and it was given on Easter Day of 1915, the 22nd of March being Easter Day in the Russian calendar.

Gibbes left Russia after the Ekaterinburg tragedy, later reached China, and through the British Embassy in Peking worked for the maritime customs there. He was converted to the Russian Orthodox Church and was eventually ordained as a priest known as Father Nicholas. He died in 1963 in Oxford, England.

ABOVE:

A diadem mounted in platinum and silver and set with brilliant and rose diamonds to form circles of leaves centered by diamond clusters similar in character to the one worn by Maria Pavlovna in the photograph on the right. This drawing, which appears on page 24 of the second volume of the Fabergé record books, is dated December 14, 1911, and measures 10½″ (26.7 cm).

RIGHT:

This fascinating photograph of The Grand Duchess Vladimir, Maria Pavlovna, born a princess of Mecklenburg-Schwerin, and an extremely strong-minded woman and enthusiastic collector of jewelry, was signed and dated by the sitter herself in St. Petersburg on December 1, 1904. It shows her wearing the well-known diamond tiara hung with large oriental pearl drops, which, it was once suggested by Eugène Karlovitch, she had ordered at Fabergé's.

Hans Nadelhoffer, in his book Cartier *reports that when this particular head ornament was left with the firm in Paris in 1911, the opportunity was taken to design three new tiaras in the same taste, each one with pendant pearls hanging from diamond-set circles. The Grand Duchess fled the 1917 Revolution and settled in Paris, and later the tiara was smuggled out of Russia by a young English admirer, the diplomat Bertie Stopford. Queen Mary acquired it after Maria Pavlovna's death in 1921.*

Upon a careful examination of the tiara, now part of the collection of Her Majesty Queen Elizabeth II, I found no maker's mark, either of Fabergé or any other jeweler, and it appears to be of marginally earlier Russian manufacture.

A watercolor drawing of an enameled Easter egg bearing the Cyrillic initials BX for Christos Voskres *(Christ Is Risen). Signed "Fabergé" in pencil. Height of egg in drawing, 3 1/16" (7.8 cm). Private collection.*

Notes

1. Arranged by Dr. Géza von Habsburg and held in the Kunsthalle of the Hypo-Kulturstiftung, December 5, 1986–February 22, 1987. The catalogue was published by Hirmer Verlag, 1986.
2. Henry Charles Bainbridge, *Peter Carl Fabergé*, 3rd ed. (London: B. T. Batsford, 1974), p. 114.
3. Ibid., p. 56.
4. At the Museum of Applied Arts, Helsinki.
5. We look forward with great interest to the article that Ulla Tillander-Godenhielm hopes to write on Alma Pihl-Klee. For the present, permission has been given to set down the relevant parts of letters sent from Helsinki.
6. Bainbridge, *Fabergé*, p. 21.
7. Marina Lopato, "Fresh Light on Carl Fabergé," *Apollo* 119 (January 1984): p. 43.
8. Bainbridge, *Fabergé*, p. 130.
9. Busaya Krairiksh, ed. *Fabergé*. Bangkok, Thailand: Chitralada Palace, probably 1986.

Select Bibliography

Bainbridge, Henry Charles. *Peter Carl Fabergé*. 3rd ed. London: B. T. Batsford, 1974.

Betteley, R. *Fabergé at Hillwood*. Washington, D.C.: Hillwood Museum, 1983.

The Burlington House Fair Handbook. The Antique Dealers' Fair. *Burlington House Magazine* (1987).

Carl Fabergé and His Contemporaries. Catalogue to exhibition at the Museum of Applied Arts, Helsinki. Articles by Christina Ehrnrooth, Max Engman, A. Kenneth Snowman, Herbert Tillander, Ulla Tillander-Godenhielm, and Géza von Habsburg-Lothringen. Helsinki: The Museum of Applied Arts, 1980.

Designs from the House of Fabergé. Auction catalogue. London: Christie, Manson and Woods, April 27, 1989.

Forbes, Christopher. *Fabergé Eggs: Imperial Russian Fantasies*. New York: Harry N. Abrams, 1981.

The Great Fabergé. Catalogue to first exhibition in U.S.S.R., at The Elagin Palace Museum, Leningrad, February 9–October 1, 1989. Foreword by Dr. Vjacheslav Muhin. Articles by Dr. M. N. Lopato, K. A. Orlova, V. V. Skurlov, N. V. Vernova, and Zavadskaya. Leningrad: The Elagin Palace Museum, 1989.

Hill, Gerard, ed. *Fabergé and the Russian Master Goldsmiths*. New York: Wings Books, 1991.

Krairiksh, Busaya, ed. *Fabergé*. Bangkok, Thailand: Chitralada Palace, probably 1986.

Lesley, Parker. *Fabergé: A Catalogue of the Lillian Thomas Pratt Collection of Russian Imperial Jewels*. Richmond: Virginia Museum of Fine Arts, 1976.

Lopato, Marina. "Fresh Light on Carl Fabergé." *Apollo* 119 (January 1984).

Nadelhoffer, Hans. *Cartier: Jewelers Extraordinary*. New York: Harry N. Abrams, 1984.

Newly Unveiled Works by Fabergé. Catalogue of exhibition in Helsinki from the collections of the A. E. Fersman Museum of Mineralogy of the Soviet Academy of Science. Helsinki: Europrint Oy, 1989.

Snowman, A. Kenneth. *The Art of Carl Fabergé*. 5th ed. London: Faber and Faber, 1974.

———. *Carl Fabergé: Goldsmith to the Imperial Court of Russia*. London: Debrett's Peerage, 1979.

———. *Easter Eggs and Other Precious Objects by Carl Fabergé*. Washington, D.C.: The Corcoran Gallery of Art, 1961.

———. *Fabergé: Jeweler to Royalty*. Exhibition catalogue. New York: The Cooper-Hewitt Museum, Smithsonian Institution, 1983.

———. "Two Books of Revelations: The Fabergé Stock Books." *Apollo* 126, no. 307 (September 1987): 150-61.

———, ed. *The Master Jewelers*. London: Thames and Hudson, 1990; New York: Harry N. Abrams, 1990.

Von Habsburg, Géza. *Fabergé: Hofjuwelier der Zaren*. Exhibition catalogue. Munich: Hirmer Verlag, 1986.

Von Habsburg-Lothringen, Géza, and Alexander von Solodkoff. *Fabergé: Court Jeweler to the Tsars*. New York: Rizzoli International Publications, 1979.

Von Solodkoff, Alexander. *Masterpieces from the House of Fabergé*. New York: Harry N. Abrams, 1984.

Waterfield, Hermione, and Christopher Forbes. *Fabergé: Imperial Eggs and Other Fantasies*. New York: Charles Scribner's Sons, 1978.

Index

Pages on which illustrations appear are in *italic* type.

Photograph Credits

Most of the photographs in this book are courtesy Wartski, London, and were taken by Gordon Robertson of A. C. Cooper, London. Following are additional photograph credits, with page numbers indicated. Photographs from the Laura Ryynänen Archive: 17, 19 below, 133; Photograph from the Print Department of the Saltikov Schedrin Public Library, St. Petersburg, reprinted with the permission of Elena Valentinova Barchatova: 29 all; Sotheby's: 79 below; Larry Stein: 115 below, 134 center; Jim Strong, Inc., New York: 61 below; Photographs from the collection of Ulla Tillander-Godenhielm: 19 above left and right.